POWL.

POWL.

THE UNIVERSITY OF CHICAGO
ORIENTAL INSTITUTE PUBLICATIONS
VOLUME 98

Thomas A. Holland • *Editor*
with the assistance of Thomas G. Urban

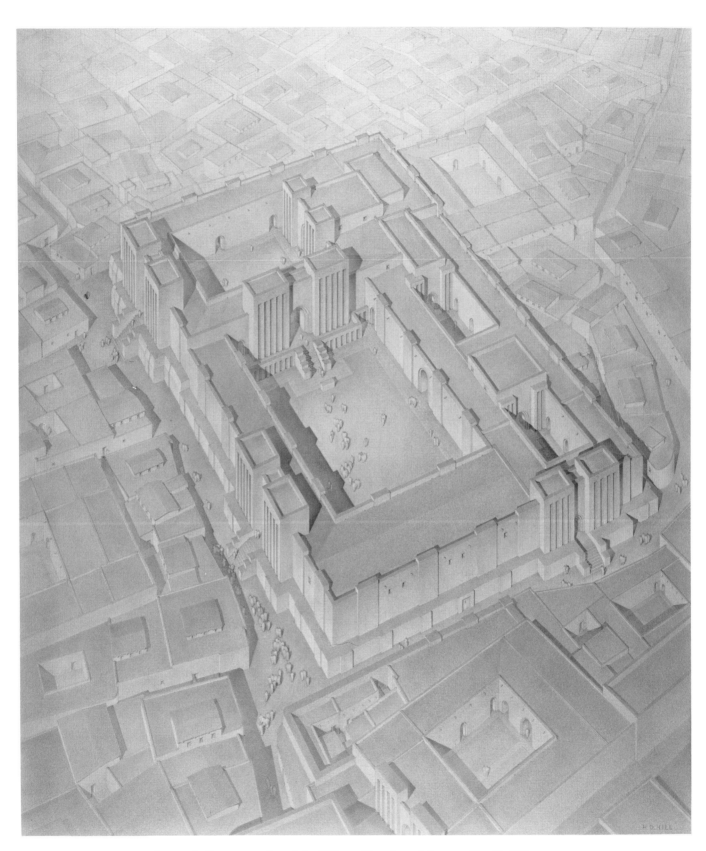

Isometric Reconstruction of the Kitûtum Temple and Surrounding Buildings
(From a water-color painting by H. D. Hill)

THE UNIVERSITY OF CHICAGO
ORIENTAL INSTITUTE PUBLICATIONS
VOLUME 98

OLD BABYLONIAN PUBLIC BUILDINGS IN THE DIYALA REGION

PART ONE

EXCAVATIONS AT ISHCHALI

HAROLD D. HILL[†] and *THORKILD JACOBSEN*

PART TWO

KHAFĀJAH MOUNDS B, C, AND D

PINHAS DELOUGAZ[†]

with contributions by
T. A. HOLLAND and AUGUSTA McMAHON

THE ORIENTAL INSTITUTE OF THE UNIVERSITY OF CHICAGO
CHICAGO · ILLINOIS

THIS PUBLICATION IS ONE OF A GROUP PLANNED TO PRESENT AS A WHOLE THE WORK OF THE ORIENTAL INSTITUTE'S EXPEDITION IN THE DIYALA REGION • THE TITLES ARE:

THE GIMILSIN TEMPLE AND THE PALACE OF THE RULERS AT TELL ASMAR (OIP 43)
SCULPTURE OF THE THIRD MILLENNIUM B.C. FROM TELL ASMAR AND KHAFĀJAH (OIP 44)
THE TEMPLE OVAL AT KHAFĀJAH (OIP 53)
PRE-SARGONID TEMPLES IN THE DIYALA REGION (OIP 58)
MORE SCULPTURE FROM THE DIYALA REGION (OIP 60)
POTTERY FROM THE DIYALA REGION (OIP 63)
STRATIFIED CYLINDER SEALS FROM THE DIYALA REGION (OIP 72)
PRIVATE HOUSES AND GRAVES IN THE DIYALA REGION (OIP 88)
MISCELLANEOUS OBJECTS FROM THE DIYALA REGION (OIP 89, Forthcoming)
STONE VESSELS FROM THE DIYALA REGION (OIP 96, Forthcoming)
OLD BABYLONIAN PUBLIC BUILDINGS IN THE DIYALA REGION (OIP 98)
FOUR ANCIENT TOWNS IN THE DIYALA REGION (Forthcoming)

Library of Congress Catalog Card Number: 89-64443

ISBN: 0-918986-62-1
ISSN: 0069-3367
The Oriental Institute

This Work Is Dedicated to the Memory of
RIGMOR

TABLE OF CONTENTS

PREFACE

The present volume forms the ninth one to be published out of the group of twelve planned to present as a whole the work of the Oriental Institute's Iraq Expedition in the Diyala region. There still remains *Four Ancient Towns in the Diyala Region, Miscellaneous Objects from the Diyala Region* (OIP 89, forthcoming), and *Stone Vessels from the Diyala Region* (OIP 96, forthcoming). However, the results of a ceramic surface survey of the region undertaken by my late wife Rigmor and myself in 1935 and scheduled to appear in the first mentioned volume were turned over to Robert McC. Adams for his resurvey of the region as a member of the Diyala Basin Archaeological Project in 1958. See Robert McC. Adams, *Land Behind Baghdad* (Chicago, 1965) and my *Salinity and Agriculture in Antiquity* (Malibu, 1982).

Work on the present volume was resumed in 1984. The report on Khafājah by Delougaz and a chapter on Ishchali by Hill were available, and Dr. Tom Holland and Miss Augusta McMahon took responsibility for some of the additional small finds mentioned in the text as well as the catalogues of objects from Ishchali and Khafājah Mounds B, C, and D.

The volume has greatly profited from Dr. Holland's careful and insightful editing and seeing it through press.

Thorkild Jacobsen
November 1989

LIST OF FIGURES

LIST OF PLATES

LIST OF PLATES xvii

24. (a) Ishchali—General View of the Period IV Well in the Northeast Part of the Main Court (2-T.30), Viewed from the West

(b) Ishchali—General View of the Shamash "Gate" (Sîn) Temple, Seen from the North

25. (a) Ishchali—Fragment of an Alabaster Carved Cylindrical Cup or Vase from Kitîtum Room 4-Q.30. Scale 1:1

(b) Ishchali—Fragment of a Limestone Stela from the Antecella 2-V.30 in the Shamash "Gate" (Sîn) Temple. Scale 1:4

26. Ishchali—Bronze Statue of a Four-Faced God from the "Serai," Top of Room 7-R.35

27. Ishchali—Side and Back Views of the Bronze Statue of a Four-Faced God from the "Serai," Top of Room 7-R.35

28. Ishchali—Bronze Statue of a Four-Faced Goddess from the "Serai," Top of Room 7-R.35

29. Ishchali—Side and Back Views of the Bronze Statue of a Four-Faced Goddess from the "Serai," Top of Room 7-R.35

30. Ishchali—Metal Objects: (a, b) Lion-Shaped Lamp, Ish. 34:51 (Top and Side Views), (c, d) Lion-Shaped Lamp Fragment, Ish. 34:52 (Side and Front View of Head), (e) Arrowhead, Ish. 34:203, (f, g) Leaf-Shaped Lamp, Ish. 35:84 (Photographs and Drawings, Side and Top Views), (h) Cup, Ish. 35:61 (Reconstruction), (i) Cup, Ish. 35:60, and (j) Bundle of Metal Bands Wrapped in Cloth, Ish. 35:69. Scale 1:2

31. Ishchali—Two Views of Mouflon Bowl Fragment (Ish. 34:117) of Bituminous Stone from 4-Q.30, Floor of Periods III-IV

32. Ishchali—Reconstruction of Mouflon Bowl Fragment (Ish. 34:117). (From water-color paintings by G. Rachel Levy)

33. Ishchali—Clay Plaques with God-Like Images: (a-d) Plaque in Four Pieces, Ish. 34:94, 102, 99, and 105, (e) Ish. 35:75, (f) Ish. 34:101, (g) Ish. 34:100, (h) Ish. 34:96, (i) Ish. 34:208, (j) Ish. 34:5, (k) Ish. 34:7, (l) Ish. 35:212, (m) Ish. 34:286, (n) Ish. 34:92, (o) Ish. 34:95, (p) Ish. 34:113, and (q) Ish. 34:59. Scale 1:2

34. Ishchali—Clay Plaques with God-Like Images: (a) Ish. 34:124, (b) Ish. 34:40, (c) Ish. 34:103 + 110, (d) Ish. 35:91, (e) Ish. 34:210, (f) Ish. 35:222, (g) Ish. 35:216, (h) Ish. 34:125, (i) Ish. 35:220, (j) Ish. 35:223, (k) Ish. 34:112, (l) Ish. 34:91, (m) Ish. 35:206, (n) Ish. 34:126, (o) Ish. 34:114, (p) Ish. 35:89, and (q) Ish. 35:62. Scale 1:2

35. Ishchali—Miscellaneous Clay Plaques: (a) Ish. 35:79, (b) Ish. 34:41, (c) Ish. 34:6, (d) Ish. 34:97-98, (e) Ish. 35:87, (f) Ish. 35:86, (g) Ish. 34:104, (h) Ish. 35:211, (i) Ish. 35:66, (j) Ish. 34:111, (k) Ish. 34:85, (l) Ish. 35:8, (m) Ish. 34:90 + 107, (n) Ish. 34:106, (o) Ish. 34:108, (p) Ish. 34:109, and (q) Ish. 35:215. Scale 1:2

36. Ishchali—Miscellaneous Clay Plaques and Figurines: (a) Ish. 34:61, (b) Ish. 35:88, (c) Ish. 35:221, (d) Ish. 34:93, (e) Ish. 35:214, (f) Ish. 35:213, and (g) Ish. 35:93. Scale 1:1

37. Ishchali—Clay Model Bed Plaques with Goddess Images: (a) Ish. 35:3, (b) Ish. 34:89, (c) Ish. 34:88, and (d) Ish. 35:204. Scale 1:1

LIST OF GENERAL ABBREVIATIONS

ag	agate	impr	impression(s)
alab	alabaster	Ish.	Ishchali (no.)
app.	appendix	Kh.	Khafājah (no.)
B.	baked brick (no.)	lgh.	length
bo	bone	lap la	lapis lazuli
brn	brown	lt	light
car	carnelian	m	meter(s)
cf.	compare	mm	millimeter(s)
ch.	chapter	N	north
cm	centimeter(s)	ND	not divided
comm.	communication	no(s).	number(s)
conglom	conglomerate	OB	Old Babylonian
cont.	continued	ob	obsidian
cry	crystal	OI	Oriental Institute
diam.	diameter	p.	page
dph.	depth	P	Pennsylvania (University Museum)
E	east	pers.	personal
Ed.	editor	pl(s).	plate(s)
exx.	examples	pp.	pages
f.	following page	rect.	rectangular
fem.	female	Ref.	reference (no.)
ff.	following pages	Reg.	registration (no.)
fig.	figure	S	south
frgm(s)	fragment(s)	sect.	section
Gen.	general	sh	shell
gm	gram(s)	st	stone
gr	grave	ste	steatite
gra	granite	var	various
hem	hematite	W	west
ht.	height	wdh.	width
IM.	Iraq Museum		

LIST OF BIBLIOGRAPHICAL ABBREVIATIONS

AASOR	Annual of the American Schools of Oriental Research
AfO	*Archiv für Orientforschung*
AHw	*Akkadisches Handwörterbuch.* Wolfram von Soden, ed. Wiesbaden: Otto Harrassowitz, 1965, 1972, 1981
AJ	*The Antiquaries Journal*
BA	*Beiträge zur Assyriologie und semitischen Sprachwissenschaft*
BagM	*Baghdader Mitteilungen*
BE	The Babylonian Expedition of The University of Pennsylvania
BIM	Bibliotheca Mesopotamica
CAD	*The Chicago Assyrian Dictionary.* Chicago: The Oriental Institute of The University of Chicago, 1956-
CH	Codex Ḫammurabi
CEšn	Codex Ešnunna
HSS	Harvard Semitic Series
HUCA	*Hebrew Union College Annual*
Iraq	Journal of The British School of Archaeology in Iraq. London
JCS	*Journal of Cuneiform Studies*
JNES	*Journal of Near Eastern Studies*
MDOG	*Mitteilungen der Deutschen Orient-Gesellschaft*
MDP	Mémoires de la Délégation en Perse
MSL	Materials for the Sumerian Lexicon
OBTIV	*Old Babylonian Tablets from Ishchali and Vicinity.* Samuel Greengus. Publications de l'Institut historique et archéologique néerlandais de Stamboul 44. Istanbul: Nederlands Historische-Archaeologisch Instituut, 1979
OIC	Oriental Institute Communications. Chicago: The University of Chicago Press
OIP	Oriental Institute Publications. Chicago: The University of Chicago Press
OLZ	*Orientalistische Literaturzeitung*
Or	*Orientalia*
PBS	Publications of the Babylonian Section. Philadelphia: The University Museum
PIHANS	Publications de l'Institut historique et archéologique néerlandais de Stamboul. Istanbul: Nederlands Historische-Archaeologisch Instituut
RA	*Revue d'assyriologie et d'archéologie orientale*

SK	Sumerische Kultlieder
StOr	Studia Orientalia, Helsinki
SUMER	Journal of the Department of Antiquities of Baghdad, Iraq
TCL	Textes cunéiformes, Musée du Louvre, Département des Antiquités Orientales
TCS	Texts from Cuneiform Sources
UCP	University of California Publications in Semitic Philology
UE	Ur Excavations
UET	Ur Excavations Texts
VAB	Vorderasiatische Bibliothek
VS	Vorderasiatische Schriftdenkmäler
WVDOG	Wissenschaftliche Veröffentlichungen der Deutschen Orient-Gesellschaft
YOS	Yale Oriental Series
ZA	*Zeitschrift für Assyriologie*
ZAnF	*Zeitschrift für Assyriologie und Vorderasiatische Archäologie, neue Folge*

BIBLIOGRAPHY

Adams, Robert McC.

1965   *Land Behind Baghdad: A History of Settlement on the Diyala Plains.* Chicago and London: The University of Chicago Press.

Alster, B.

1980   "Sumerian Proverb Collection XXIV," in I. M. Diakonoff, U. Jeyes, B. Alster, E. Møller, and A. M. Bisi, *Assyriological Miscellanies* 1, pp. 33-50. Copenhagen: Institute of Assyriology.

Andrae, W.

1927   "Haus-Grab-Tempel in Alt-Mesopotamien," *OLZ* 30: 1033-1043.

1930   *Das Gotteshaus und die Urformen des Bauens im alten Orient.* Berlin: Hans Schoetz and Co.

Baqir, Taha

1946   "Tell Harmal: A Preliminary Report," *Sumer* 2: 22-30.

Basmachi, Faraj

1975-76   *Treasures of the Iraq Museum.* Baghdad: Ministry of Information, Republic of Iraq.

Bauer, Theo

1957   "Ein Viertes Altbabylonisches Fragment des Gilgameš-Epos," *JNES* 16: 254-62.

Bergmann, E.

1953   *Codex Ḫammurabi: Textus Primigenius.* 3rd ed. Rome: Pontificial Biblical Institute.

Bernhardt, Inez and Kramer, S. N.

1975   "Die Tempel und Götterschreine von Nippur," *Or* 44: 96-102.

Buchanan, Briggs

1981   *Early Near Eastern Seals in the Yale Babylonian Collection.* New Haven and London: Yale University Press.

Castellino, G. R.

1972   *Two Šulgi Hymns (BC)*. Studi Semitici 42. Rome: Istituto di Studi del Vicino Oriente.

Chiera, Edward

1934a   *Sumerian Epics and Myths*. OIP, vol. 15. Chicago: The University of Chicago Press.

1934b   *Sumerian Texts of Varied Contents*. OIP, vol. 16. Chicago: The University of Chicago Press.

Civil, Miguel (ed.)

1971   Izi = *išātu,* Ká-gal = *abullu* and Níg-ga = *makkūru*. MSL 13. Rome: Pontificium Institutum Biblicum.

Cooper, Jerrold S.

1983   *The Curse of Agade*. Baltimore and London: The Johns Hopkins University Press.

Cros, Gaston

1910-14   *Nouvelles Fouilles de Tello*. Paris: Ernest Leroux.

Deimel, P. Anton

1947   *Šumerisches Lexikon* I, 3rd ed. Rome: Pontificium Institutum Biblicum.

Delougaz, Pinhas

1940   *The Temple Oval at Khafājah*. OIP, vol. 53. Chicago: The University of Chicago Press.

1952   *Pottery from the Diyala Region*. OIP, vol. 63. Chicago: The University of Chicago Press.

Delougaz, P., Hill, H. D., and Lloyd, S.

1967   *Private Houses and Graves in the Diyala Region*. Oriental Institute Publications, vol. 88. Chicago: The University of Chicago Press.

Delougaz, P. and Lloyd, S.

1942   *Pre-Sargonid Temples in the Diyala Region*. Oriental Institute Publications, vol. 58. Chicago: The University of Chicago Press.

Ferrara, A. J.

1973   *Nanna-Suen's Journey to Nippur*. Studia Pohl, Series Maior 2. Rome: Biblical Institute Press.

Figulla, H. H. and Martin, W. J.

1953 *Letters and Documents of the Old-Babylonian Period.* UET 5. London and Philadelphia: The Trustees of The British Museum and The Museum of The University of Pennsylvania.

Finkel, Irving L.

1982 The Series SIG$_7$.ALAN = *Nabnītu.* MSL 16. Rome: Pontificium Institutum Biblicum.

Frankfort, H.

1933 *Tell Asmar, Khafaje and Khorsabad: Second Preliminary Report of the Iraq Expedition.* OIC, no. 16. Chicago: The University of Chicago Press.

1936 *Progress of the Work of the Oriental Institute in Iraq, 1934/35: Fifth Preliminary Report of the Iraq Expedition.* OIC, no. 20. Chicago: The University of Chicago Press.

1939 *Cylinder Seals: A Documentary Essay on the Art and Religion of the Ancient Near East.* London: Macmillan and Co.

1943 *More Sculpture from the Diyala Region.* OIP, vol. 60. Chicago: The University of Chicago Press.

1955 *Stratified Cylinder Seals From the Diyala Region.* OIP, vol. 72. Chicago: The University of Chicago Press.

1956 *The Art and Architecture of the Ancient Orient.* Harmondsworth: Penguin Books, Ltd.

Frankfort, H., Lloyd, S., and Jacobsen, Th.

1940 *The Gimilsin Temple and the Palace of the Rulers at Tell Asmar.* OIP, vol. 43. Chicago: The University of Chicago Press.

Gadd, C. J. and Kramer, S. N.

1963 *Literary and Religious Texts: First Part.* UET 6/1. London and Philadelphia: The Trustees of The British Museum and The Museum of The University of Pennsylvania.

1966 *Literary and Religious Texts: Second Part.* UET 6/2. London and Philadelphia: The Trustees of The British Museum and The Museum of The University of Pennsylvania.

Gadd, C. J. and Legrain, Léon

1928 *Royal Inscriptions.* UET 1. London and Philadelphia: The Trustees of The British Museum and The Museum of the University of Pennsylvania.

Gibson, McGuire; Franke, Judith A.; Civil, Miguel; Bates, Michael L.; Boessneck, Joachim; Butzer, Karl W.;
Rathbun, Ted A.; and Mallin, Elizabeth Frick

1978   *Excavations at Nippur: Twelfth Season.* OIC, no. 23. Chicago: The Oriental Institute of The
University of Chicago.

Goetze, Albrecht

1956   *The Laws of Eshnunna.* AASOR 31. New Haven: Department of Antiquities of the Government
of Iraq and the American Schools of Oriental Research.

Green, M. W.

1978   "The Eridu Lament," *JCS* 30: 127-67.

Greengus, Samuel

1979   *Old Babylonian Tablets from Ishchali and Vicinity.* PIHANS 44. Istanbul: Nederlands
Historisch-Archaeologisch Instituut.

1986   *Studies in Ishchali Documents.* BIM 19. Malibu: Undena Publications.

Gurney, Oliver R.

1974   *Middle Babylonian Legal Documents and Other Texts.* UET 7. London: British Museum
Publications, Ltd.

Harris, R. B.

1954   "The Archive of the Sin Temple in Tutub (Khafājah)." Ph.D. diss., The University of Chicago.

1955   "The Archive of the Sin Temple in Khafajah (Tutub)," *JCS* 9: 31-88.

Heinrich, Ernst

1982   *Tempel und Heiligtümer im alten Mesopotamien,* Text und Abbildungen. Berlin: Walter de
Gruyter and Co.

Heinrich, Ernst and Seidl, Ursula

1967   "Grundrißzeichnungen aus dem Alten Orient," *MDOG* 98: 24-45.

Hilprecht, Herman V., ed.

1903   *Explorations in Bible Lands During the 19th Century.* Philadelphia: A. J. Holman and Co.

Jacobsen, Thorkild

 1970 *Toward the Image of Tammuz and Other Essays on Mesopotamian History and Culture.* (William L. Moran, ed.) HSS 21. Cambridge: Harvard University Press.

 1982 *Salinity and Irrigation Agriculture in Antiquity: Diyala Basin Archaeological Projects: Report on Essential Results, 1957-58.* BIM 14. Malibu: Undena Publications.

 1987 *The Harps That Once . . . : Sumerian Poetry in Translation.* New Haven and London: Yale University Press.

Kärki, Ilmari

 1980 *Die Sumerischen und Akkadischen Königsinschriften der Altbabylonischen Zeit I: Isin, Larsa, Uruk.* StOr 49. Helsinki: Finnish Oriental Society.

Koldewey, R.

 1911 *Die Tempel von Babylon und Borsippa.* WVDOG 15. Osnabrück: Otto Zeller.

Kramer, Samuel Noah

 1944 *Sumerian Literary Texts from Nippur in the Museum of the Ancient Orient at Istanbul.* AASOR 23. New Haven: American Schools of Oriental Research.

 1969 *Sumerian Literary Tablets and Fragments in the Archaeological Museum of Istanbul, I.* Türk Tarih Kurumu Yayinlarindan VI/13. Ankara: Türk Tarih Kurumu Basimevi.

Landsberger, B.

 1931 Review of *Royal Inscriptions,* by Gadd, C. J. and Legrain, Léon, Ur Excavations Texts 1, *OLZ* 34: 115-36.

Langdon, Stephen

 1912 *Die Neubabylonischen Königsinschriften.* Vorderasiatische Bibliothek 4. Leipzig: J. C. Hinrichs.

Legrain, Léon

 1926 *Royal Inscriptions and Fragments from Nippur and Babylon.* PBS 15. Philadelphia: The Museum of The University of Pennsylvania.

 1947 *Business Documents of the Third Dynasty of Ur.* UET 3. London and Philadelphia: The Trustees of The British Museum and The Museum of The University of Pennsylvania.

Lenzen, Heinrich J.

    1955   "Mesopotamische Tempelanlagen von der Frühzeit bis zum zweiten Jahrtausend," *ZAnF* 17: 1–36.

Levine, Baruch A. and Hallo, William W.

    1967   "Offerings to the Temple Gates at Ur," *HUCA* 38: 17-58.

Lutz, Henry Frederick

    1919   *Selected Sumerian and Babylonian Texts*. PBS, vol. I, no. 2. Philadelphia: The University Museum.

    1931   *Legal and Economic Documents from Ashjâly*. UCP, vol. 10, no. 1. Berkeley: University of California Press.

Macmillan, Duncan

    1906   "Some Cuneiform Tablets Bearing on the Religion of Babylonia and Assyria," *BA* 5: 531-712.

McCown, D. E., Haines, R. C., and Hansen, D. P.

    1967   *Nippur I: Temple of Enlil, Scribal Quarter, and Soundings*. OIP, vol. 78. Chicago: The University of Chicago Press.

Meissner, Bruno

    1925   *Babylonien und Assyrien II*. Heidelberg: Carl Winters.

Moorey, P. R. S.

    1982   *Ur 'Of the Chaldees': A Revised and Updated Edition of Sir Leonard Woolley's Excavations at Ur*. Ithaca: Cornell University Press.

Moortgat, A.

    1969   *The Art of Ancient Mesopotamia*. London and New York: Phaidon.

Myhrman, David W.

    1911   *Babylonian Hymns and Prayers*. PBS, vol. 1, no. 1. Philadelphia: The University Museum.

Nougayrol, J.

    1947   "Textes et Documents Figurés," *RA* 41: 23-53.

Poebel, Arno

    1923   *Grundzüge der Sumerischen Grammatik*. Rostock.

    1924   "Zum Ruhmeslied der Ištar SK 199 III 8-41," *ZAnF* 1: 52-56.

    1933-34   "Eine sumerische Inschrift Samsuiluna über die Erbauung der Festung Dur-Samsuiluna," *AfO* 9: 241-92.

Porada, Edith

    1947   *Mesopotamian Art in Cylinder Seals of the Pierpont Morgan Library*. New York: The Pierpont Morgan Library.

    1965   *The Art of Ancient Iran*. New York: Crown Publishers, Inc.

Porada, Edith (ed.)

    1948   *The Collection of the Pierpont Morgan Library*. Text and Plates. The Bollingen Series 14. Washington D.C.: Pantheon Books, Inc.

Powell, Marvin A., Jr.

    1978   "Ukubi to Mother . . . The Situation is Desperate: A Plaidoyer for Methodological Rigor in Editing and Interpreting Sumerian Texts with an Excursus on the Verb t a k a : da$_x$-da$_x$(TAG$_4$)," *ZA* 68: 163-95.

Pritchard, James B.

    1955   *Ancient Near Eastern Texts Relating to the Old Testament*. 2nd ed. Princeton: Princeton University Press.

Radau, Hugo

    1911   *Sumerian Hymns and Prayers to God NIN-IB from the Temple Library of Nippur*. BE, Series A: Cuneiform Texts, vol. 29, pt. 1. Philadelphia: Department of Archaeology, University of Pennsylvania.

Reisner, George

    1896   *Sumerisch-Babylonische Hymnen nach Thontafeln griechischer Zeit*. Mittheilungen aus den orientalischen Sammlungen 10. Berlin: W. Spemann.

Salonen, Erkki

    1966   *Die Waffen der Alten Mesopotamier: Eine Lexikalische und Kulturgeschichtliche Untersuchung*. StOr 33. Helsinki: Societa Orientalis Fennica.

Schneider, Nikolaus

    1924-30   *Das Drehem und Djohaarchiv 2: Heft der Götterkult.* Rome: Pontificio Istituto Biblico.

Scheil, V.

    1900   *Textes Élamites-Sémitiques.* MDP II. Paris: Ernest Leroux.

Seidel, Ursula

    1968   "Die babylonischen Kudurru-Reliefs," *BagM* 4: 7-220.

Sjöberg, Åke W.

    1960   *Der Mondgott Nanna-Suen in der sumerischen Überlieferung I.* Uppsala: Almqvist & Wiksell.

    1973   "Nungal in the Ekur," *AfO* 24: 19-46.

Sjöberg, Åke W. and Bergmann, E.

    1969   *The Collection of the Sumerian Temple Hymns.* TCS 3. New York: J. J. Augustin.

Sollberger, Edmond

    1965   *Royal Inscriptions: Part Two.* UET 8. London and Philadelphia: The Trustees of The British Museum and The Museum of The University of Pennsylvania.

Thureau-Dangin, François

    1898   "Un Cadastre Chaldéen," *RA* 4: 13-27.

    1903   *Recueil de tablettes chaldéennes.* Paris: E. Leroux.

    1907   *Die Sumerischen und Akkadischen Königsinschriften.* VAB I/1. Leipzig: J. C. Hinrichs.

    1922   *Tablettes d'Uruk à l'usage des prêtres du Temple d'Anu au temps des Séleucides.* TCL 6. Paris: P. Geuthner.

    1925   *Les Cylindres de Goudéa découverts par Ernest de Sarzec à Tello.* Paris.

van Buren, E. D.

    1930   *Clay Figurines of Babylonia and Assyria.* YOS, Researches, vol. 16. New Haven: Yale University Press.

Weadock, Penelope N.

    1975   "The *Giparu* at Ur," *Iraq* 37: 101-28.

Woolley, Leonard

    1926   "The Excavations at Ur, 1925-26," *AJ* 6: 365-401.

    1939   *The Ziggurat and Its Surroundings.* UE 5. London and Philadelphia: The Trustees of The British Museum and The Museum of The University of Pennsylvania.

    1962   *The Neo-Babylonian and Persian Periods.* UE 9. London and Philadelphia: The Trustees of The British Museum and The Museum of The University of Pennsylvania.

Woolley, Leonard and Mallowan, Max

    1976   *The Old Babylonian Period.* UE 7. London and Philadelphia: The Trustees of The British Museum and The Museum of The University of Pennsylvania.

Zimmern, Heinrich

    1912   *Sumerische Kultlieder aus Altbabylonischer Zeit: Erste Reihe.* VS 2. Leipzig: J. C. Hinrichs.

    1913   *Sumerische Kultlieder aus Altbabylonischer Zeit: Zweite Reihe.* VS 10. Leipzig: J. C. Hinrichs.

PART ONE:

EXCAVATIONS AT ISHCHALI

CHAPTER 1

GENERAL ACCOUNT OF THE EXCAVATIONS AT ISHCHALI 1934-1936[1]

by H. D. Hill†

A. DESCRIPTION OF THE TELL

The tell known as Ishchali is, as shown in the sketch plan (see fig. 1), an irregularly shaped mound, a little over 600 meters long and approximately 300 meters wide, with a low spur reaching northward at the northwest corner. Small outlying mounds lie to the north and south. The highest elevation and sharpest contours were at the southeast end of the mound, where our excavations were located. In this part, also, there were many holes left by illicit digging, from one of which, located south of the Kitîtum building in the "Serai," were said to come the bronze statues now [in the museum of The Oriental Institute].

B. ACCOUNT OF DIGGING PROCEDURE

[Regular excavations began in the fall of 1934 under the overall direction of Henri Frankfort with Thorkild Jacobsen in charge, assisted by Harold Hill as architect, and

1. [The original publication plan for the Ishchali materials called for Harold Hill to furnish the architectural drawings and to give final form to my notes and detailed write-ups of both seasons, 1934-35 and 1935-36. He was able to finish the drawings, but in the case of the text, a fatal illness allowed him only to set down an outline and to write the draft for its sections IA and C, IIA.1, 2, and 3, and IIB.1. His outline is as follows: I. General. A. Description of Tell, B. Account of Digging Procedure, C. Brief Enumeration of the Architectural Finds; II. The Kitîtum Complex. A. General, 1. The Plan, 2. Stratigraphy, 3. History of the Building, B. Original Building, 1. The Plan, 2. Construction, 3. Secondary Occupation, 4. Rebuilding of the North Wing, 5. Fourth Occupation, C. Second Building Period, 1. The Plan, 2. Construction, D. Third Building Period, E. Detailed Description of the Architectural Remains. 1. Facade and Kisû, a. South side, b. East side, c. North side, d. West side, 2. Upper Temple, a. South rooms, b. Court, cella, and adjoining rooms, c. West rooms, d. East rooms, 3. Lower Building, a. North wing, (1) western unit, (2) eastern unit, b. main lower court, c. south wing, d. east wing; III. Shamash Temple; IV. Town Wall; V. Serai.

   We give here the draft for sections I to IIB.1 as written with only minimal editing indicated by square brackets; we also follow Hill's outline in general, adding some further sections and partially reordering sections II to IV. Th. Jacobsen, 1987.]

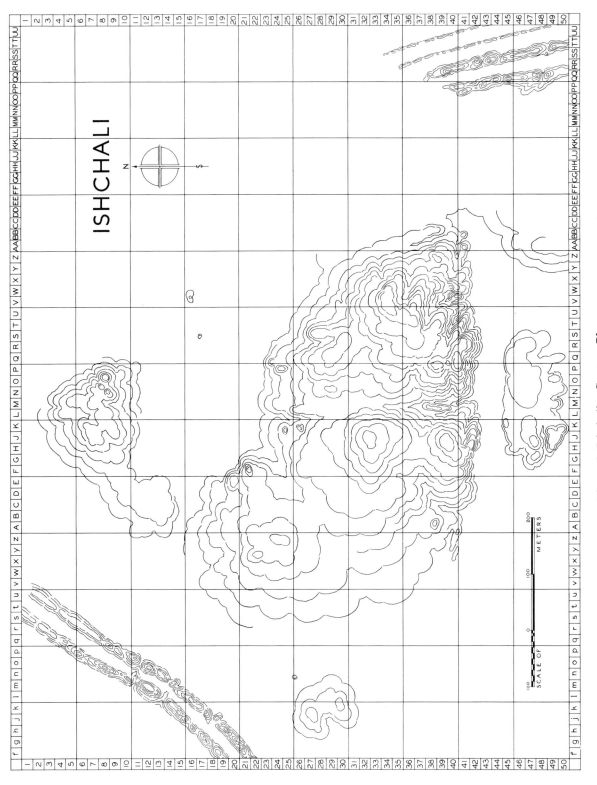

Figure 1. Ishchali—Contour Plan.

Rigmor Jacobsen as photographer. Work was started at 7-R.35 (see fig. 23) where the bronzes just mentioned had been found. As excavation proceeded it soon became clear that the area was one of the private houses linked to form what seemed to be a larger administrative unit. We named it "The Serai."[2] Extending our area of work northward we soon encountered walls of far more massive character, suggestive of a major public building. They proved to belong to a monumental temple complex dedicated to the goddess Inanna Kitîtum.[3] We also explored the area to the east of this temple.]

The structures uncovered lay near a gate in the city wall which ran along the east edge of the mound (see general contour plan of the excavations, fig. 2). The chief of these were the Kitîtum complex (A on the plan), the "Shamash" [Sîn?] temple (B), and the "Serai" (D). With these were traced the faces of buildings outlining two streets: the east-west thoroughfare leading to the gate (C on the plan) on which the Kitîtum complex was situated, and a long street running south from the center of the complex, and curving toward the west. There was, of course, also a third street between the Kitîtum complex and the subsidiary buildings attached to the west side of the "Shamash" temple. Beyond this, to the north, were thick walls too fragmentary to indicate a plan; but a curved front close to the northeast corner of the Kitîtum complex suggested another street leading off to the northwest.

C. BRIEF ENUMERATION OF THE ARCHITECTURAL FINDS

The combination of these features sketches a part of the town plan, even though all the structures were not contemporaneous. The Kitîtum complex and the "Shamash" temple were roughly of the same period, judging from [dated tablets and] the similarity of objects produced. The "Serai" as discovered could be dated to one of the upper levels in the Kitîtum complex by tablets found within the complex. It appears that the city wall and the south outline of the street east of the "Serai" were later, since the city wall filled up the east rooms of the "Shamash" temple, and the face of the buildings along the street crowd so very close to the stairs of the complex. But the gate and that part of the city wall which lies north of the "Shamash" temple may have been contemporary with the temples. That this is possible is suggested by the manner in which the gate forms a forecourt to the "Shamash" temple with the lighter structures surrounding the latter; for these structures appear to have been built when the Kitîtum complex was in its original form, since their facades carefully parallel the side of that building, and swing back to make room for the stairs at its northeast corner.

However this may have been in detail, it is likely that the monumental Kitîtum building, with its fine towered facade and broad stairways, was hemmed in by narrow

2. [The designations "Serai" and "Shamash" temple were coined early in the first season for easy reference. They are probably misnomers. The "Serai" was more likely a large private establishment made up of two adjoining originally separate houses, the "Shamash" temple is, to judge from tablets found in it, more likely to have been a temple for the Moongod Sîn.]

3. See below pp. 88f. and Frankfort 1955, p. 52, no. 917, pl. 87, no. 917, description on opposite page and pp. 46 and 47.

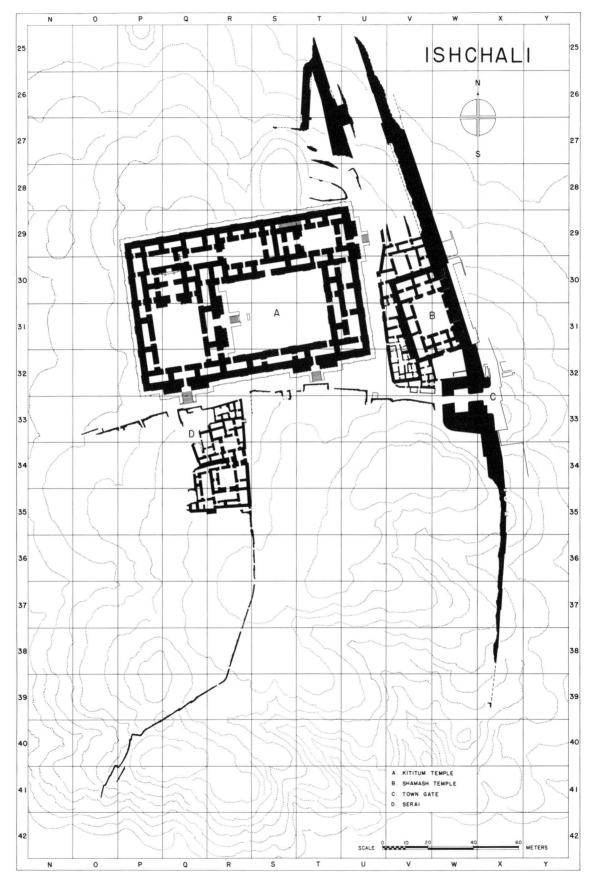

Figure 2. Ishchali—General Plan of the Kitûtum Temple, the Shamash "Gate" (Sîn) Temple, the City Gate and City Wall, and the "Serai."

streets such as suggested by the plan (see fig. 2) and shown in the isometric reconstruction (see frontispiece) even in its original period, for there is every indication that the monumental axis of approach, while understood and employed within the building (as illustrated by the features along the north-south axis of the upper temple) was not used in town planning until long after this period.

As for the rest of the city, superficial observation indicated that the area just west and south of the Kitîtum complex were occupied by smaller buildings of lighter walls, apparently private houses. It seems likely, also, that the city wall turned toward the west to bound the south edge of the mound, as suggested by the contours. However, after rain, traces of building could be seen on the ground for some distance east of the wall, suggesting that the city at one time was larger than indicated by the contours and was probably enclosed by an outer city wall. It should be added, though, that the shallow digging for the foundations of a field house, some thirty meters east of the gate, showed no walls or other signs of occupation.

CHAPTER 2

THE KITÎTUM COMPLEX AT ISHCHALI
by H. D. Hill[†] and Th. Jacobsen

A. GENERAL

1. THE PLAN

Much the most important building uncovered at Ishchali was the Kitîtum complex. A comparison of the building with the surrounding structures on the general plan (see fig. 2) emphasizes its large scale and monumental character. By the multiplication of a familiar unit (that of the enclosed court, with an important element emphasized by towers at one end) and the use of two levels, the builders arrived at an imposing and dignified building.

The plan as shown on the general plan is that of the original building, as restored. This went through several rebuildings, and had been somewhat changed before it reached its final phase; but fortunately, the evidence for the original plan is so conclusive as to allow little doubt that it was as shown. In fact, much of the original work was preserved through the rebuildings; and generally where it had been replaced by later construction, there was evidence that the later work followed the original plan. Thus it appears that throughout its history the building generally followed the original scheme as represented here, which consisted essentially of the following elements: an upper temple with its forecourt, antecella, and surrounding rooms, and an adjacent large lower court, enclosed on its north side by a wing comprising two temple-like units each with its own court, and on two sides by rooms of secondary importance. The entire complex was set up on a brick-faced platform above the surrounding buildings, and approached by broad stairways at the entrances. Another stairway connected the two levels within the building.

2. THE STRATIGRAPHY

Three chief "building periods," in which there was construction substantially affecting the whole building, could be distinguished in the remains of the building. In addition there were several intermediate re-floorings, and one rebuilding of a large part of the north wing of the lower building. These periods are given the following designations:

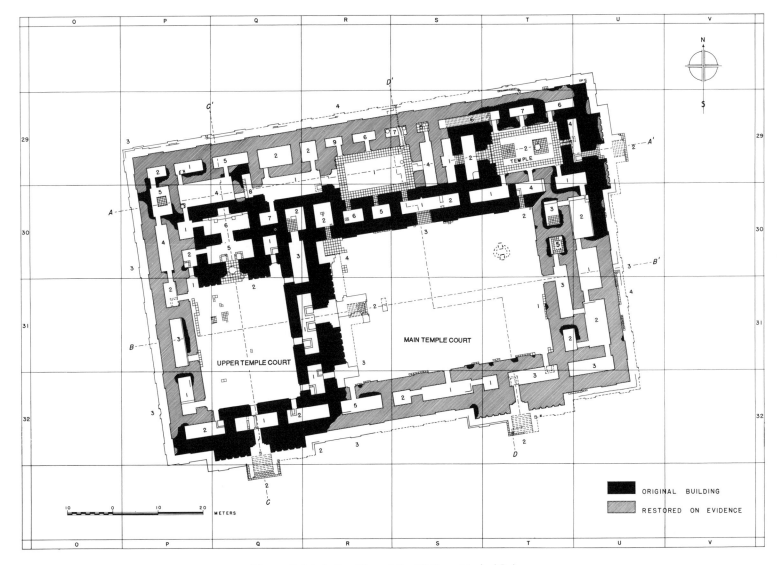

Figure 3. Ishchali—Plan of the Kitûtum, Period I-A.

I-A   Original building
I-B   Second occupation of the original building
II-A Rebuilding of the north wing (also elsewhere third occupation of the original
         building)
II-B Fourth occupation of the original building
III   Second building period
IV   Third building period

3. THE HISTORY OF THE BUILDING

The history of the building as determined from the archaeological investigations is as
follows. The original building, after use for some time, was re-floored in the lower parts by
means of a clay fill on top of the original floor, which raised the level by a few centimeters
(I-B). Some time later, the outer part of the north wing, which lay along the north side of

the larger lower court, was entirely rebuilt, and again the floor in the entire lower part was raised (II-A). A later re-flooring (II-B) within these same walls, raised the level further, but only within the north wing. At this time, the westernmost of the two units making up this wing lost its monumental character with the addition of many fireplaces for cooking in the main room and court.

A general conflagration, which extended as far as the neighboring "Serai," brought this period to an end, and necessitated the general rebuilding (III) which followed. In this rebuilding, about half the complex was rebuilt, the old walls being torn down to below floor level to make room for clay foundations on which the new walls were set. For the first time, the floor level was raised in both the upper and lower parts of the complex. This was probably made advisable by the general rise in the surrounding town. From the evidence of the burnt layer within the "Serai," for example, the floor level within that building was nearly at the same height as the floor of the upper temple. Thus, the level of the street in front of the complex must have risen considerably also, spoiling the effect of the platform on which the building was set. The extensive changes in level made it necessary to raise the top of the *kisû* facing in the lower part, and to construct new staircases to the outer entrances and connecting the upper and lower parts of the building. The north wing was further [raised].

Another general rebuilding (IV) followed, indicating that for some reason the one just described was unsatisfactory, since it occurred wherever the recent work had been done. The old walls were cut down to their clay foundations and replaced by the new ones of this period. The level of the lower part of the complex was again raised, this time sufficiently to bring it to nearly the level of the upper temple.

Traces of burning throughout the building indicated that this occupation also was brought to an end by a general fire. That the complex was restored after this and again occupied is evidenced by traces of a still higher floor, but these, being approximately at the level of the surface of the mound, were so fragmentary as to be negligible.

B. THE ORIGINAL BUILDING PERIOD (I-A)

1. THE PLAN (BY H. D. HILL)

The extent to which the original walls of the complex were preserved can be seen on the plan of the original building (see fig. 3). In many of the places where the walls had disappeared, they had been replaced by walls of a later period which had obviously been built along the original lines. An example is the north half of the north wing (rooms 2-Q.29 to 5-S.29), where the walls as found make a plan so logically completing the part of the original which still remained that it seems evident that they were simply rebuildings of the original plan. This was the case in the large lower court, at the south edge, where a very few baked bricks of the original pavement, which still remained in place, indicated enough of the breadth of the buttress and the interval between to make it quite safe to assume that the buttressing system was the same here as on the opposite wall, as would be expected. It is true that in much of the part which had to be restored, few doors were preserved, since the walls of the succeeding period had been destroyed to their

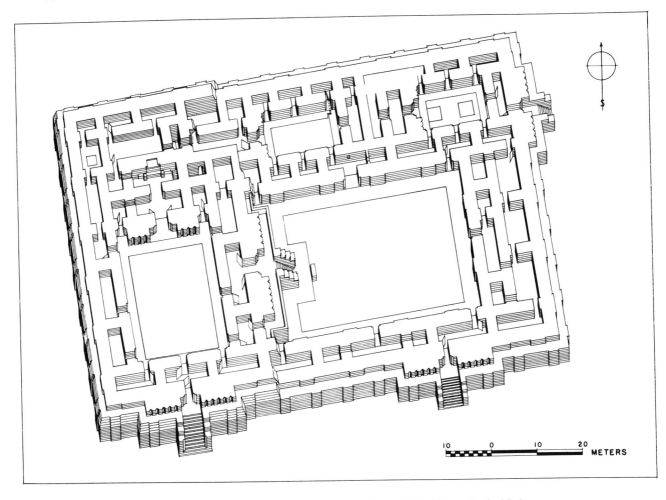

Figure 4. Ishchali—Isometric Reconstruction of the Kitîtum, Period I-A.

foundations, and later walls were so close to the surface that they had frequently been eroded to below the sills of the doors. However, as will be found on close examination, there were few places where even the position of the door was not indicated by some fairly conclusive evidence. For example, the doors in the courts could be assumed to have been on an axis with those on the opposite wall, on the evidence of those courts which were preserved; or, in the case or rooms 3-T.30 and 5-T.30, although the actual doors were not found, there was no other wall where they could have been.

Detailed evidence for the reconstruction will be given in the discussion of each room, but it may be assumed that the original plan was certainly substantially as shown (cf. figs. 3 and 4). In this plan, the division into parts at different levels has been mentioned above. The lowest part was set about two meters above the general surrounding level, but the upper part was two meters above that. This upper part formed in effect the culminating point of the whole plan; it was the focus of the entire lower building, and as such occupied the important position at the end of the large court of the lower building, typically the location of the cella.

Its importance is marked by the large towers flanking the entrance to it from the lower court and the entrance was further embellished by a terrace the full width of the lower court, and a broad stairway of monumental proportions connecting the two levels.

There seems little doubt that the upper temple was thus emphasized because it housed the chief shrine of the complex, and was, in itself, the Kitîtum temple. The finding of an inscribed seal [dedicated to Kitîtum] in the cella only gives corroboration to the evidence of the architecture (see ch. 1, n. 3).

Taken as a unit in itself, the upper temple presents no features unusual in a Babylonian temple, except for its triple entrances. The plan is essentially a simple rectangle formed by a court surrounded on three sides by single rows of rooms, with the cella and its adjuncts at one end. It could be entered both from its east side (through 1-R.31 or 1-R.32) and from the south (through 1-Q.32). This latter entrance is noticeable not so much for affording access from the street in addition to that from the lower court, which is understandable, as for representing a new trend first observable in temples of the Ur III period: it presents an opening to the outside directly on an axis with the inner doors to the antecella, and the cella itself. In this it stands alone in the complex, for although the small temple in the eastern unit of the north wing has its entrance at the end opposite the cella (or focal point), there the interior of the temple is screened from the outside by means of the doors of the gate room which are not opposite each other. It will be seen from the plan that all other entrances to the courts are thus placed.

The street entrance, flanked by the imposing five-slotted towers, and at the head of the broad staircase, constituted a truly monumental gateway to the temple. Within the broad vestibule (1-Q.32) was a single pivotstone box to house the pivots on which the two doors, exterior and interior, swung.[1] These led to the spacious court, which was dominated at its further end by the features making up the entrance to the antecella. These were essentially the same as those constituting the outer entrance, but here the doorway was much wider, and the towers only wide enough to accommodate three vertical slots. The symmetry of the northern facade of the court was furthered by the two smaller entrances to the rooms at the sides of the antecella (see reconstructed section B-B´, fig. 6). The other three sides of the court were simple walls with three entrances in each. (The west side has been restored as identical with the east, on the assumption that here, as in the later periods, there were three rooms at the west, and that the doors to these rooms would undoubtedly have been placed opposite those in the east wall.) The court was paved with large baked bricks (52 × 52 × 9 centimeters), probably in a walk around the edges in a manner similar to that in the smaller courts of the north wing. There were also remnants of a paving of smaller bricks (36 × 36 × 8.50 centimeters) toward the center of the court at the north end, which may have been from squares similar to those in 2-T.29.[2] Within the door of the antecella, at least, this paving was covered with a layer of bitumen.

---

1. The doors would have cleared one another with almost no distance to spare between them.
2. In fact it is possible, to judge by a few bricks of the large size which were at the south end of the court, that the entire courts was paved, but it has not been so restored because the rule seems to have been otherwise.

The antecella (5-Q.30) had no unusual features. Two pivotstone boxes, one still containing its pivotstone, indicated double doors by which the room could be closed off from the court (pl. 1a). Similarly, the small connecting room, 2-P.30, had a pivotstone box at its door to the court.

The cella itself (6-Q.30) was a "broadroom,"[3] that is, with the entrance and cult-niche on the long sides of the room. Considering the breadth of the niche (2.50 meters, the same as the door), which suggests a recess of considerable height, it is surprising that the room should have been so narrow (3.60 meters) on its short axis (see section C-C′, fig. 7 and pl. 1a). Pedestals stood before the niche, at each side, with their inner faces flush with the edges of the rebate of the niche. These pedestals were constructed of mudbrick, were 70 centimeters square in plan, and, as found, stood to a height of 40 centimeters above the original floor. However, there was definite evidence that they had been shaved off at the top so that the new floor which was later laid in this room could pass over them (i.e., the top course of brick had been cut off horizontally at a level just below that floor).

The niche had been partly filled with a dais of baked brick. The evidence for this existed in the clearest impressions of the brick courses on the walls of the niche, frequently with traces of the bitumen which had been used for mortar still adhering to the wall. The actual brick had been removed, except for two fragments which still remained in the rebate at the east side (pl. 1b). In front of the niche, other impressions of brick were found in a groove, the bottom of which was 15 centimeters (the equivalent of two courses) below the floor level, and which was clearly two bricks (75 centimeters) in width, between the columns. The groove extended beyond these, narrowing down to the distance between the columns and the wall (one and one-half brick, or 54 centimeters) and continuing to a distance of about 1.20 meters from each side wall. Here it abutted a low bench of mudbrick on each side.

The combination of the evidence for the dais within the niche with the pedestals in front of it led Dr. Jacobsen to a comparison with the representation of a shrine on a clay plaque published by Mrs. van Buren.[4] Here, if one assumes the horizontal lines to represent brick courses instead of steps (a reasonable assumption considering how literally the texture of mats, for example, is indicated on other terracottas), are the niche with its dais, and the two, exactly as found in the plan. The pedestals would have borne statues of guardian beings (or sculptured stelae) which in turn supported the poles bearing a canopy which stretched above and across the front of the niche (see section C-C′, fig. 7). In the restoration, because it was felt that to have carried the face of the dais out along the walls would have been awkward and unsound structurally (since there was no bonding with the wall behind), the brickwork which occupied the groove in front of the niche has been reconstructed as a low step or bench in front of the dais. The curious shape of the top of the niche as represented on the plaque has not been repeated in the restoration, as it is not clear how such a form would have been possible in brick, even assuming the use of wood lintels. The statue in the niche is, of course, purely restoration and could easily have been a seated figure such as is represented on the plaque.

3. [The term translates W. Andrae's term *Breitraum* (1930, p. 16). We use it here to denote a typical shape of cella only.]

4. See van Buren 1930, pl. 53, fig. 255 (see also below, p. 79).

Other bench-like constructions of mudbrick were found at the east wall. These were similar to those mentioned above, in the corners at the ends of the groove. These may have been intended to receive votive objects.[5]

A door in the west wall led to a small room (1-P.30) by which the cella was connected with a group of rooms at the back. The largest of these, 4-Q.30, may have been a sort of sacristy for the temple, at least in period III-IV it contained an unusually large number of valuable objects such as cylinder seals, beads, and fragments of stone vessels, which may have been cult objects or votive offerings (pls. 31, 32, 40g, h, 41e, and 43b).[6] Some of these were buried beneath the later floor; and since they range in time from the Early Dynastic period down to the Larsa period, it seems probably that they had been collected over a long period of time, and were buried here at the time of the rebuilding, since, according to custom, they could not have been thrown away. A pivotstone box at the south door indicated that this room could be closed off from the cella, possibly for protection for the valuable objects kept there. It will be noted that in the reconstructed section (see sections A-A´ and C-C´, figs. 5 and 7) this room is represented as lighted by a clerestory raised above the row of rooms in the back. It was necessary that this method of construction be used for both this room and the cella, if they were to have received outside light. The alternative which suggested itself, that 4-Q.30 was actually a court (from which the cella could have been lighted) was rejected because of the nature of the finds in the room, and the absence of any paving or means of drainage. Also, the use of a clerestory, for which there was good evidence in the Private House Area at Tell Asmar, would have been a very simple matter here, where it could have been effected by raising the walls of the antecella, cella, and 4-Q.30, and roofing these rooms with a single pitch toward the north, as illustrated in the section.[7]

The small rooms adjoining 4-Q.30 (1-P.29 and 5-Q.29) had no remarkable features except for the traces of a pivotstone box for the door to 1-P.29, a rather surprising indication of a door in this apparently unimportant room.

At the east end of 4-Q.30 was one of the two links between the upper temple and the lower part, a narrow stairway leading down into the north wing. Since the connection was closed off in the later remodelings, which also destroyed the original wall to well below the original floor level (see section A-A´, fig. 5), no door was found at the top of these stairs; however, one has been restored, as the stairs could hardly have led elsewhere than to this room. The stairs, which were both narrow and precipitous, having a riser of 27 centimeters to a tread of 36 centimeters, were certainly not intended for public use. It seems likely that they were intended for the use of priests coming from their private quarters to the sacristy, to prepare for the ceremonies in which they were to take part.[8]

It will be seen from the plan that much of the wall in this part has been restored. This is because original construction has been largely replaced by later walls in this part (see

5. [Further examination during the 1935-36 season showed that the benches were mere blocks of masonry forming part of the fill to heighten the floor.]

6. [Similarly Frankfort 1936, p. 85.]

7. [For a different interpretation of this part of the plan arrived at more recently, see below, p. 74. It could thus, unfortunately, not be discussed with Mr. Hill.]

8. [See now pp. 74f.]

sections A-A´ and C-C´, figs. 5 and 7), and existed only at a very deep level. Wherever these remnants of the original walls were investigated by soundings, they followed the upper walls so closely that it seemed quite safe to assume that they were as in the upper plan. Specifically the inner face of the outer wall, having been found in 5-P.30, a corner of 1-P.32, and all along 2-P.32, could be assumed throughout to have been on a line made by connecting these known points. The thickness of the original wall was tested in both 5-P.30 and 2-P.32 and found uniform; thus the outer face could be restored for its full length. The resulting face was parallel to that of the *kisû* facing, as would be expected. The wall as preserved showed no buttressing, because it was not preserved to the height where the buttresses would have begun. Buttresses have therefore been restored following the system discovered in the north wall, in a later rebuilding.

The points indicating the direction of the east wall of this row of rooms may be seen on the plan (see fig. 3). In room 2-P.31 a face found at a very low level (36.65 meters) corresponded in level and direction to a ledge found in the foundation wall of 3-P.31 (see section B-B´, fig. 6). It was therefore possible to assume that the actual face of the upper wall would have been somewhat back from the line, which put it along the line of walls found farther south. The thickness of the wall was shown at 2-P.30, but it was also indicated, along with the direction of the east face of the wall, by the existing baked brick of the original paving. Although the actual row which had lain along the face of the wall was preserved for only a short distance, it was apparent that its continuation would have run next to the course farther north and the location of the inner face could be located in that part.

The other adjacent rooms here belong to the row of rooms along the west side of the temple. Except for a paved floor and a few pieces of wall where the investigation was carried deep enough to uncover the remaining foundations, there was little here which belonged to the original period. This entire part had been rebuilt in the succeeding periods, and the existing walls were the clay foundations of one of these periods, and the brickwork of a later period on top of these. Even in the latter there were no preserved doors, since the floor level must have been just at or above the existing surface of the mound. However, the position of the walls was certain, and there were enough soundings to the deep level where the original walls still remained to indicate their position.

The location of the doors was similarly indicated with some definiteness, in most cases. The interior doors in 2-P.29, 5-P.30, 4-P.30, and 2-P.31 were all actually found, at least in part. The three doors into the court were placed opposite those in the east wall, following the symmetrical examples in the two courts of the north wing. There was also more tangible evidence for the restoration of the northernmost of these doors. A pivotstone box belonging to an intermediate rebuilding immediately following this period was found where it should have been for a door in this location. This was probably a repairing of the original box. A single thin wall across 1-P.32 may have marked the side of a similar pivotstone box of the door there.

Even the floors of the original building in these rooms had been largely destroyed. There remained only a rectangle of baked brick covered with bitumen in room 5-P.30. This did not entirely fill the room, but its being bordered on all sides by half bricks suggests that it was complete as found. There was no drainage hole in this paving.

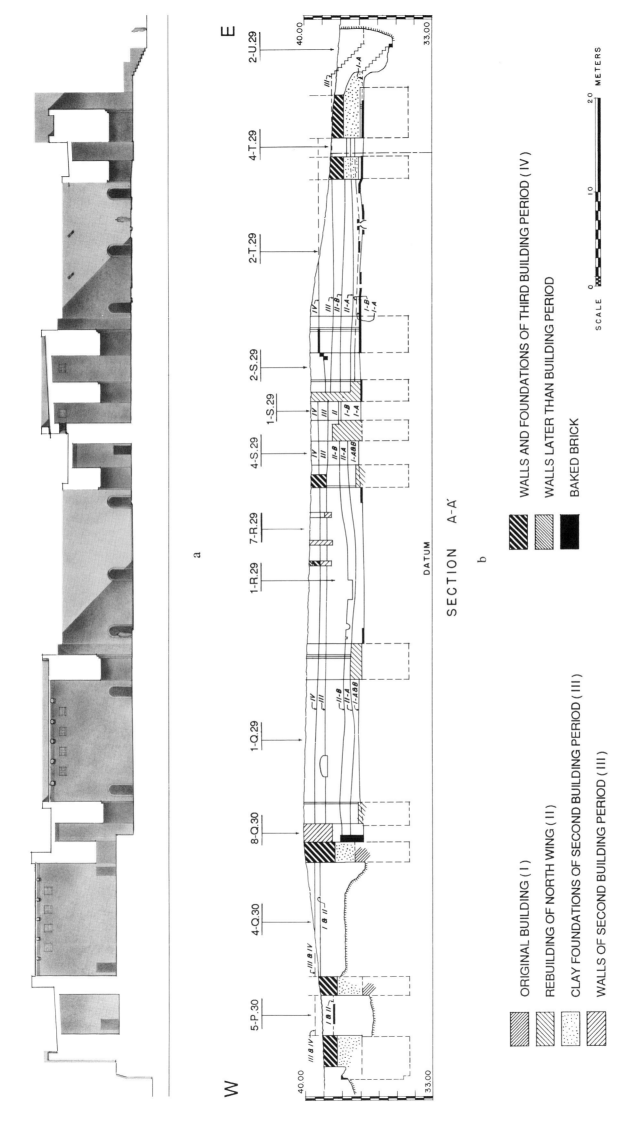

W   E

a

SECTION   A-A'

b

ORIGINAL BUILDING (I)

REBUILDING OF NORTH WING (II)

CLAY FOUNDATIONS OF SECOND BUILDING PERIOD (III)

WALLS OF SECOND BUILDING PERIOD (III)

WALLS AND FOUNDATIONS OF THIRD BUILDING PERIOD (IV)

WALLS LATER THAN BUILDING PERIOD

BAKED BRICK

SCALE

METERS

Figure 5. Ishchali—(*a*) Reconstructed Facade and (*b*) Stratigraphical Section of the Kitītum, A-A'.

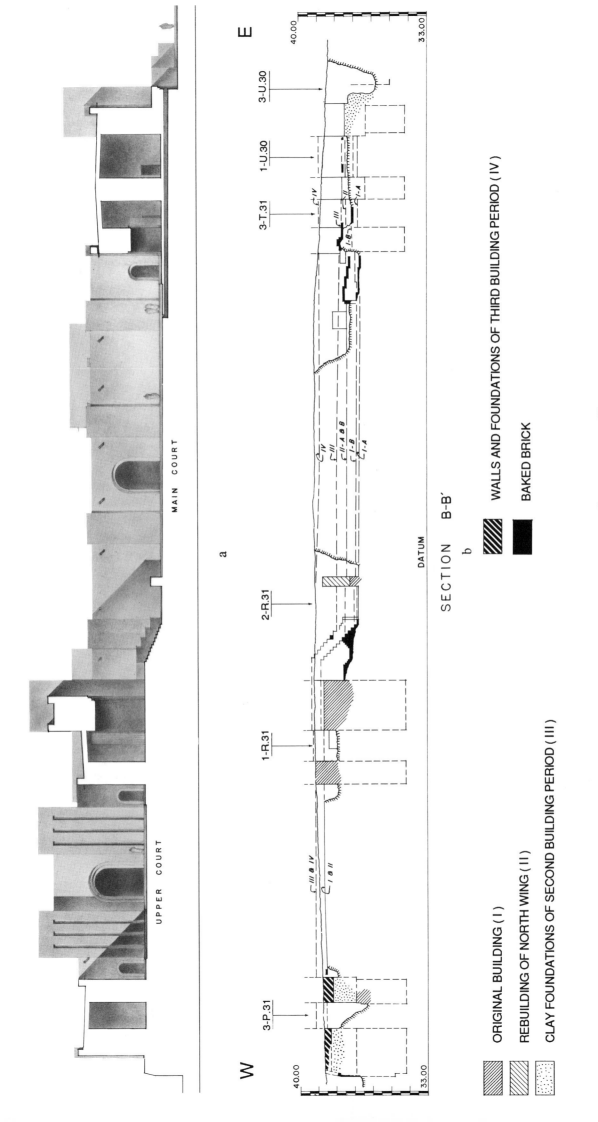

MAIN COURT

UPPER COURT

a

W

E

SECTION B-B'

DATUM

b

40.00

33.00

40.00

33.00

3-P.31

1-R.31

2-R.31

3-T.31

1-U.30

3-U.30

ORIGINAL BUILDING (I)

REBUILDING OF NORTH WING (II)

CLAY FOUNDATIONS OF SECOND BUILDING PERIOD (III)

WALLS AND FOUNDATIONS OF THIRD BUILDING PERIOD (IV)

BAKED BRICK

SCALE

10   0   10   20

METERS

Figure 6. Ishchali—(a) Reconstructed Facade and (b) Stratigraphical Section of the Kitītum, B-B'.

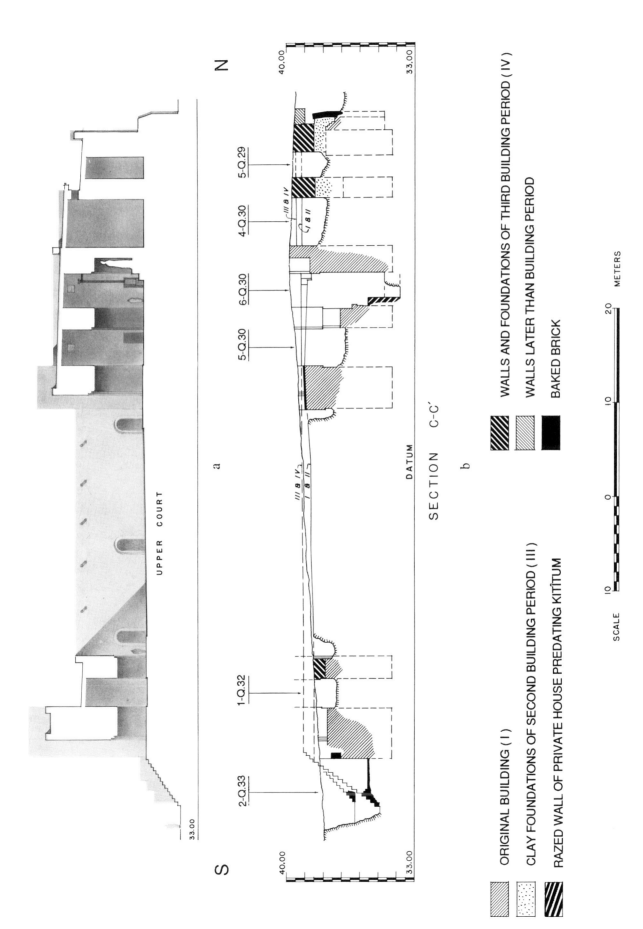

Figure 7. Ishchali—(*a*) Reconstructed Facade and (*b*) Stratigraphical Section of the Kitîtum, C-C'.

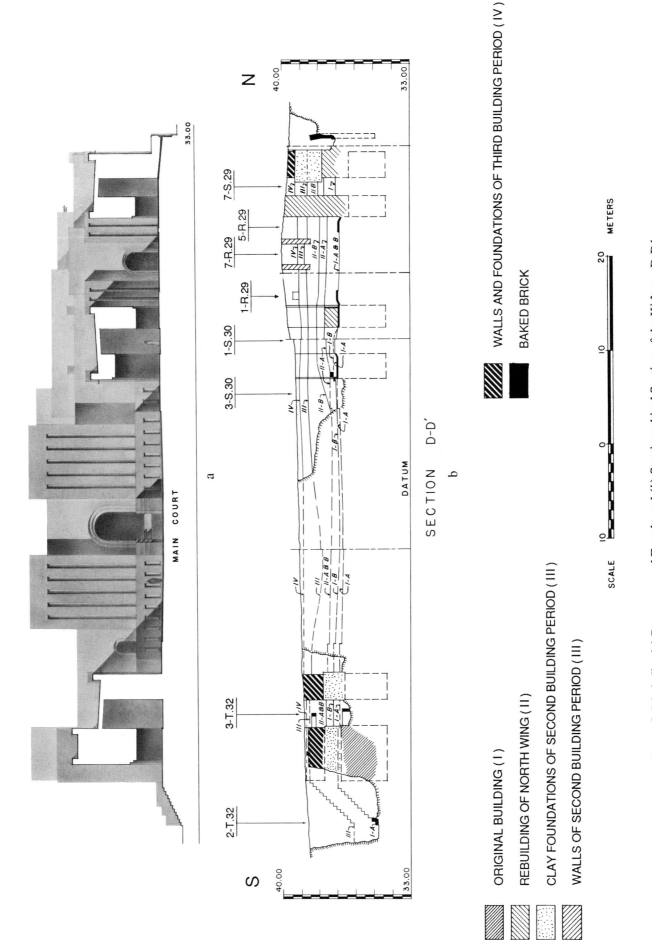

MAIN COURT

33.00

a

SECTION D-D'

b

DATUM

N

S

ORIGINAL BUILDING (I)

REBUILDING OF NORTH WING (II)

CLAY FOUNDATIONS OF SECOND BUILDING PERIOD (III)

WALLS OF SECOND BUILDING PERIOD (III)

WALLS AND FOUNDATIONS OF THIRD BUILDING PERIOD (IV)

BAKED BRICK

SCALE

METERS

Figure 8. Ishchali—(*a*) Reconstructed Facade and (*b*) Stratigraphical Section of the Kititum, D-D'.

On the east side of the court, where the original construction had not been marred by later rebuilding, the surface was fortunately higher (see section B-B´, fig. 6), so that the entrances were all preserved. The chief room on this side was of course the vestibule, 1-R.31, which formed the public connection between the upper and lower part of the complex. Here the inner and outer doors were nonaligned, i.e., were placed so as not to be opposite each other, a principle referred to above (p. 11) in a curious contrast to those at the south entrance, considering that here the doors merely gave onto the large court, a fairly protected area. The wide outer door, like the one to the cella, had two pivotstone boxes, indicating double doors. The small door to the upper court would also be close. Bitumen traces on the jambs of the larger door indicated the original paving within the opening and the approximate level of the floor within the room.

An extraordinary feature of this side of the temple was that there was a second vestibule (1-R.32) next to the large one. This duplication of entrances into the upper court is similar to that in the Kitîtum sanctum, except that here there was no communication between the two vestibules. It appears possible that in both cases the larger doors were opened only during ceremonies to which the public was admitted, while at other times the smaller entrances were used. The doors in the smaller vestibule, which both had pivotstone boxes were also nonaligned.

At the other end of this wing were the two connecting rooms, 2-Q.30 and 3-Q.30. The smaller of these was paved with baked brick, some of which had been removed. Toward the center of the room stood a block of mudbrick masonry approximately 35 centimeters high. There is no explanation as to why this room should have been paved.

A curious result of the intertwining of the plan of the upper temple with the lower western unit in the north wing was that the room next to this, 7-Q.30, although between two rooms of the upper temple, belongs to the lower building. Its original floor was nearly 2 meters below those in the upper rooms. Similarly it will be seen on figure 3 that the plan of the upper temple failed to occupy the rectangle usual in such plans, because of the encroachment of rooms 1- and 2-Q.29 and 8-Q.30 of the north wing.

The relation of the upper temple to the lower building has been compared with that of the cella to the rest of the ordinary temple plan. In accordance with this concept of the plan, the great lower court was the center around which all the elements of the complex were grouped. Thus, the exterior approach to this part was as impressive as that to the actual shrine, in the upper temple, and consisted of the same elements: the wide stairway and five-slotted towers. The vestibule was about the same size as that to the upper temple, but the privacy of the court was carefully insured by the two doors which could be closed, and which were nonaligned.

The court's great size (a width of 32 meters and length of more than 48 meters) made it predominant in area in the plan. The architectural treatment of the wall surfaces, which were broken into bays by wide spaced buttresses, gave scale to the court and accentuated its size (see perspective restoration, fig. 4). But the massiveness and elaboration of detail of the entrance to the upper temple at the west end, made it overpower the rest of the court. Here again, the five-slotted towers were used, at the head of a wide stairway. But the stairs, in themselves more elaborate than those at the exterior entrances, led to a terrace of baked brick, the face of which was enriched with slot decoration (pl. 2b). Also, the door, double rabbeted like the other important entrances in the building was a wide gateway like that leading to the antecella of the upper temple. The effect was truly monumental, as can be seen from the drawing of the restored building on the frontispiece of this volume.

As found, the entire front of the staircase was preserved, as well as a large part of the baked brick core behind this (pl. 2a). A broad rabbeted face on each of the balustrade plinths indicated a decorative treatment which it has been assumed was used throughout the length of the staircase. The row of baked brick (52 × 52 × 9 centimeters) on the ground in a line connecting the faces of the two plinths was not a step, but the remnants of the paving of the court. The first step started on top of this, and was broadened at each end by the width of a single brick, apparently purely for decoration. The steps were one brick wide and two courses high. For the steps here a special brick (different from that used in the plinths), 33 centimeters square, was used. Thus the tread was 33 centimeters, while the risers averaged 16.50 centimeters high. The five risers preserved reached a height of 80 centimeters above the court paving. Traces of bitumen within the door to the upper temple indicated the sill, which was 1.97 meters above the court. Thus, to span the remaining 1.17 meters of height, seven more risers would have been required. Restoration of the steps accordingly in plan brought the edge of the top step to approximately the face of the terrace, where the steps might normally be expected to begin.

The location of this face of the terrace was fixed by a remaining remnant at the south end (see plan, fig. 13, p. 33). Here the front was preserved for a stretch of a little over 2 meters. Between here and the stairs, excavations disclosed a trench, the interior of which was filled with softer earth than the rest, which had been put down in a later period, after the floor of the court had risen, for the removal of the baked bricks of the terrace. The east side of this trench continued roughly the line of the terrace face as established by the remnant of the south end. At the north end (4-R.30), the terrace had unfortunately been largely destroyed; however, here the remaining edge of a patch of the court paving, as well as some remaining bricks, indicated the north edge of of the terrace (pl. 3). At this point, also, remained a piece of a later addition to the terrace, from which came the clue to the decoration of the terrace front. This addition, which was an extension of the terrace face to the north wall of the court (see figs. 4 and 13 and p. 54), bore the shallow recesses which have been taken as indication of vertical slot decoration (as explained later, see pp. 36f.), and which must have been used in this addition only because it was made to match the existing original face.

It will be seen that the terrace was narrowed at each end; that is, its outline receded to accord with that of the towers, in the same manner as the face of the *kisû* followed that of the building. However, although the towers were symmetrical about the center of the court, the terrace was not, being somewhat longer at the south end. This irregularity was obviously resorted to in order to bring the wide part of the terrace opposite the entrance to the upper temple. The face of the recessed part, at the south end, was preserved to a height of about one meter, and was not decorated with the slots assumed to have been used on the terrace face. However, it is probable that the builders would have confined the decoration to the projecting face in agreement with the facade behind the terrace, where the decoration was applied only to the fronts of the projecting towers.

As will be seen from the plan, the south and east facades of the court had to be restored. This was because here again, the original building had been replaced by the clay foundation and upper walls of succeeding periods. However, here also, the restoration could be made on good evidence. The walls are assumed to have been the same as those of the third building period. Where the excavations were carried deep enough to strike the existing foundations of the original walls, this assumption was borne out. Also, remnants of paving remained to indicate that the buttressing had been the same as in the later walls, which, in the case of the south wall, corresponded to that of the opposite original wall. It was established by fragments remaining along the north wall that the row of brick which originally ran along the wall was made up of half-bricks where this row passed the buttresses although it was of whole bricks elsewhere. Thus, for example, the first buttress at the east, on the south wall, was located definitely by the six half-bricks which had lain along its face, and which were flanked on the east by two whole bricks. Investigation at a lower level disclosed the west corner of the actual buttress. Similarly, the third buttress from the east was marked by the six half-bricks, next to which were two fragments of the whole bricks which had evidently been broken at the time when the original wall was cut down for rebuilding.

The evidence for the locations of the doors was less definite. The door in the east wall existed in the later rebuilding. The easternmost door in the south wall was also at least partly traceable in the rebuilding, and was marked by a pivotstone box. The others in the south wall were placed in the restoration opposite those existing in the north wall. This was in accordance with the symmetrical examples of the small courts in the north wing.

The paving of the court, which helped so greatly in the restoration of the walls, was preserved in its greatest extent in the northeast corner of the court, at 4-R.30 (pl. 3). It seems likely that the width of six courses along the north wall here represents the original walk which probably ran around all sides of the court, as in the smaller courts of the north wing. This walk would probably have been carried across the front of the terrace, and widened to come in front of the stairway, as indicated in the restoration. In this connection, it is noteworthy that the distance between the brick course at the foot of the stairs, and the face of the block of mudbrick which stood in front of them was exactly the width of the six brick walk.

The masonry block just referred to is an enigma. The original masonry was preserved to a height of only about 0.50 meters; but a rebuilding apparently dating to the period immediately following stood nearly 1.50 meters above the floor to which it is ascribed (see section B-B′, fig. 6). The part preserved was square at the south end, where it was finished with plaster. It had been broken away at the north. It has been assumed that originally it was a rectangular block placed symmetrically in front of the stairway. Too high (at least in the rebuilt form), to have served as an altar, it had the appearance of a screen wall; although why the broad and open approach to the upper temple should have been blocked off by a rectangle of mud masonry is certainly not clear.[9]

9. [See now the suggestion made below on pp. 70f.]

The center of the large court was not excavated, due to limitations on the funds available. The Oriental Institute was closing down the Iraq Expedition at the time, and it seemed unlikely that any features of importance would have been uncovered there. [At the eastern end, a well, lined with baked bricks of a later period was located (pl. 13a). It seems likely that it was an original feature later relined.]

There is little to be said about the actual rooms of the south and east wings. As has been explained, they are shown as found in the later rebuilding, and, in general, have been corroborated by soundings to the level of the remains of the original foundation at only a few points. In 5-R.32 and 1-T.32 in the south wing, and 3-T.30, 2-U.30, and 2-U.31 in the east, parts of the wider foundation wall were found, as indicated by the single outlines on the plan (see fig. 3). There were some floors of tamped earth which could be traced, particularly in the south wing, and in rooms 3- and 5-T.30 there were fragments of baked brick pavement. In the former room, there was a hole for drainage, toward the center of the paving.

The doors in the south wing are discussed above. The doors in the east wing had been largely destroyed, even in the later building. In the plan, they have been restored in what seems to have been likely positions. The entrance to the north wing through 2-U.30, which was actually preserved, as well as being marked by a pivotstone box, was a significant connection between the two wings (see below p. 53 to 1-T.29).

The north wing was of considerably more interest than the other two wings of the lower building, since it was composed of more complex units, and more formal in plan. In fact, both units of this wing followed so closely the typical temple plan that it seems likely that they were originally planned for ritual use. It is quite clear, however, that the western unit was not a temple; and the eastern unit acquired an actual niche to identify its cella, only in a later remodeling.[10]

The western unit was given much the greater prominence in the court facade in that it had an entrance (3-S.30) as wide as that to the upper temple. This door, centrally placed in the north wall of the court, led to a long vestibule (1-S.30), the east end of which (2-S.30) was cut off by a light partition. There were no pivotstone boxes here to indicate doors by which the opening could be closed, but the cubicle at the end of the vestibule suggests a sort of guard's room. An unusual feature of the vestibule (1-S.30) was a small rectangular recess in the north wall, directly on an axis with the wide entrance (pl. 4a). This recess, the bottom of which was 90 centimeters above the floor, was 49 centimeters square overall. A second box-like recess within this was 35 centimeters square and 19.50 centimeters deep. Thus there was a face all around within the larger recess, about 7 centimeters wide, and set back 8 centimeters from the wall face. The effect was of a square opening which was bordered all around with the same sort of rabbet which was generally used on the doors of the building. This recess, although finished with plaster, may have been intended to receive a plaque of carved stone or terracotta.

The court of this unit was entered through a smaller door which was not opposite the entrance. Although the north half of the court (and of the entire building) had been rebuilt in the period immediately following, the rebuilding obviously followed the original plan, so

10. [See pp. 25f. for assuming that the temple character of this unit was original. Hill concurred in a letter to me of March 13, 1937.]

that the court as it was found must have been much as it was originally built (see fig. 3 and pl. 4b). It was, in effect a smaller version of the court of the upper temple. Here, again, there were three symmetrically placed doors on each of the long sides, an important towered entrance in one of the shorter sides and a door opposite it at the other end. The court was paved in the form of a walk around the edges, with the same large baked bricks. Paving was also found within the doors on the south side. Here the brick was coated with bitumen. The other doors were presumably originally paved in the same way. A fragment of brick and traces of bitumen still remained at the south edge of the large west door to show that this had once had a brick sill.

The rooms to which the large west door led were strangely unimpressive, consisting only of a long narrow room (1-Q.29), at the end of which was a small paved room (8-Q.30). Of the three small rooms on the north side of the court, only the easternmost (7-S.29) was of particular interest. Here was found part of a drain which obviously was originally the connection between a small channel in the paving at the northeast corner of the court and a hole in the *kisû* facing just outside this room. The channel in the paving, which was 25 centimeters wide, was formed by the manipulation of brick rows, as indicated in the photograph (pl. 5a). It was only as deep as the thickness of the bricks, the bottom being the tamped earth upon which the bricks were laid. The sides and bottom of the channel were coated with bitumen. The drain within the room, which was approximately the same size, and also lined with bitumen, was formed in a strip of clay which crossed the room. The connection of this drain with the opening in the *kisû* face is discussed elsewhere (see pp. 39f.).

This room also contained two bread ovens (*tanoors*) and a third was found in the court. These, particularly the latter, appear to have been afterthoughts and are significant as early indications of the domestic use to which this unit of the north wing was put, and which resulted in the ultimate deterioration of the unit in later periods.

Room 6-R.30, on the south side, also contained equipment for cooking; there was a small U-shaped hearth of unbaked clay in the southwest corner (see fig. 3). The remaining room on this side, 5-R.30, contained no remarkable features.

The entrance to the large room, 1-Q.29 (pl. 5b), is referred to above. Here, instead of the projecting towers at each side found elsewhere in important entrances such as that of the antecella of the upper temple, the masses of masonry which contained the vertical slot decoration abutted the side walls of the court (1-R.29 and 30), and appeared, in plan, to form the wall surface at the west end of the court. However, because of the emphasis given this part by the vertical slots, it has been assumed that these faces actually rose slightly above the tops of the side walls, forming in effect low towers which were imperfectly expressed in plan, and which were limited in thickness to that of the east wall of room 2-R.30 (see perspective restoration [frontispiece] and restored sections A-A´ and D-D´, figs. 5 and 8). Between these towers was a wide doorway, decorated with the additional rabbeted face usually accorded to entrances of importance in this building. A pivotstone box proved that the door could be closed.

All these features indicated an important room; the size of the room (approximately 12.80 × 4.80 meters) made it the largest in the complex. It is remarkable, also, in that its long axis continues that of the court in front of it, and that it has connecting rooms around it, in the manner of a court. However, the room itself contained no features to indicate its use; the wide door at the west end, beyond which one would expect to find the focal point of the entire unit, led only to a small stairway connecting this part with the upper temple, which is discussed above. This stair was in a room (8-Q.30) so small that it could accommodate little else, and was certainly not a shrine, such as one might expect in this location on the plan. The disparity between the breadth of the doorway which led to this room, the cramped proportions of the room itself, and the stairway which it contained is striking. Neither of the rooms on the north of the large room (2-Q.29 and 2-R.29), nor the one room on the south side (7-Q.30) seem particularly important because of size or any particular feature. Therefore, it appears that the large room, 1-Q.29, was in itself the chief room of the unit, to which the smaller rooms adjoining were accessories. The room must also have been dignified by additional height, since it would have required a clerestory for lighting (see restored section A-A´, fig. 5).[11]

It is true that the original walls of the northern half of this room, and of the rooms north of it, had been replaced by those of the rebuilding of the north wing. However, the original floor existed and, particularly in 1-Q.29, it had been so little disturbed as to indicate that the walls had been rebuilt in their original position.

Perhaps more should be said of the stairs, since they constituted an important link between the upper and lower parts of the complex. They were constructed of baked brick, and as found were preserved to a height of 1.35 meters above the original floor (see fig. 3 and section A-A´, fig. 5). This represented five risers, each riser being consistently 27 centimeters in height. The risers were constructed of three courses of bricks, which were 8 centimeters in thickness. The remainder of the height of the riser was made up of the mortar between courses. Each tread was covered with a coating of bitumen about 1 centimeter thick. The breadth of the stair was one and one-half bricks, or approximately 58 centimeters. Three additional risers would have been required to bring the stair to the level of the floor within the upper temple at the door to 4-Q.30. Restoration accordingly allowed an adequate landing at the top outside this door.

The other unit which made up the north wing, centering around the court, 2-T.29 (see fig. 3 and pl. 6a), resembled the upper temple more closely in plan. Here, again, was a court which could be entered either from the large court or from outdoors, and the entrances were placed in positions similar to those in the upper temple. The outer entrance was similar to those on the south side of the complex, with its stairs and towers. However, the towers were smaller, being wide enough to accommodate only four slots, and the projection of the *kisû* in front of them, of which the north half was still completely preserved in outline, was simplified by the omission of the buttresses. The face of the towers was too poorly preserved to show the actual slots. However, the doorway itself containing its original paving still existed, with a pivotstone box behind it. The door to the court from the vestibule was not opposite the street door, but was in the middle of the wall of the court. There was a pivotstone box at this door in an intermediate period immediately following the original occupation, as well as in the later rebuilding.

The nonaligning of the doors was also employed in the entrance to the unit from the lower court (4-T.30). In 4-T.30 there was also a pivotstone box to indicate that the outer

---

11. [For a suggestion about the original function of 1-Q.29, see below, pp. 69f.]

door could be closed. The north and east walls had been destroyed to below floor level, but at the east end of the room the face of the wider foundation wall was found, as shown on the plan (see fig. 3).

There was still another entrance to this east unit, from the east wing of the lower building, through room 1-T.29. This peculiar duplication of entrances suggests that it was desired to have a connection leading directly from the east wing to this unit, so that the occupants could avoid passing through the public lower court. It heightens the probability that the east wing contained living quarters for the personnel of the temple, by whom this entrance could be used when the unit was closed to the public by the doors in its other entrances.

The court of the eastern unit (2-T.29) was like that of the west (1-R.29) in design (see frontispiece and section A-A´, fig. 5), except that it was somewhat shorter. There were the same balanced triple entrances on the long sides, and the wide towered entrance at the west end. The court was also bordered by a walk of baked brick; in addition there were two squares of baked brick in the otherwise unpaved area (see fig. 3). The easternmost of these had been broken into by a drain which was set down from a later floor. Two of the bricks were pierced with small holes, as for drainage, and below were remnants of vertical pottery drains. The presence of these led to the assumption, in the reconstruction, that the roofs immediately around the court were pitched toward the court, and drained into it by means of terracotta spouts.[12] In the middle of the western rectangle of paving was a single brick sunken to one course below the others. The depression in which it was set was bordered by half-bricks. Investigation below this feature gave no clue as to its purpose. A similar feature was a gap in the walk near the door to 7-T.29, created by the omission of one brick, and lined on two sides by narrow strips of brick. The bottom of this recess was the clay fill on which the bricks were laid. There was nothing in the earth just below this hole.

Except at the west end, the walls surrounding the court, like most of those in this unit, had been cut down to pavement level. However, they were traceable below this, where even the rabbeting of the doors was preserved. At the east end, the original towers and the entrance wall stood to the surface of the mound. Also, the walls of room 1-T.30, which had not been cut down for rebuilding, remained to this height. This room completed the row of rooms along the south side of the unit.

On the north, the rooms 6- and 7-T.29 had been largely destroyed down to floor level. But room 6-S.29, from the door westward, had not been leveled quite so low as this. Just west of the door there remained three steps of a mudbrick stairway, the treads of which were covered with baked brick. Behind this, mudbrick core extended some 4.50 meters, and beyond this the room was filled with debris. If, as seems probable, the stairs led to the roof, they would have extended the full length of the room, except for some room for a landing (see restoration, fig. 3). Probably the sill of debris behind the mudbrick core was covered above, originally, with mudbrick to form the steps; or, it is possible that the upper end of the stairs was finished in wood.

[The west wall of the court was occupied entirely by the monumental entrance mentioned earlier. This entrance duplicated in all respects the similar entrance in the west

12. [Part of such a roof drain was found in 7-S.29. See below, p. 50.]

wall of the court in the western unit described earlier; it had the same decoration with additional rabbeted face and was flanked on either side by the same kind of slotted simulated towers abutting the side walls of the court (pl. 6b). The sill was paved with baked bricks in extension of the paved walk of the court outside. The entrance gave access to a "broadroom," 2-S.29, which, in the original building period had not yet been made into a cella but seems rather to have served as antecella with the room behind it, 1-S.29, constituting the cella. Its most notable feature in its original form was a rectangular patch of bitumen covering the floor at the southeastern corner (fig. 3). This patch measured some 2 meters in length along the east wall and 1.50 meters in width along the south wall; its free northwestern corner was rounded. Apparently it was there for a purpose, for it was continued for some considerable time, as shown by the fact that it had been recoated ten times. Evidently it served to protect the floor from liquids spilt or seeping from cult vessels used or located here.]

[A rabbeted door of the same width as the entrance door and on the same axis, led through the west wall into 1-S.29, a slightly narrower room which presumably was the original cella. The western part of the original wall and all of the west wall which would have contained the cult niche had been destroyed anciently to make room for the clay foundations of the second building period. However, the later wall built to replace it followed its lines faithfully and even shows a niche of the width and at the point where the cult niche should have been. Since this niche would serve no purpose in the rebuilt room it can hardly be other than a conscientious reflection of a feature of the original wall.]

2. THE CONSTRUCTION OF THE SUBSTRUCTURE (BY TH. JACOBSEN)

The Kitîtum complex in its original form was built with sun-dried mudbricks laid in a mud mortar. These bricks measured 38 × 40 × 8 centimeters except directly inside the baked brick *kisû* where mudbricks of 40 × 40 × 9 centimeters were used (see below in section E.2 on the *kisû*). Baked bricks were employed sparingly, in stairs, and for protection against water as, e.g., in the *kisû*, in drains, in pavements, et cetera. There were two sizes, one of 36 × 36 × 8 centimeters for general use, and a larger one of 52 × 52 × 9 centimeters used for paving the sidewalks around the courts of the complex. The baked bricks, when exposed to the weather were generally laid in a bitumen mortar, and they could have bitumen coating on top. Bitumen alone, without underlying bricks, was used as protection for a patch of floor in 2-S.29, but that seems to have been an isolated case. Wood was presumably used for roofing and for doors, but no trace of wood of the original building periods survived.

Of special interest is the construction of the foundation terraces on which the temple complex stood. It was investigated in soundings put down at various points in the complex, the most important of which were at 6-Q.30, 2-P.31, and 2-R.31. From these soundings it appeared that the first thing done after the site for the complex had been chosen and marked out, was a rough leveling. The upper parts of standing structures—apparently mostly private houses—were torn down and filled into the lower parts, producing a low flat-topped mound of debris and stumps of razed walls a little less than a meter high. On the surface of this mound the plan of the complex was then laid out, and wherever walls were to be, narrow foundation trenches were cut through the layer of debris and into the ground below. In these trenches the mudbrick foundations of the buildings of the complex were then laid. In the deepest one of the soundings, the one in 6-Q.30, we encountered the razed tops of earlier walls belonging to a private house at a level of about 35.83; this was a little less than a meter above the ground level at that period, which was 34.85 (see section C-C′, fig. 7). The filling between the wall stumps was house debris and, below the debris, a succession of floors with traces of occupation. Where the wall stumps were cut by the foundations for the temple above, practically no space was left between the surface of the cuts in the earlier walls and the faces of the foundation walls cutting through them. Similar observations were made at the "Southern Building" at Tell Asmar[13] and, as there, these findings are only explicable if we assume that the foundation trenches were cut down from above exactly on the lines of the foundations. When the foundations were then laid in the trenches the bricks were laid all the way out to the side of the trench. How deep below the then general level of the ground the foundation trenches for the Kitîtum complex had been cut we could not ascertain, but it was certain that they went below it.

The mudbrick foundation walls built in the trenches were carried up above the surface of the debris mound all the way to the level of the main platform at 36.50 to 36.80 (see section B-B′, fig. 6). Their existence was verified in many deep soundings all through the complex. In all soundings, further, we found that the space between these foundation walls had been filled in with a filling of tamped clean earth. The top of this filling represented, in the eastern and lower part of the complex, the floor of rooms and courts, and had been treated accordingly. Also under the upper temple, however, this floor at a level of 36.80 meters seemed to carry through, for we encountered at that level an even mud surface resembling that of a floor except that—although exposed by us over a considerable area—it showed none of those traces of occupation always found on a floor that has been in use.

In the lower eastern part of the complex the actual above ground walls of the building stand on top of the foundation walls, which stop at the 36.80 to 36.50 meter level. They differ from the foundation walls by being somewhat narrower, by being plastered, and by showing a number of features uncalled for, or undesirable in a foundation, such as doorways, decoration by vertical T-shaped grooves, rabbeting, et cetera. Rather surprising was, however, to find that remarkably similar walls stood on the foundations also in the western part of the complex, under the upper temple, and formed the skeleton of the second, upper, platform. These walls, which are what is generally known as substructure walls, resemble walls above ground in so far as they too are narrower than the foundations, that they show every doorway of the building above even to the rabbeting, and that they repeat decoration with vertical T-shaped grooves found above. The only points in which they differ are that they are not plastered, that all doorways have been carefully blocked up with bricks to floor level, and that at least one very vital element of the building on top, the cult niche, is not repeated in the substructure. One should mention also that no traces of details like sills of baked bricks, pavements, et cetera, were found. The whole of the substructure was filled with tamped clean earth as was the

13. See Frankfort 1933, p. 31.

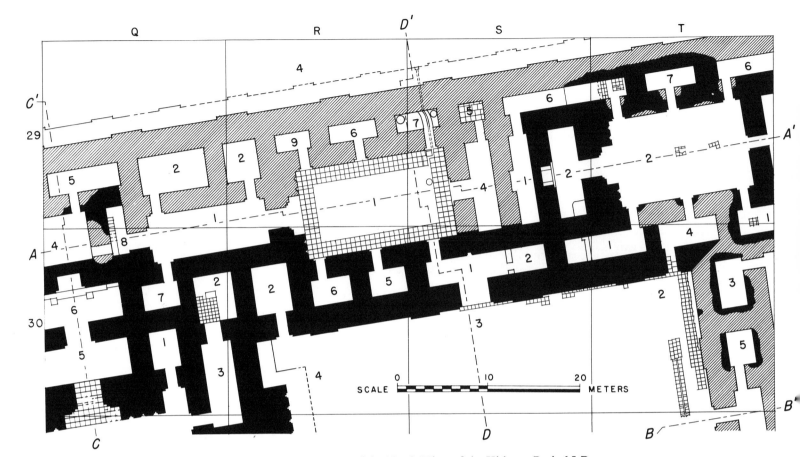

Figure 9. Ishchali—Plan of the North Wing of the Kitîtum, Period I-B.

foundation terrace below.[14] A possible reason for the use of this elaborate and seemingly quite unnecessary mode of construction is suggested below in section F on the history of temple plans.

3. SECONDARY OCCUPATION, PERIOD I-B (BY TH. JACOBSEN)

After the complex had been in use for a while, a re-flooring of the lower parts of it appears to have been needed and accordingly the floors were raised a few centimeters. At the same time the plan of the eastern unit of the north wing was changed from that of a temple with cella and antecella to one with cella only. The door in the west wall of 2-S.29 was blocked at the back to turn it into a niche and in the niche thus formed, on the original sill of baked bricks, a stand resembling an armchair was built with sun dried bricks and covered with a coat of mud plaster three centimeters thick (see fig. 9 and pl. 7a and b). The tops of the "armleans," which may have been rounded in toward the side walls of the niche, had unfortunately been cut by the later floor of the succeeding period, II-A. If the proposed restoration is correct one may compare the similarly shaped Early Dynastic

14. Other such substructures were found under the Sîn Temple IV at Khafājah (see Delougaz and Lloyd 1942, p. 21), under the Ur III Giparu at Ur (see Woolley 1926, p. 397), under the temple kitchen at Nippur (see McCown, Haines, and Hansen 1967, pp. 6, 19, and 27), and under the Harbour temple at Ur, which dates as late as Neo-Babylonian times (see Woolley 1962 and Moorey 1982, pp. 245ff.).

"altar" in "House D" in the Oval, in the Sîn and Nintu temples at Khafājah, and perhaps the Assyrian stand for a divine symbol of Tukulti-Ninurta.[15]

The blocking of the west door of 2-S.29 left the room behind it, 1-S.29, the original cella, with no means of access. Here, therefore, a door was opened in the north wall to a space freed through demolition of the stairway in 6-S.29, which was leveled down to the height of its third step only. Instead of carrying the debris from the demolished stairs out through the city for disposal, the remodeler simply spread it on the floor of 1-S.29, thus heightening it to the level of 6-S.29.

As the reasons behind the curious change from temple with cella and antecella to temple with cella only, one may surmise a change from a major to a minor deity as occupant. In its changed state the temple did, apparently, belong to a minor deity, Inanna's handmaiden Ninshubura (Ilaprat), for in the niche of room 1-S.29 west of the cella, a tablet (Ish. 35-T.99)[16] listing her treasures was found from the I-B period. Which major deity may have preceded her when the temple had both cella and antecella is a moot question. One might guess at the city god, or personal god, of the original builder of the temple, whose cult might well have been discontinued for political reasons when the city changed hands.

4. REBUILDING OF THE NORTH WING, PERIOD II-A

The third occupation of the original building (II-A) was marked by a rebuilding of the northernmost row of rooms of the north wing of the complex, and by a raising of the floor level in the lower part of the complex.

The reason for the rebuilding was apparently a settling of the walls in this part of the complex, testified to by the condition of the paved walks around the edges of the courts in both the western and eastern units of this wing (1-R.29 and 2-T.29). In both, the bricks laid against the walls were found tilted sharply down toward the wall, evidently forced into that position by the wall settling (see section D-D´, fig. 8 and pl. 8a). It seems reasonable to assume that the settling of the walls in the extreme northern row of rooms will have been even more severe, since they were the ones that were rebuilt.

The rebuilding followed conscientiously the lines of earlier walls that were replaced, so no change of plan was involved. A new feature was a flight of stairs in room 2-R.29 leading up to the roof (see fig. 10). The stairs were built of mudbrick with their upper flights supported on a corbeled arch.

5. FOURTH OCCUPATION, PERIOD II-B

The fourth occupation of the original building saw yet another re-flooring of the north wing. There was little change of plan except for the opening of a door in the wall between 7-S.29 and 5-S.29. The western unit of the wing, which earlier had been empty of special features was in this period found to be full of fireplaces for cooking, bread ovens, and other kitchen gear (see figs. 11 and 12). The fireplaces for cooking were, as natural in view of

15. See Delougaz 1940, p. 47, fig. 44 and p. 73, fig. 65 (Shrine of "House D" in the Oval). Also see Delougaz and Lloyd 1942, p. 17, figs. 79-81 (Nintu temple) and Meissner 1925, pl. 24.

16. [See OBTIV 106 in Greengus 1986, pp. 46-47 and p. 48, n. 29. Note that the findspots for OBTIV 104-106 listed as 2-S.29 in Greengus 1979 on p. 54 should read 1-S.29.]

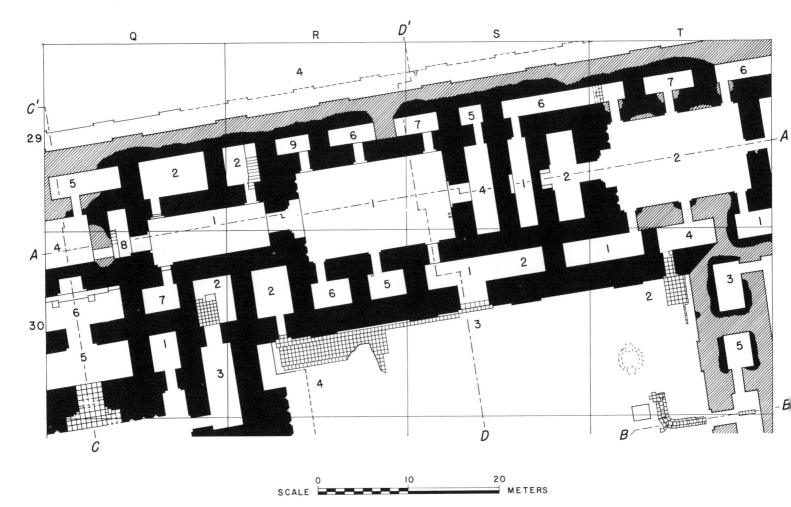

Figure 10. Ishchali—Plan of the North Wing of the Kitîtum, Period II-A.

their size, restricted to the courtyard (1-R.29, pl. 19a) and to the main room (1-Q.29, pl. 18b) west of it. The size of the fireplaces also suggests that food could have been prepared for a considerable number of people at any time.

In the central court of the complex the well in the northeast corner (2-T.30) was lined in its lower parts with baked bricks of this period ($40 \times 40 \times 9.50$ centimeters). It is not clear whether this represents an original lining of the well or, as seems more probably, merely a relining. Built into the period I pivotstone box in nearby 4-T.29 were segmental bricks which could well be surplus of bricks used in the original well.

A few meters south of the well was a block of mudbrick masonry measuring 2 meters square in plan and 1.50 meters high. It seems to have been served by a drain constructed of baked bricks with the stamp of Ipiq-Adad II and measuring $40 \times 40 \times 9.50$ centimeters. The drain began slightly north of the block, ran south along its east side and then east toward the door to 3-T.31 where it was cut by the clay foundations of period III (see fig. 11 and pl. 9a and b). Originally the drain must have passed through at this point all the way to the outside of the building, but it had been destroyed anciently and only a line of fragments of bitumen remained to indicate its course. The purpose served by this block of

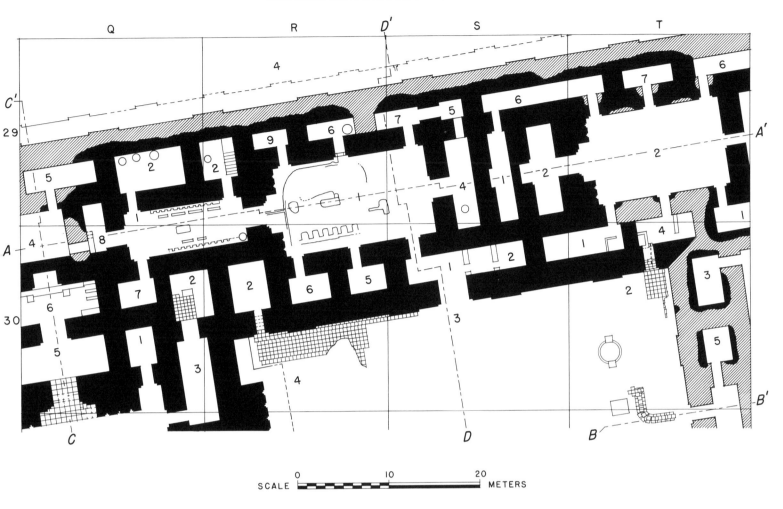

Figure 11. Ishchali—Plan of the North Wing of the Kitîtum, Period II-B.

masonry and its drain is not clear except for the obvious suggestion that liquid, probably water from the nearby well, was involved.[17]

The period ended in a general conflagration extending beyond the complex and affecting the buildings of the town around it. How far it raged was not ascertained.

C. THE SECOND BUILDING PERIOD (III)

1. THE PLAN

The conflagration which ended the fourth occupation of the original building made extensive rebuildings necessary. They involved the westernmost row of rooms of the upper temple, the northwest corner with the unit around 4-Q.30, as well as all of the north wall, the east wing, and the south wing of the lower part of the complex.

As before, the rebuilding followed the earlier walls faithfully and so brought no changes in plan of any significance. A number of flimsy shacks were built in the court of the western unit of the north wing, seemingly to serve as living or working quarters for

17. A conjecture is offered below on p. 70.

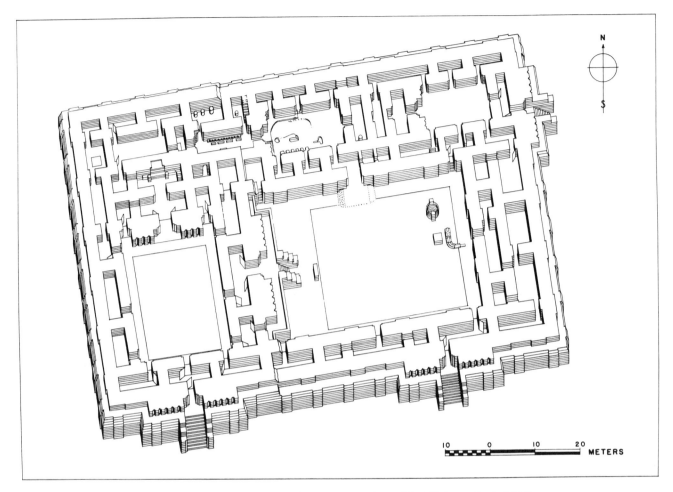

Figure 12. Ishchali—Isometric Reconstruction of the Kitîtum, Period II-B.

personnel. They have rooms of 2×2, 2×3, and 3×3 meters and in these rooms were pots, numerous potsherds, fireplaces, bread ovens, et cetera, and the floors were covered with ashes as in the private houses (see plan, fig. 13, and pl. 10a).

In the adjoining room to the west, 1-Q.29, the fireplaces for cooking were in this period replaced by two standard clay kitchen ranges (cf. pl. 10b) and three circular bread ovens (fig. 14).

2. THE CONSTRUCTION

The rebuilder took pains about the founding of the new structure. The old standing walls were removed to far below floor level and the resultant trenches—usually dug a little wider than the removed walls—were filled with substantial foundations made of solid clay (pl. 11a). On these foundations the new walls were then set.

In connection with the rebuilding, the floor level was raised both in the lower and upper parts of the complex and new outer stairs were built at 2-Q.33, 2-T.32, and 2-U.29 to accommodate to a notable rise in the street level outside. This rise, which had occurred gradually since the time of the original building, also necessitated a heightening of the *kisû* around the lower part of the complex.

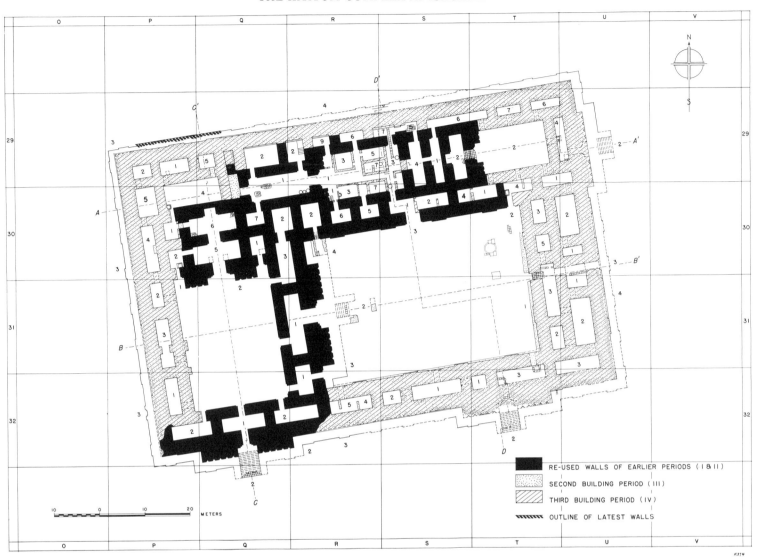

Figure 13. Ishchali—Plan of the Kitîtum, Periods III-IV.

The general raising of the floors brought the north wing up higher than the central court to the south of it, and short stairs were accordingly built in the south doors of 2-R.30 and 4-T.30 while the monumental entrance in the middle of the court wall, the south door of 1-S.30, was served by an upward slope of the floor of the court at this point.

D. THE THIRD BUILDING PERIOD (IV)

The walls of the second building period must have proved defective in one way or another, for in the following third building period they were all replaced with new walls throughout the complex. As usual, the general plan remained unchanged in all essentials and only minor adjustments were made (figs. 13 and 14).

In the eastern unit of the north wing, a narrow door was cut through the niche in the west wall of 1-S.29 to 4-S.29. At the same time the wide west doorway of the latter room was blocked up, presumably to shield the room from the noise and bustle of the adjoining court 1-R.29, where the shacks of period III were still in use. There was still access to

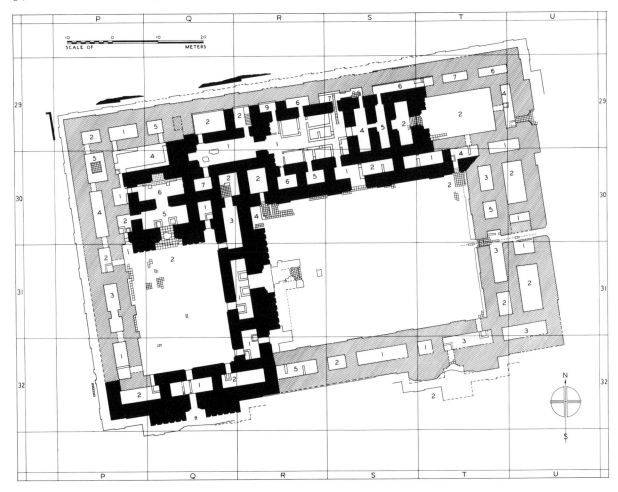

Figure 14. Ishchali—Plan of the Kitîtum, Period IV (Uppermost Level).

court 1-R.29 if needed through 5-S.29 and 7-S.29 (see fig. 13). In its new form, however, 4-S.29 now looked to the east rather than to the west. It was part of a unit consisting of 4-S.29, 1-S.29, and 6-S.29 (see figs. 14 and 15) which seems to have housed an accounting unit of the temple, for tablets dealing with the handing out of agricultural implements to workmen were found scattered over the floors of both 4-S.29 and 1-S.29 and some had even spilled over into the court 2-T.29.

In the eastern unit of the north wing to which the accounting unit belonged, and which apparently still functioned as the temple of Ninshubura, the floor of the cella 2-S.29 was, curiously enough, not raised with the other floors of the building. Perhaps there was a reluctance to interfere with arrangements in the cult niche. As a result the floor remained some 25 centimeters lower than that of the court and steps of baked bricks led down to it. These bricks bore the stamp of Ibal-pî-el II to whom the rebuilding of the third building period (IV) may plausibly be assigned. The steps, the cella floor, and the standing stumps of the walls all show traces of fire from the conflagration that ended this period of occupation. On the floor of the room were fragments of charred beams fallen from the roof (pl. 12a and b). The best preserved piece was oblong in section, 0.12 centimeters high to 0.20 centimeters wide, but probably the oblong section was due to pressure exerted by the ground above and the beam was originally a round one. The cult niche had in this

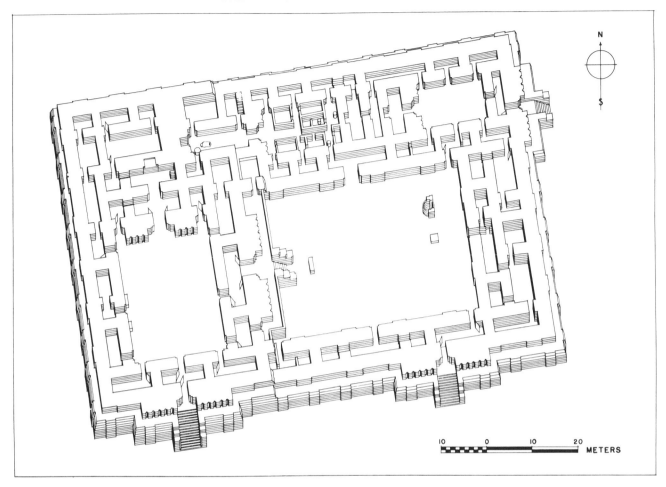

Figure 15. Ishchali—Isometric Reconstruction of the Kitîtum, Periods III-IV.

period a single rabbet but nothing similar to the earlier "armchair" arrangement. Across it we found on the floor remnants of three charred planks lying side by side. The best preserved piece measured 3 × 13.50 × 100 centimeters. It was not preserved to its original length. All the planks had been carefully planed and the texture of the wood differed from that of the roofing beams found out in the room. To judge from the position in which these planks were found they probably had constituted a lintel for the niche. This should therefore be reconstructed with a flat top and not arched.

Besides the charred remains of beams there were also a few thin pieces that looked like rafters, and the floor was to its full extent covered with a thin layer of white ashes above which was a layer of charred powderish substance showing no pattern. Above that came a heavier layer of relatively clean clay. These findings—although hardly definite enough to allow any actual conclusions—would be naturally explained if the roof had consisted of heavy beams supporting thinner rafters and covered first with a tight layer of palm leaves and above that with a layer of clay.

In the east wing of the complex, a minor and yet notable adjustment of the earlier plan was made. Here, in the east wall of 1-U.31 (see fig. 14) a cut was made to create an additional rabbeted entrance to the complex from the outside. Consonantly with later architectural preference this entrance was placed in the medial axis of the central court and led through the aligned doors of the two gaterooms, 1-U.30-31 and 3-T.30-31, into the court directly opposite the stairs to the upper temple. Due to the rise in street level at this period no outer stairs were apparently needed.

In the northeastern corner of the main court (2-T.30, fig. 13) the well was carried up above the new floor level and was lined with baked bricks measuring 32 × 32 × 8.50 centimeters and carrying the stamp of Ibal-pî-el II. In the north and south sides of the lining two earlier brick pillars for carrying a winch or other hoisting apparatus was built in. They were preserved only in their lower parts which were part of the lining (pl. 13a).

The floor level at the well and to the south of it seems to have remained much the same as it was in the preceding period III, probably the floor of this part of the central court was not raised with the rest, so the square block of mudbrick masonry was apparently still in use. The drain beside it, however, was replaced with an open drain at higher level with a flooring of baked bricks with Ibal-pî-el's brick stamp. This open drain carried into 3-T.31 under a pavement and sill of baked bricks in the west door (pl. 9b). These bricks likewise had Ibal-pî-el's stamp.

The third building period perished, like the second, in a conflagration. It was the last of which any substantial traces remained, but there may have been still later rebuilding—or attempts at rebuilding—of the complex, for a fragment of a still later wall face could be traced at the north west edge. There was nothing left, however, to connect with it.

E. DETAILED DESCRIPTION OF THE ARCHITECTURAL
REMAINS AND SMALL FINDS

1. THE FACADE

The original outer walls of the complex are preserved in the northeast and southwest corners and at a few other disconnected points. Everywhere else they have been cut away by later foundations of periods II-A and III. Fragmentary as is this evidence, it suffices, though, to reconstruct the line of the walls with a fair degree of certainty, and to establish the fact that they were decorated all along their course with alternating buttresses and bays in the manner typical of Babylonian sacred architecture.

a. South Side

The western half of the south facade of the complex is original wall, the eastern is foundations of periods II-A and III (see fig. 3). In the western half is the gate giving access to the upper temple from the south. The gate is flanked by two towers each of which is decorated at the front with a panel of five vertical T-shaped grooves. The doorway itself has a double rabbet. On either side of the towers the nearest wall buttress was broadened so that it would abut the tower and thus the gate is emphasized by a solid projection of the wall for a distance of some five meters to both sides. The vertical T-shaped grooves of the towers are here, as elsewhere in the building, constructed partly of mudbrick and partly of plaster. U-shaped grooves were first spaced out in the brick work of the wall, and the two innermost corners of these grooves were then filled in with square panels of plaster changing them into T-shaped grooves. This method of constructing vertical T-shaped grooves has to my knowledge not been found elsewhere (cf. pl. 13b). The normal way of constructing such grooves is to build them all through with mudbrick cut to shape.

Corresponding to the gate of the upper temple and balancing it is a second gate in the eastern half of the south wall leading into the central court of the lower part of the complex. Also this gate has towers and the wall projects on either side of them as at the gate in the western half; this time, however, only for a distance of 2.50 meters at each tower; otherwise the dimensions are practically the same. The decoration of these towers was presumably the same as on the other gate, but the original wall is almost completely cut away by later foundations.

As to the original height of the wall one must rely on conjecture. The considerations which guided Mr. Hill in his reconstruction (see figs. 5–8 and frontispiece) he set out in a letter to me of October 13, 1936 as follows:

> You can judge by the figures of the men, whom I have made about 1.70
> centimeters tall [on original drawings—Gen. Ed.], the scale of the building.
> I arrived at the wall height by comparison with other construction drawings
> and by what seemed a logical proportion in the sections of the rooms.

As will be seen it led him to assume the height of the wall of the gate towers of the upper temple were three times that of the *kisû* which is exactly the proportion of the temple wall and *kisû* given by Ur-Baba in his description of the temple for Ningirsu he built at Girsu.[18]

b. East Side

The east facade of the complex has in its northern part a gate leading into the eastern unit of the north wing (see fig. 13). The gate, except for the fact that the towers are narrower with only four vertical T-shaped grooves each, and that the projections of the wall on either side are not of the same width, resembles closely the gates of the south facade. That the northernmost projection is narrower than that to the south is evidently due to the fact that the gate does not come exactly in the middle between two buttresses, for the projections are merely the two buttresses nearest to the towers widened so as to abut them.

At 3-U.30, slightly to the south of the middle point of the wall, a secondary entrance was cut in period IV (above, pp. 35f.). It had a rabbeted doorway but no towers and led through 1-U.30-31 and 3-T.30-31 into the main court.

---

18. See Thureau-Dangin 1907, p. 60, Statue, iii. 3-7.

^{3}uš murub-bi mu-ak ^{4}ugu$_x$(SAG × ugu$_4$)-bi-a ki-sá-a 10 kùš-àm bí-dù
^{5}ugu$_x$(SAG × ugu$_4$)-ki-sá-a-ka ^{6}É-ninnu-bar$_6$-bar$_6$ 30 kùš-àm ^{7}mu-nà-dù

... in its midst I constructed foundations and on their tops I built a ten ell *kisû* and on its
top I built for him (i.e., Ningirsu) Eninnu, the flashing thunderbird being 30 ells

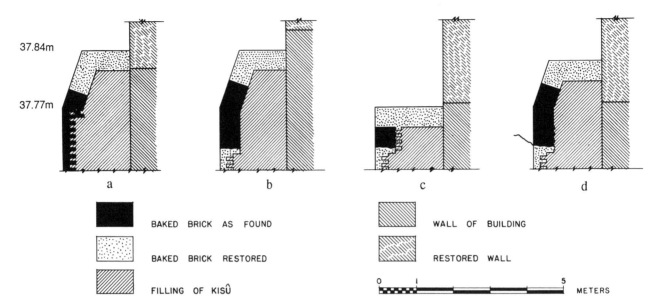

Figure 16. Ishchali—Architectural Sections through the Kitītum *Kisû*: (*a*) High *Kisû* as Originally Built (Based on Section as Found, Next to First Buttress from West, North Side of Building), (*b*) High *Kisû* as Repaired in Period II-A (Based on *Kisû* as Found Next to Third Buttress From West, North Side), (*c*) Low *Kisû* as Originally Built (Based on *Kisû* as Found Next to Drain, North of 7-S.29, combined with Remnants at 3-U.30), (*d*) Low *Kisû* as Raised in Period II-A (Based on *Kisû* Next to Drain, North of 7-S.29).

c. North Side

Only a single buttress of the original north wall of the complex remained in grid square T.28 (see fig. 3). Of the walls of later periods, however, since the mound is higher at this side than elsewhere, we found not only the foundations but also—from 6-S.29 and westward—the lower part of the actual wall. This wall is decorated with plain buttresses varying slightly in width and also somewhat irregularly spaced. Only the actual wall is buttressed, the foundation is plain and its face is aligned with the front faces of the buttresses. The wall belongs to period IV and the foundations to period III.

d. West Side

On the west side of the complex only the foundations of the wall of period IV remained.

2. THE *KISÛ*

The main platform, formed of the filled in substructure on which the complex rested, was enclosed on all sides with a retaining wall or *kisû* which consisted of a mudbrick core with a facing of baked bricks (see fig. 16a). This *kisû* was fairly well preserved all along the west side of the complex (cf. pl. 14), but had suffered considerable damage at the hands of brick robbers elsewhere. Fortunately, however, the brick robbers had been content to work their way down removing the bricks one by one without disturbing either the core of mudbrick or the accumulated layers of the street on the other side. By clearing away the loosely packed, easily distinguishable mixture of fallen earth and broken bricks left where the robbers had worked, we were able to obtain, therefore, what amounted to an exact cast of the facing, often so clear that impressions of individual bricks were discernible. From this evidence the existence and contours of the *kisû* could be ascertained even when every single actual brick had been removed.

As mentioned, the *kisû* consisted of a mudbrick core with a facing of baked bricks. The baked bricks were uninscribed, measured 36 × 36 × 9 centimeters and were bonded with the mudbricks of the core. These mudbricks were considerably larger, measuring 40 × 40 × 9 centimeters. They abutted the face of the outer wall of the substructure of the complex without being bonded into it. The mortar used for the baked bricks was bitumen, so that the casing formed a watertight mantle protecting the mudbrick behind it against rainwater. An exception formed a point at the northwest corner where the *kisû* dipped down some 85 centimeters below the surface of the ground, probably because the builders encountered a soft spot of ground that had to be dug through to firmer footing. Here the lowest courses of the facing which would be underground and not exposed to rain were laid in clay mortar. The mudbricks of the core were laid in clay mortar throughout. The *kisû* had no foundation but was built directly on the ground at ground level.

In its original form the part of the *kisû* that enclosed the lower parts of the complex rose to the level of the floors inside the building, some 3.50 meters above the ground outside. It ended in a thick pavement of baked brick laid flat from the top of the casing into the outer wall of the building (see section, fig. 16c). Remnants of this pavement were found at 3-U.30.

In the higher, western part of the complex, the *kisû* shows, at the level where the lower *kisû* ends, the beginning of a batter (pl. 15b). The bonding of facing and core is here discontinued and the facing, which is now built as a separate wall one and one-half bricks deep, is tilted inward at an oblique angle (pl. 16a). The inner half of the first tilted course does not rest directly on the mudbrick of the core, but is supported by baked half bricks (see section, fig. 16a). The top of the battered *kisû* is nowhere preserved intact but it seems logical to assume that it ended with a flat pavement level with the floor level inside the buildings of the upper part of the complex. This is supported by the fact that the towers at the south gate have vertical T-shaped grooves beginning at floor level. It seems unlikely that this decoration would have been concealed in its lower parts by the *kisû*.

In the rebuilding of the north wing in period II-A the low *kisû* of that area was rebuilt too. The casing was raised and given a batter similar to that of the high *kisû* further west and a new core filling was put in behind it (see sections, fig. 16c and d). Lastly, in the general rebuilding in period III, the new clay foundations were widened to serve also as the new core for the *kisû*.

The face of the *kisû* was decorated with alternating buttresses and bays along the walls; the buttresses measure 2.30 meters, the bays 5.45 meters in width. The spacing makes the four corners of the complex fall each at the middle of what would have been a bay between two buttresses. Curiously enough no attempt to relate the buttressing of the *kisû* to that of the similar scheme of decoration in the wall of the building about it appears to have been made.

At several points along the *kisû* there were vertical slots. The best preserved one occurred on the north side of the complex outside room 7-S.29 (see section, fig. 17 and pl. 16b). It is some 40 centimeters wide to 15 centimeters deep in its lower, original, part; but some 20 centimeters deep from the level of the II-A rebuilding and up. At the bottom, it is

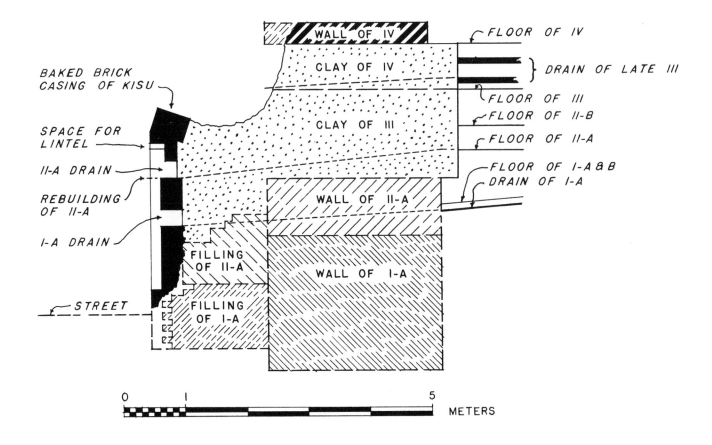

Figure 17. Ishchali—Architectural Section through the *Kisû* and Outer Wall of the Kitîtum Building at 7-S.29.

closed with a bitumen covered sill and at the top it ended against a wooden sill that has now disappeared. Two square holes in the back wall of the slot served as outlets for drains of two different periods leading from the court 1-R.29 out through 7-S.29 (see fig. 3). The lowest of these outlets served the drain of the original building, period I-A. The upper one served a drain of period II-A, lost in the period III rebuilding and, still higher, in a part of the *kisû* now lost will have been the outlet for the well-preserved drain of period III (see fig. 13).

A similar slot with a hole in its back wall and closed above with a wooden sill occurred in the third buttress east of the northwest corner of the *kisû* and still another example— less well preserved—was found in the third buttress west of the northeast corner. In none of these cases however, did we find traces of drains inside the buildings with which they could have been connected. It is not excluded, though, that such drains may once have existed and may have subsequently been lost in one or other of the extensive rebuildings.

On the west side of the complex the third buttress of the *kisû*, from the southwest corner, shows at a level of 37.86 meters a horizontal row of five square holes partially filled with bitumen (pl. 17a). This feature is as yet unexplained. Also puzzling is a shallow rabbeted niche in the second buttress from that corner, closed at the bottom with a lintel of baked brick at level 35.91 meters. The top of the niche is not preserved.

The three towered entrances to the original complex were served by stairs faced with baked bricks which unfortunately made them a target for brick robbers. Thus at 2-U.29, at the entrance in the east side, nothing is left of the stairs, and at 2-T.32, on the south side, only fragments of two steps have survived. Better, fortunately, is the situation at the third staircase, the one to the upper part of the complex at 2-Q.33. Here enough remains to give a general idea of what the outside stairs were like. The *kisû*, following the outline of the two massive gate towers forms a square bastion in front of the gate and from the face of this bastion remnants of the original staircase stretch south for 2.90 meters. They show that the staircase had a clay core encased in baked bricks that were of the same kind as those in the *kisû* and were bonded into it. Only the two lowest courses of this casing remain except at the front where the first four steps are preserved. They consist of two courses of baked brick each and are protected by a covering of bitumen. A brick of the inner face of the western casewall still remained in position, indicating that the casewall was four bricks wide and that it only started with the third step, leaving the first two free in their full length.

At high level, ca. 36.20 meters, remnants of three further steps were found. They belong to period III when the complex was rebuilt and the rise that had occurred in the street level called for the construction of new outer stairs.

3. THE UPPER TEMPLE

a. South Rooms

2-Q.32, Rectangular room. The walls were plastered and a door was situated in the west part of the north wall to the upper court. A pivotstone box was located at the west jamb (see fig. 3). Both the door and the room were filled in solid with mudbrick.

1-Q.32, Rectangular gateroom. The plastered walls of period I rested on unplastered substructure walls. The doors in the middle of the north and south walls led to the upper court and outside respectively. Both doors were blocked with mudbrick to the surface of the mound. A single pivotstone box stretching from the south to north wall at the west jambs of the doors served both. The box was built with mudbricks, $38 \times 38 \times 10$ centimeters and baked bricks, $34 \times 34 \times 7.50$ centimeters. A pot was located in the northwest corner of the room. A terracotta model bed fragment (Ref. 34:145) was found in the top levels belonging to period III or IV.

2-P.32, Rectangular room. Plastered walls of period I rested on unplastered substructure walls. The door in the east part of the north wall to the upper court was blocked with mudbrick to the surface of the mound. A pivotstone box at the east jamb was built of mudbricks measuring $38 \times 38 \times 10$ centimeters. The north wall was cut by the clay foundation of period III from a point 40 centimeters east of the northwest corner to the middle of the door down into substructure.

b. Court

1-P.31 and 2-Q.31, Rectangular court. At the northern end are remnants of a common
floor of periods III and IV; otherwise the floor is one common to periods I and II. The
period III rebuilding of the west wall shows irregular buttressing. There are remnants of
paving of a period I floor with baked bricks of 52 × 52 × 9 centimeters at the west wall,
and probably remnants of a paved walk along the edges of the court. Other remnants of
paving on the floor south of the west tower in the north wall have baked bricks of 36 × 36
× 8.50 centimeters. At the center of the court were two bricks, 40 × 40 × 9.50 centimeters,
both with the stamp of Ipiq-Adad II (period IV). In the north wall is a towered and double
rabbeted gate leading to the antecella 5-Q.30. The towers are decorated with three
vertical T-shaped grooves each. The entrance is paved at the floor of period I with baked
bricks, 52 × 52 × 9 centimeters, covered with a thick layer of bitumen. Two cylinder seals,
Ish. 34:128 and Ish. 34:68 (OIP 72, pl. 86:902, 903), were found in the northwest corner of
the court (1-P.31) on the floor of periods I and II. At the northeast corner (2-Q.31), on the
same floor, were three letters, Ish. 34-T.95 (to the "bishop" [*sangû*] Abizum), Ish. 34-
T.94 (to sangû),[19] and Ish. 34-T.93 (from Dingir-ré-ma-an-sum, name of addressee
damaged), and also a list of commodities, Ish. 34-T.87.

c. Cella and Adjoining Rooms

2-P.30, Almost square room. The western half of the room was cut by the wall and clay
foundation of period III. The cut runs through the door in the south wall and cuts the north
wall ca. 10 centimeters west of the northeast corner. Doors are located in the original east
wall leading to the antecella, 5-Q.30, and in the south wall to the court. Two pivotstone
boxes, one of baked bricks at the west jamb of the door, and another, later one, of
mudbrick, apparently replaced it at the east jamb (see fig. 14). In the south door there
were remnants in bitumen of a sill of baked brick. A bronze lamp in the shape of a lion
(Ish. 34:51) and the head of another were found in this room and are dated to period III-IV
(pl. 30a-d).[20]

1-Q.30, Almost square room. A door is located in the south wall leading to the court
with a pivotstone box of mudbrick at the east jamb. Along the east wall is a facing of
baked bricks placed flat up against it.

5-Q.30, Rectangular "broadroom" antecella (pl. 17b). Two doors are located at the
centers of the south and north walls to the court, 2-Q.31, and cella, 6-Q.30, respectively.
The one to the cella is rabbeted. Another door is located in the west wall leading to 2-
P.30. At both jambs of the south door were pivotstone boxes of baked brick (pl. 18a).
Both showed traces of fire on their insides, presumably the fire at the end of period II-A.
In the eastern box, which was undisturbed, the pivotstone was still in position; it rested
on a layer of sand and was held in position by a 15 centimeters thick layer of stamped
earth surrounding it on all sides. Above this layer the box was filled with granulated clay

19. See OBTIV 4 in Greengus 1986, p. 11.
20. See also Frankfort 1936, p. 98 and figures 75-76 on p. 97. For "in the antecella" read "in a room next to the
     antecella."

mixed with straw similar to the floor filling of periods III and IV in the rest of the room and in the cella. In the southeast corner of the box, level with the surface of the pivotstone, period III, was a collection of twenty beads (Ish. 34:71), two Old Babylonian cylinder seals (Ish. 34:69 and 72),[21] and an early stamp seal (Ish. 34:73, pl. 42c). In the floor fill (III-IV) of period IV was an unfinished cylinder seal (Ish. 34:47, OIP 72, p. 61), a stamp seal (Ish. 34:56, pl. 42a), and an Early Dynastic cylinder seal (Ish. 34:46, OIP 72, pl. 86:901). Other objects found in the room in that fill were a clay plaque depicting two dancers (Ish. 34:41, OIC 20, fig. 73b and pl. 35b here), two plaques depicting walking lions, one nearly complete (Ish. 34:57, OIC 20, fig. 72d and pl. 38a here), the other missing the rear half (Ish. 34:58, pl. 38b), a stone macehead, 2.90 × 4.00 centimeters (Ish. 34:55), and a tablet dated to MU GUD-APIN KÙ-GI. (Ish. 34-T.70).[22]

6-Q.30, Rectangular "broadroom" cella. One door in the south wall leads to 5-Q.30 and another in the west wall to 1-P.30. The east jamb of the door to 5-Q.30 was damaged in period III or IV and was repaired with a facing of fragmentary baked bricks starting from the floor. The cult niche is situated in the center of the north wall directly opposite the south door, to which it corresponds in width. It has a single rabbet at the sides and is 2.50 meters deep. In front of the niche, their inner faces aligned with the outer side of the rabbet, stand two square columns built of mudbrick which are plastered. These columns belong to the original floor and rose, when found, to the level of the floor of periods III and IV above. It was clear, however, that originally they had been higher, for the leveling of the floor of periods III and IV had cut in half the thickness of the bricks of their uppermost course. Between these columns and in the niche behind them were traces of a dais built of baked bricks laid in bitumen. Practically all of the bricks had been removed anciently, but the imprint they had left on the walls of the niche and in the floor-filling of periods III and IV were definite enough to show the plan and to give also some idea of the height of the dais. In plan the dais formed a rectangular block extending from the niche out between the two columns where it ended in a plain vertical face, the imprint of which was clear in the filling of periods III and IV. As to height, pieces of bitumen mortar on the wall of the niche at a height of 80 centimeters above the original floor indicate a minimum, but general considerations might well favor as much as a meter and a half as reasonable. From the sides of the niche a shallow groove with the imprint of a row of baked bricks stretched out along the wall for a length of two meters to either side. Whether this represented a single line of bricks only, or, as seems more likely, low bench-like structures, must be left open. For a discussion of the reconstruction of this part of the cella see above p. 12 and below p. 73.

A marble stamp seal (Ish. 34:135, pl. 42f) was found on the floor of the cella along with a number of other recorded finds (not illustrated) listed in the *Catalogue of 1934 Reference Numbers* (app. 2) with the designation "Ref."

The features and objects mentioned above all belong to periods I and II. The later of these periods ended in a conflagration, traces of which were observable in the debris

21. See Frankfort 1955, pl. 86:912 and 911. Note that the designation Ish. 34-127 given to Ish. 34:69 in Frankfort 1936, p. 88 and fig. 68 is incorrect.
22. See Greengus 1979, pl. 73:219.

covering the common floor of these periods. In the following periods III and IV the floor seems to have stretched evenly all through the room. Whether it also continued into the niche or whether there was a dais of baked bricks here as in the preceding periods could not be ascertained since the floor stopped against the outlines of the hole dug when the bricks of the original dais were removed. In the floor of period IV were a shell ring and other shell fragments (Ish. 35:21, pl. 46d).

At the southwest and northeast corners of the 6-Q.30 room were remnants of periods III and IV pavements of baked brick. On the former of these pavements lay the cylinder seal of Mattatum with a dedication to Inanna Kitîtum (Ish. 34:45, OIP 72, pl. 87:917), and two lion-shaped amulets or (?)weights (Ish. 34:42 and 43, pl. 44a, b). On the upper floor of period III-IV were a letter with seal impression of Abizum, sangû of Kitîtum and servant of Ibal-pî-el (Ish. 34-T.74), an account of gold dated to *šanat* ÍD-ŠÀ-URU^{ki} [*ip*]-*pé-tu-ú* (Ish. 34-T.64),[23] a record of cattle (Ish. 34-T.63),[24] and one of fields (Ish. 34-T.67). Robber dumps at this locality yielded tablets dated to MU ^{giš}GIGIR-GAL-NU-DI ^dUTU (Ish. 34-T.111), *šanat* ^{giš}*narkabat šēpi ša* ^d*Adad* (Ish. 34-T.109), and MU GUD-APIN KÙ-GI (Ish. 34-T.110) as well as a letter (Ish. 34-T.73).

1-P.30, Square room. Doors are located in the east wall leading to the cella, 6-Q.30, and in the north wall to 4-Q.30. The western part of the north wall and the west and south walls were cut by the clay foundations of period III to a level of 37.98 meters and below that lay the substructure walls. On the clay foundations, on a layer of ashes, were the walls of period IV. Floors of I and II were made of lumps of pure clay. Against the east wall in periods III and IV was a facing or bench of mudbrick one brick deep. The period IV finds from this room included an Old Babylonian hematite cylinder seal (Ish. 34:121, OIP 72, pl. 87:916).

4-Q.30, Rectangular room. There are doors in the south wall to 1-P.30, and in the north wall to 1-P.29 and 5-Q.29. The doors belong to period IV except for the east jamb of the south door that forms part of the south wall, which is original from the door to the southeast corner. The other walls all belong to period IV. They rest on a layer of ashes which in turn rests on clay foundations of period III. The line of the layer of ashes is covered up with a layer of heavy plaster except at the doors and on the west wall, where the ashes were left exposed. The south wall shows marked traces of fire. They were covered by a period IV filling of pure clay and mudbrick from the level of the plaster and up. At the west jamb of the door in the south wall is a pivotstone box of baked brick of period I or II. In the room on floor I-II was found a fragment of a carved cylindrical cup of alabaster (Ish. 34:30, pl. 25a) showing parts of two robed figures walking toward a gate held open for them by an attendant. Below the figures is the conventional design representing mountains. On this floor also were four stamp seals (Ish. 34:133-137, pl. 42b, d, e, and g). On the III-IV floor was a pig-shaped amulet (Ish. 34:130), a carved bowl

23. Greengus 1979, pl. 43:98 and OBTIV 98 in Greengus 1986, pp. 44-45.
24. Greengus 1979, pl. 50:120 and OBTIV 120 in Greengus 1986, p. 54.

fragment with mouflon heads (Ish. 34:117, see OIC 20, figs. 78, 79, and pls. 31-32 here), a bowl base (Ish. 34:32, pl. 40g, h), a fragment of ostrich shell (Ish. 34:31), forty-three beads (Ish. 34:33, pl. 43b), eight cylinder seals (Ish. 34:37, 38, 39, 48, 49, 50, 86, and 87; for Ish. 34:39, 48, 49, 50, 86, and 97 see OIP 72, Ish. 34:39, 48, and 49 = pl. 87:923, 922, 925; Ish. 34:50 = p. 61; Ish. 34:86 = pl. 86:910; and Ish. 34:87 = pl. 87:924), a round school tablet (Ish. 34-T.92), and an account of sheep lost (Ish. 34-T.59).[25] An unstratified alabaster bowl fragment (Ish. 34:44, pl. 40d) also came from this room as well as a plaque fragment (Ish. 34:201, pl. 41a) dated to period IV.

1-P.29, Rectangular room. A door is in the south wall to 4-Q.30. The walls belong to period IV and rest upon clay foundations of period III. In the south wall was a layer of ashes between the wall and foundation. Below the clay foundations are walls of the substructure. A pivotstone box at the east jamb of the door was built of fragments of baked bricks and belonged to period II-A. In the room at the level of period I-II, were found accounts of gold and precious stones (Ish. 34-T.69a,[26] Ish. 34-T.88, and Ish. 34-T.90), the latter dated to MU ᵍⁱˢGU-ZA. Also there was a list of disbursements to individuals (Ish. 34-T.91).[27] These finds and the fact that the room could be closed, unusual in an inside room, suggest that it served as depository for the goddess' jewelry and other treasures. Three cylinder seals are dated to period III-IV (Ish. 34:34, 35, and 36; see OIP 72, pl. 86:915, p. 60, and pl. 86:914).

5-Q.29, Square room. A door in the south wall leads to 4-Q.30 (see fig. 13). The walls belong to period IV and rest on the clay foundations of period III. Between the walls and foundations were ashes. The floor filling was of mudbricks made with sand.

d. West Rooms

1-P.32, Rectangular room. All walls were replaced with the clay foundations of period III. Below the clay foundations (at ca. 36.35 meters) are walls of the substructure (at ca. 36.40 meters), and below that the foundation. Across the room at the south end runs the mudbrick wall of a pivotstone box (see fig. 3) that served a door to the court in periods I and II.

3-P.31, Rectangular room with door in south wall to a small square room considered part of locus 3-P.31 (see fig. 13). The walls consist of two to three courses of mudbrick that remained from the period IV walls. These courses dwindle to only a single course at the south end of the room. Below the bricks are clay foundations of period III, and below these substructure walls and foundations.

2-P.31, Rectangular room. The walls of period IV rest on the clay foundations of III. In the southeast corner is a pivotstone box of mudbrick that served a door to the court in the original wall (see fig. 3). There is also a door in the north wall to 4-P.30.

25. Greengus 1979, pl. 50:119 and Greengus 1986, p. 53.
26. Greengus 1979, pl. 46:107 and Greengus 1986, pp. 48-50.
27. Greengus 1979, pl. 80:242.

4-P.30, Rectangular room. The walls belong to period IV and rest on the clay foundations of III. Under these, at 36.95 meters, were walls of the substructure with a door in the south wall into 2-P.31 (see fig. 3). Another door in the north wall gives access to 5-P.30.

5-P.30, Wide rectangular room. The walls belong to period IV and rest on the clay foundations of III. In the east and south walls is an intervening layer of ashes. Below the clay foundations, at 36.92 meters, were the walls of the substructure. In the middle of the room is a square pavement of baked bricks, $36 \times 36 \times 7$ centimeters, covered with bitumen (fig. 3). It belongs, as indicated by the brick size, to period I-A. Its purpose is not clear. Above it was the pure clay fill of the I-B re-flooring. There are doors in the north wall to 2-P.29 and in the south wall to 4-P.30.

2-P.29, Small rectangular room. The walls belong to period IV and are built of mudbricks measuring $35 \times 35 \times 10$ centimeters. They rest on the clay foundations of III. One door is situated in the south wall to 5-P.30.

e. East Rooms

2-Q.30, Almost square room with original walls and a door in the south wall to 3-Q.30. The southwest quarter of the floor had a paving of baked bricks which originally may have extended over the entire floor (see fig. 3). At the center of the room was a "bench" of mudbrick masonry 35 centimeters high and approximately 1×0.50 meters in plan. The purpose of this "bench" and the reason for the paving are not clear.

3-Q.30, Rectangular room. The walls are original; a door in the north wall leads to 2-Q.30 and a narrow one in the southwestern wall allowed access to the court. Traces of bitumen suggest that this latter door originally had a sill of baked bricks.

1-R.31, Rectangular gateroom. The walls are original (see fig. 3). The gate in the east wall, slightly north of center, opens onto the terrace and stairs of the main lower court. There is also a narrower, nonaligned door, in the west wall, well south of the center, opening upon the upper court. At either jamb of the gate in the east wall was a pivotstone box of mudbrick and a few baked bricks. The boxes were filled with sand. On top of the north box, but out of position, was a marble slab that had served as a pivotstone. A similar second slab was found lying on the surface near the south box. In the gate itself was a bitumen ledge, indicating that the gate had had a sill of baked bricks two courses thick. At the door in the west wall, at its south jamb, was a single pivotstone box built both of mudbricks and baked bricks. Also this door had had a sill of baked bricks, as shown by the remaining traces of bitumen. Under the sills of both doors were the corresponding blocked up doors of the substructure. A stone relief fragment (Ish. 34:207, pl. 41b) is dated to period IV.

1-R.32, Rectangular room. There are two nonaligned doors, one in the east wall to the terrace and main lower court and a second one in the west wall to the upper court. The door in the east wall has a pivotstone box of mudbrick at its north jamb, and the door in the west wall has one of both mudbrick and baked brick. The pivotstone was still in position and showed remnants of bronze from the shoe of the doorpost in the socket. Under the sills of both doors were the corresponding blocked up doors of the substructure. A cylinder seal (Ish. 35:5, OIP 72, pl. 87:926) was found on the surface of this room. A fragment of a terracotta model bed with a female figure (Ish. 34:89, pl. 37b) dates to period I-II.

4. THE LOWER BUILDING

a. North Wing (Western Unit)

1- and 2-S.30, Rectangular gateroom. A gate in the south wall leads to the main lower court 3-S.30 and a narrower nonaligned door in the north wall connects with court 1-R.29 (see figs. 3 and 9). The walls are original. The walls settled in period I-B carrying the pavings in the doors down with them and tilting the bricks of the adjoining pavement of 1-R.29 (see section D-D′, fig. 8). A thin screenwall with a door at its end partitions off the east end of the room (see fig. 9). In the north wall, centered on the south gate, is a small rabbeted square niche measuring 48 × 48 centimeters at the outer edge of the rabbet and 35 × 35 centimeters at its inner edge. The depth of the niche from the face of the wall is 27.50 centimeters with the rabbet accounting for 8 centimeters. The bottom of the niche is 90 centimeters above the floor (pl. 4a). In period II-B a further screenwall was built running north from the east jamb of the south gate (see fig. 11). This screenwall also had a door near its south end with a sill of baked bricks and was lined in its north part with baked bricks set on edge. The floor and walls show traces of fire, apparently the fire at the end of period II-B. In period III the doors in the screen walls were moved to their north ends (see fig. 13). Objects found in 2-S.30 dating to period I-B include the following: a cylinder seal (Ish. 35:71, OIP 72, pl. 86:900), a fragment of a plaque with a lion and a man (Ish. 35:86, pl. 35f), and a plaque depicting a goddess (Ish. 35:222, pl. 34f). A duck-shaped weight (Ish. 34:62, pl. 44m) and a terracotta rider-type plaque (Ish. 34:107, pl. 35m) were among the objects in 2-S.30 dating to period IV.

5-R.30, Almost square room. There is a door in the north wall to court 1-R.29. All walls are original. In period III thin walls built in the court in front of its door made it part of a three room unit composed of 3-, 5-, and 7-R.30 (see fig. 13). A cylinder seal (Ish. 34:127, OIP 72, pl. 86:908) and a terracotta god plaque (Ish. 34:124, OIC 20:67 and pl. 34a here) are dated to period III.

6-R.30, Almost square room. There is a door in the north wall to court 1-R.29. All walls are original. In the southwest corner was a small U-shaped fireplace for cooking (see fig. 3). In period III the door was narrowed by thin walls projected into it from both sides. A number of plaques and other terracotta objects were found dating to periods I-II and III-IV (see app. 4).

1-R.29, Rectangular court. There are rabbeted doors in the south wall to 1-S.30, 5-R.30, 6-R.30 and in the north wall to 9-R.29, 6-R.29, and 7-S.29. There was an unrabbeted gate in the east wall to 4-S.29 during periods III and IV (figs. 13 and 14) which was probably rabbeted in earlier periods (figs. 3, 9, and 10). There also was a rabbeted gate in the west wall which gave access to 1-Q.29. Only the south wall and the south part of the west wall are original. The north part of the west wall, the north wall, and the east wall belong to the rebuilding in period II-A (see fig. 10). The original walls were built of mudbrick measuring 38 × 38 × 8 centimeters. Those belonging to II-A are of mudbrick that measure 34 × 34 × 8 centimeters. The court has a three row paved walk around its edges, laid with baked bricks measuring 52 × 52 × 9 centimeters. The bricks along the south wall and south part of the west wall were tilted down when the wall settled (pl. 8a). In the east end of the court was a vertical pottery drain (see fig. 3). An open drain of baked bricks and bitumen led outside the complex through 7-S.29 to a hole in the *kisû* (see above pp. 39f.). This drain was cut by the mudbrick sill of the II-A door to 7-S.29.

Centered in the west wall is the gate to 1-Q.29 flanked by two simulated towers (see above p. 23) as well as double rabbets. Each tower had two vertical slots as decoration (pl. 8a). Those in the southern one, built in period I-A, were regular vertical T-shaped grooves; those in the northern one, part of the period II-A rebuilding (see fig. 10), were U-shaped. Whether this was intentional, or whether the clay panels used to produce the T-shape were accidentally omitted, or later destroyed, could not be decided (see pp. 36f. above, and pl. 4b). The bottom part of the original T-shaped grooves in the southern "tower" was well preserved. The width of the groove at the face of the wall was 36 centimeters. Into it a baked brick measuring 36 × 36 × 8 centimeters had been placed in an upright position, its edge resting on the floor. In the central groove, level with the upper edge of this brick and supported by a clay filling a suitably shaped fragment of baked brick had then been inserted.

On the floor of the court, 1-R.29, in period II-B was a number of cavities and shallow grooves for drainage (see plan, fig. 11). The cavity at the center of the court was filled with green earth suggesting that animal remains, perhaps blood, had accumulated there (see pl. 19a). A terracotta plaque depicting a man on a bovine (Ish. 35:8, pl. 35l) and a number of other unillustrated objects (see app. 4) were found on the period II-B floor. At floor II-A or high I-B was a cylinder seal (Ish. 35:24, OIP 72, pl. 86:904). On floor I-B were the head of a clay female figurine (Ish. 35:214, pl. 36e) and a fragment of a clay plaque (Ish. 35:215, pl. 35q); also two tablets, a house sale (Ish. 35-T.2)[28] and a school text (Ish. 35-T.11).[29]

To period II-A belongs a small fireplace (see fig. 10), made of two baked bricks placed parallel with their edges against the east wall, just south of the east gate. In the following period II-B a multiple fireplace for cooking was built in the southwest corner of the court, and other cooking facilities were placed further out in the court (pl. 19a), all suggesting that food for a considerable number of people was prepared here. During the third building period (IV) finally, a number of shacks constructed of thin mudbrick walls were erected in the court (see fig. 13). Some of these had facilities for cooking. Cylindrical bread ovens (*tanoors*) were found in 7-R.29, 3-S.29, and east of 7-R.30. Fireplaces were situated in 3-R.30 and 1-R.30 in the southwestern corner of the court. The floor at this period was full of

28. Greengus 1979, pl. 16:30.
29. Greengus 1979, pl. 95:283.

ashes and potsherds. A hematite cylinder seal (Ish. 34:64, OIP 72, pl. 87:918) was found in shack 5-R.29.

1-Q.29, Rectangular room (pl. 18b). There are doors in the east wall to 1-R.29, in the south wall to 7-Q.30, in the west wall to 8-Q.30, and in the north wall to 2-Q.29 and 2-R.29 (see fig. 3). The southern wall and the south parts of the east and west walls are original and built with mudbrick measuring 38 × 38 × 8 centimeters. In the wall were traces of matting at irregular level-intervals such as 29 centimeters and 49 centimeters. The north wall was built of mudbricks measuring 34 × 34 × 8 centimeters. It showed layers of matting 69 centimeters (i.e., 6 courses) apart. On the floor of I-A was a layer of ashes 33 centimeters thick, and over this lay a 7 centimeters thick clay floor of I-B and over that 20 centimeters of ashes; then a 20 centimeters clay filling of II-A and a continuous succession of ash layers. To period II-B dates a cooking range built against the north wall (see fig. 11). It consists of two parallel benches, the rearmost of which has eleven square bays while the foremost is divided into four equal parts with narrow gaps in between. In the center of the room was a rectangular oven, and along the south wall a range similar to that on the north wall, but with the front bench divided into two only and the back one with ten bays only. In the southwest corner of the room was a bread oven (*tanoor*). In the following period III the cooking ranges were replaced with two oval kitchen stoves built in the middle of the room (pl. 10b), and instead of a single bread oven (*tanoor*) in the southeastern corner there were now three (see fig. 13). A terracotta plaque (Ish. 34:108, pl. 35o) and a model wheel from 1-Q.29 date to period IV.

7-Q.30, Almost square room. There is a door in the north wall to 1-Q.29. All the walls are original. There are no special features.

8-Q.30, Small rectangular room (see fig. 3). A door in the east wall leads to 1-Q.29. The north wall and north part of the west wall, in their lowest courses, and the south wall are original. The east wall, north of the door, is the rebuilt wall of period II-A (see fig. 10), and the upper part of the west wall is the clay foundation of III with the mudbrick foundation of IV on top. Along the west wall are stairs built of baked bricks measuring 36 × 36 × 8.50 centimeters (pl. 19b). Each step is one and one-half brick wide and three bricks high and is covered with bitumen ca. 1 centimeter thick. Only four complete steps remain. The upper part of the stairs was removed in period III and the room was filled in with mudbricks. The lowest part of the filling consisted of a course of mudbricks which stood on edge, and above it was a section ca. 40 to 50 centimeters high of mudbricks laid flat. The door to 1-Q.29 was not filled in. Here the filling in the room was plastered over so that the door became a deep niche in the west wall of 1-Q.29. The upper torso of a male terracotta figurine (Ish. 35:213, pl. 36f) is dated to period I-B.

2-Q.29, Rectangular room. The door in the south wall gives access to 1-Q.29. All of the walls rebuilt in period II-A had mudbrick measuring 34 × 34 × 8 centimeters. The top part of the west and south walls were cut by the clay foundations of period III. Along the north wall in period II-B were three cylindrical bread ovens, *tanoors* (see fig. 11). A cylinder seal (Ish. 35:26, OIP 72, pl. 86:906) is also dated to this period.

2-R.29, Almost square room. There is a door in the south wall to 1-Q.29. All walls rebuilt in period II-A had mudbricks measuring 34 × 34 × 8 centimeters. In the north wall the top is cut by the clay foundation of III. Along the east wall is a period II-A staircase (see fig. 10 and pl. 20a) built of 34 × 34 × 8 centimeters mudbrick leading up to the roof and supported in its upper part by a corbeled arch (pl. 20b). On the floor of the room in period II-B was a cylindrical bread over, *tanoor* (see fig. 11). On the floor of period I-A a clay plaque (Ish. 34:40, pl. 34b and OIC 20, fig. 31, left side) was found. Another clay plaque (Ish. 34:106, pl. 35n) is dated to period III. See appendix 4 for other finds from these and other periods.

9-R.29, Small rectangular room. A door in the south wall leads to 1-R.29. The walls were rebuilt in period II. There are no special features. However, a terracotta cylinder seal (Ish. 35:78, not illustrated) is dated to period I-B (see OIP 72, p. 60).

6-R.29, Small rectangular room. A door in the south wall gave access to the court 1-R.29. All walls were rebuilt in period II-A. The top of the north wall was cut by the clay foundation of period III. In the southeast corner were remnants of a ribbed vertical pottery drain belonging to period II-B (see fig. 11), which probably served as an ending point for the groove in the floor in the western half of 1-R.29. At some time in period II-B a narrow high sill was built across the door opening. A fragment of a terracotta god plaque (Ish. 34:101, pl. 33f) and a bone pin (Ref. 34:157, not illustrated) from this room are dated to period IV.

7-S.29, Small rectangular room. Doors are located in the south wall to 1-R.29 and in the east wall to 5-S.29 in period II-B. The walls were all rebuilt in period II-A (see fig. 10). On the floor of period I-A (see fig. 3) was an open drain of baked bricks and bitumen coming from 1-R.29 and originally continuing to the outside (see above pp. 47f.). In the northeast and northwest corners were cylindrical bread ovens (*tanoors*). On the floor, part of a roof drain of baked clay was found. In period III a covered drain of baked bricks followed the line of the earlier open one (see fig. 13).

4-S.29, Rectangular room. A wide doorway was situated in the west wall leading to 1-R.29 and a narrow door in the north wall led to 5-S.29. The south wall was original, but the others were rebuilt in period II-A. A cylindrical bread oven (*tanoor*) was found on the floor of II-B in the south end of the room (see fig. 11). In period III the doorway in the west wall was blocked up and a narrow door cut through the center of the east wall to 1-S.29 (see fig. 13). A stone cylinder seal (Ish. 34:74, OIP 72, pl. 87:921) and a figurine (Ref. 34:207, not illustrated) date to period IV.

5-S.29, Small, almost square, room. A door in the south wall gave access to 4-S.29. All walls were rebuilt in period II-A. They were cut on the north and east sides by the clay foundations of period III. The floor of I-A was paved with baked bricks, measuring 36 × 36

× 8.50 centimeters, which were covered with bitumen. In period II-B another door was opened in the west wall to 7-S.29 (see fig. 11). In period III the room was again paved with baked bricks (see fig. 13).

b. North Wing (Eastern Unit)

4-T.30, Rectangular gateroom. A door in the south wall gave access from the main court at 2-T.30 and the nonaligned door in the north wall opened onto the court of the eastern unit, 2-T.29. The walls are original except the extreme northwest corner of the north wall which is the clay foundation of period III with the wall of period IV on top. In period I the south door had a paving of baked bricks (36 × 36 × 8 centimeters) laid in bitumen; and at its west jamb a pivotstone box of the same kind of baked bricks (see fig. 3). In period II-B this door had a pavement of baked bricks measuring 40 × 40 × 9.50 centimeters with a stamp of Ipiq-Adad II (see fig. 11 and pl. 23). In period III, when the floors of the complex were raised, three steps of baked bricks leading up to the room from the main court were built in this doorway. A pivotstone box at the west inner jamb of the door, its top even with the new raised floor, had a brick with the stamp of Ibal-pî-el II built into its wall. A thin screenwall running south from the east jamb of the north door, with an opening at its south end, partitions off the east end of the room. The III filling in the room is of solid clay. To period IV belongs a new pivotstone box at the west jamb of the south door and a rebuilding of the screenwall (see fig. 14). Between it and the east wall is an amorphous mass of baked bricks. A stone cylinder seal (Ish. 35:70, OIP 72, pl. 86:905) is dated to period II-A.

2-T.29, Rectangular court (see fig. 3 and pl. 21b). There are doors in the south wall to 1- and 4-T.30 and 1-T.29; a "towered" gate in the west wall to 2-S.29, and there are doors to 6-S.29, 7-T.29, and 6-T.29 in the north wall, and to 4-T.29 in the east wall. The west and east walls, as well as part of the north and south walls, are original; although all, except the west wall, were cut by the clay foundations of period III. In period I-A a pavement of three rows of baked bricks, measuring 52 × 52 × 9 centimeters, was laid around the edges of the court. The bricks along the north side were tilted down toward the wall, tipped when the wall settled at the end of period I-B. Those along the south wall were less affected (pl. 6a). In the middle of the court were two small square pavements of baked bricks measuring 36 × 36 × 8 centimeters. The easternmost one had two bricks with holes pierced in them for drainage into two vertical pottery drains beneath them (see fig. 3, and section A-A′, fig. 5, and p. 25). In the middle of the western one was a brick sunk one course below the others. Nothing was found under it. All doors which faced onto the court were rabbeted. The gate in the west wall was double rabbeted. It was flanked by the same kind of simulated towers that were found at the gate into 1-Q.29 in the eastern unit of the north wing. Each tower was decorated with two vertical T-shaped grooves. In the northeastern corner was a ribbed vertical pottery drain belonging to the floor of period II-A. Terracotta plaques and other objects were recovered from the floors of periods I-A, II-B, and IV (Ish. 35:93, pl. 36g; Ish. 35:219, pl. 38e; and Ish. 34:109, pl. 35p).

1-T.30, Rectangular room. There is a door in the east end of the north wall to 2-T.29. The walls are original. A thin screenwall partitioned off the west end of the room in period I-B (see fig. 9). In period II-B (see fig. 11) a screenwall, half a brick thick, partitioned off a two meter square cubicle in the southeastern corner of the room. This cubicle was open at the east end of its north wall.

2-S.29, Rectangular "broadroom" antecella, later changed into a cella. It has a wide door in the east wall to court 2-T.29. All walls are original. The door in the west wall to 1-S.29 is doubly rabbeted, has a bitumen covered paved sill, and plastered sides. In the southeast corner the floor was covered with a layer of bitumen. This layer was long in use as ten successive coats of bitumen could be distinguished. In period I-B the doorway to 1-S.29 was blocked at the back, changing it into a niche, and in this niche a mudbrick structure resembling an armchair was built (see fig. 9 and pl. 12a) possibly to serve as a seat or base for a statue or symbol of the deity. Since the "arms" were cut by the floor of II-A it is impossible to tell how they were finished on top or how high they originally were. In period II-B the niche was cleared, possibly for a wooden dais, and remained so. In period IV the gate in the east wall was repaved with baked bricks bearing the stamp of Ibal-pî-el II and a pivotstone box was put in at its southern jamb (see fig. 13). The pivotstone, resting on a pavement of baked bricks, was still in situ. In the paved sill two steps led down to the floor of 2-S.29 which had been left low. The walls showed traces of burning, and remnants of charred wood lay on the floor of IV (see above pp. 34f.). On the floor of I-B a perforated gold bead (Ish. 35:51, pl. 43c) was found and on the floor of II-A lay a small alabaster monkey with inlaid eyes (Ish. 35:48, pl. 40e, f).[30] At the eastern door was a tablet with a seal impression of a servant of Ibal-pî-el II (Ish. 35-T.25[31]) and in the pivotstone box was a tablet (Ish. 35-T.53) with dates for three successive years (8-10) of Ibal-pî-el II: MU É-s á-ğar-ra-a-⌈ni é⌉ ᵈEn-líl(!?) ba-an-⌈x⌉, MU Ra-pí-qum^{ki} ba-gul, and MU erín Su-bir₄^{ki} ᵍⁱˢtukul ba-an-sìg. On the floor of IV was also a fragment of a clay plaque (Ish. 34:91, pl. 34l).

1-S.29, Rectangular room. In period I this room served as a broadroom cella with 2-S.29 as its antecella. The west wall and the western part of the north wall belong to the rebuilding in period II. The other walls are original. A door in the east wall led into 2-S.29. This door was blocked in period I-B. The original west wall is lost but the niche it will have had opposite the door to 2-S.29 was repeated in the new period II wall that replaced it. This niche was carefully bonded at its corners and not formed by the blocking of a door. In period IV a narrow door to 4-S.29 was cut through the northern part of this niche.

When the floor in the east wall to 2-S.29 was blocked in period I-B a new door was cut in the north wall. It gave access to 6-S.29 and debris from an original stair in that room was used to raise the floor level in 1-S.29. See p. 29 above.

In the niche of period I-B was a clay tablet with an inventory of precious stones, jewelry, et cetera, belonging to the goddess Ninshubura (Ish. 35-T.99[32]). On the floor of

30. See Frankfort 1943, p. 35, no. 335 and pl. 74A and B.

31. Greengus 1979, pl. 99:298.

32. Greengus 1979, pl. 45:106 and OBTIV 106 in Greengus 1986, pp. 46-48.

IV two further inventories of ornaments, one fragmentary, were found (Ish. 34-T.98[33] and Ish. 34-T.104[34]).

6-S.29, Rectangular room. The west wall and western part of the north wall belong to the rebuilding in period II-A (fig. 10). The other walls are original. A door at the east end of the south wall led to 2-T.29. In the east end of the room was a pavement of 'baked' bricks. One of the bricks was perforated and covered a pot sunk beneath it. From this pavement stairs originally went up to the roof but only three steps remained. They were built of mudbrick with baked bricks on top. In period I-B (fig. 9) the stairs were razed down to the remaining three steps, a new door was cut in the west end of the south wall to 1-S.29, and the debris from the upper part of the stairs was used to raise the floor level in 1-S.29.

7-T.29, Rectangular room. There is a door in the middle of the south wall to court 2-T.29. All walls are original except for the inner corners of the door jambs. Later, all the walls were cut by the clay foundations of period III. There are no special features.

6-T-29, Rectangular room. There is one door in the western part of the south wall to court 2-T.29. The west and south walls are original except for the inner corners of the door jambs. The north and east walls were destroyed by the clay foundations of period II. There are no special features. Two figurines (Ref. 34:218 and 237, not illustrated here) are dated to period III-IV.

4-T.29, Rectangular gateroom. One door is located near the middle of the west wall which leads to court 2-T.29 and there is a nonaligned gate at the south end of the east wall which gives access from the street. All walls are original but were cut almost to the floor by the clay foundations of period III. The door in the west wall was paved with baked bricks, measuring $52 \times 52 \times 9$ centimeters, and with brick fragments at the center line of paving. The paving was covered with a layer of bitumen. At the north jamb of the door was a pivotstone box of mudbrick. The door in the east wall had a paving of baked bricks, measuring $36 \times 36 \times 8$ centimeters, covered with bitumen. At its south jamb was a pivotstone box of baked bricks. In period II-A the pivotstone box at the east door was rebuilt, in part with segmented bricks. On top of it are remnants of the lower parts of the period IV box. Joining fragments of a terracotta god plaque (Ish. 34:94, 99, 102, and 105, pl. 33a-d) were found on the period IV floor.

1-T.29, Rectangular room. One door is situated in the western end of the north wall leading to court 2-T.29, and another one in the eastern end of the south wall to 2-U.30. All walls are original but cut almost to the floor by the clay foundations of period III. In period I-B there was a small square pavement of baked bricks in the west end of the room (see fig. 9). Remnants of a pivotstone box at the west jamb of the door in the north wall was built of unbaked and baked mudbricks.

33. Greengus 1979, pl. 44:104.
34. Greengus 1979, pl. 45:105.

c. Main Lower Court

(West Side)

The west side of the main lower court is bounded by the east facade of the upper temple. A terrace of baked bricks laid in bitumen was built against the upper platform on which the west part of the complex rested. Most of the bricks were removed anciently. There are two entrances: a door leading to 1-R.32 and, north of that, a main towered gate, giving entrance to 1-R.31, which was served by a monumental staircase. See the discussion of these features as they appeared in period I-A given above on pp. 19–21.

3-R.31, Southwest corner of main court. There are remains of the south end of the terrace. See above p. 20.

2-R.31, Stairs to terrace and 1-R.31. See description above on pp. 19f. for remains dating to period I-A and the reconstruction. The masonry block in front of the stairs discussed on pp. 21f. stood on an irregularly built pillar which descended to the substructure floor.

Above the stairs of period I were remains of a later staircase starting from the floor of period III at a level of 38.01 meters. Only one step and part of the south casewall remains. The casewall is recessed in front as was that of the original stairs. Both casewall and steps of these later stairs are built of fragmentary bricks of varying size, clearly in secondary use. Some bear the stamp of Ipiq-Adad II. A clay mortar was used in the construction. The head of a painted stone statuette (Ish. 34:139, pl. 40a-c)[35] was found on the period III floor.

4-R.30, Northwest corner of main court. In period I-A a pavement of baked bricks, measuring $52 \times 52 \times 9$ centimeters, was laid along the north wall of the court. Apparently it was part of a paved walk around the edges of the court (see above p. 21). Remnants of baked brick stairs, built early in period III in front of the door to 2-R.30, led up to the north end of the terrace. Later in this period a slotted retaining wall of baked bricks was built along the face of the terrace up to the north wall of the court and the space behind it was filled in.

(North Side)

2-R.30, Almost square room. A door in the south wall opened onto the main court at 4-R.30. All of the walls are original. In period III stairs were built in the door down to the main court (see fig. 13). On the floor of that period, at level 38.76 meters, were the following clay tablets: Ish. 34-T.145,[36] a disbursement of grain dated MU GUD-APIN KÙ-GI; Ish. 34-T.146,[37] a delivery of cattle and sheep dated MU É-s á-ğ[ar-ra-n]i é ᵈEn-líl-lá m[u-un]ʳ-naʳ[-dù]; and Ish. 34-T.144, a *hubullu* loan of grain from

---

35. See also Frankfort 1943, pp. 20, 35, no. 333, pl. 73.

36. Greengus 1979, pl. 66:179.

37. Greengus 1979, pl. 48:112.

^{d}*Kitîtum ú* ŠÀ-TAM-MEŠ witnessed by ^{d}Sîn, ^{d}Šamaš, ^{d}Adad and dated MU R a - p í - q u m^{ki} ⌐b⌐a - g u l. The last two dates are dates of Ibal-pî-el II. On the higher level (top) a school text (Ish. 34-T.55),[38] a letter (Ish. 34-T.58),[39] and a fragment of a clay stand with a painted relief of a musician (Ish. 34:79, pl. 39c) dated to period III were found. A duck-shaped weight (Ish. 34:29, pl. 44d), and a terracotta animal plaque fragment (Ish. 34:60, pl. 38g) dated to period IV also were found.

3-S.30, Space in front of gate to 1-S.30. From the floor of period I-B a step of baked bricks leads up into the gate from the court. On the period III floor was a seal of a servant of [Ipiq]-Adad II, Ish. 35:42 (OIP 72, pl. 86:909). On the floor of period IV two fragments of clay plaques were found (Ish. 34:104 and Ish. 34:114, pls. 34o and 35g). Here also was a large eye for a statue (Ish. 35:217).

2-T.30, Northeast corner of main court. Against the wall of the court was a pavement of baked bricks, measuring $36 \times 36 \times 8$ centimeters, belonging to period I-A, apparently remnants of the paved walk around the sides of the court (see fig. 9). A later pavement above it at level 37.46 meters, belonging to period II-B, was laid with baked bricks, measuring $40 \times 40 \times 9.50$ centimeters, with the stamp of Ipiq-Adad II (see fig. 11 and pl. 23). Above that, just under the surface, was a pavement of bricks, each measuring $41 \times 41 \times 8$ centimeters, with the stamp of Ibal-pî-el.

(East Side)

The main features of the east end of the main court, the well and the block of mudbrick with nearby drain, are discussed above (see pp. 29ff., fig. 10 and pl. 24a). The east wall is formed by the clay foundations of period III with mudbrick foundations of period IV on top. A terracotta plaque of a male figure (Ish. 35:221, pl. 36c) dating to period II-A was found in the southeastern corner of the main court.

(South Side)

The south wall of the main court is formed by the clay foundations of period III with mudbrick foundations of period IV on top. It has no special features.

d. South Wing (see fig. 13)

The wall enclosing the rooms of the south wing in the lower part of the complex had all been removed anciently to make room for later foundations so that what we found were merely mudbrick foundations of period IV resting on clay foundations of period III, which in turn clearly followed the lines of still earlier walls. As this is the case with all rooms in the wing it seems unnecessary to repeat the information for each separate one. We did not excavate to below the clay foundations of III.

5-R.32, Rectangular room. The door in the north wall was restored on the plan (see fig. 3) on the assumption that it was situated opposite the door of 2-R.30 in the north wing

38. Greengus 1979, pl. 96:285.
39. Greengus 1979, pl. 10:19.

during the original building period. Two narrow screenwalls (see fig. 13) running north-south across the room are earlier than, and cut by, the foundations of period III; they probably belong to period II-B. The west screenwall, dividing 4-R.32 and 5-R.32, has a narrow door with a single baked brick as a sill at its south end; the east screenwall has a similar door and sill at its north end. In the west end of the room were two storage pots sunk beneath the floor. An Old Babylonian cylinder seal (Ish. 34:82, OIP 72, pl. 87:919) was found dating to the period IV remains of 4-R.32.

2-S.32, Small, almost square room. The door shown on the plan (fig. 3) in the east wall to 1-S.32 is a logical conjectural restoration by Hill.

1-S.32, Rectangular room. A door is restored on the plan (see fig. 3) in the north wall to match the gate to 1-S.30 in the north wing. In the floor filling, just under the surface, was a fragment of a baked brick with the stamp of Ibal-pî-el II.

1-T.32, Small square room. A door in the west wall to 1-S.32 is another logical conjectural restoration by Hill.

3-T.32, Rectangular gateroom. The room had a door in the south wall leading to the outside. It had remnants of a sill of baked bricks with the stamp of Ibal-pî-el II and a pivotstone box of baked bricks at the inner west jamb of the south door. Traces of a nonaligned second door lead to the main court at the east end of the north wall. This door has a pivotstone box, likewise of baked bricks, with the pivotstone still in place situated at the inner east jamb of this door. There were traces of fire in this door. A cylinder seal (Ish. 35:73, OIP 72, pl. 60) came from the remains of period II-B and a white stone 'goddess' figurine (Ish. 34:80, pl. 41d) was found on the floor of period IV.

e. East Wing

The walls of the East wing of the complex, like those of the south wing in the lower part, are represented only by the mudbrick foundations of period IV and the clay foundations of period III, and it seems unnecessary to repeat this information for each separate room.

3-U.31, Rectangular room. The door on the plan (see fig. 3) in the northeastern end of the north wall is a conjectural restoration. There are no special features and no recorded finds.

2-U.31, Rectangular room. Doors are a conjectural restoration on the plan (see fig. 3) in the north wall to 1-U.30, the west wall to 3-T.31 and 2-T.31, and in the south wall to 3-U.31. There are no special features.

1-U.31, Almost square room (figs. 13 and 14). Beside the conjectural door in the south wall to 2-U.31, the room had two aligned doors at its north end, in the west wall to 3-T.31, and in the east wall to the outside at locus 3-U.30. This latter door, lacking a proper gateroom, is clearly secondary, opened up in period IV or, less likely, III to obtain an easier entry to the main court on its central east-west axis. It follows the line of a drain of baked bricks coming from the main court and 3-T.31. This drain was originally built with baked bricks with the stamp of Ipiq-Adad II, then renewed with bricks with the stamp of Ibal-pî-el (see above pp. 29ff.). In 1-U.31 its bricks were removed and only a line of fragments of bitumen indicates its course. Sediments from this drain were observed outside the door on the east side. Across the room, along the south side of the drain a narrow wall of baked bricks, one brick wide, had been sunk into the floor.

3-T.31, Rectangular room. Beside the conjectural doors in the east wall to 2-U.31 and in the north wall to 5-T.30, the room has two aligned doors in its north end, one in the west wall to the main court, and one in the east wall to 1-U.31. Through the former an open drain cut through the top of the clay foundation and was covered in the door with a "sill" of baked bricks with the stamp of Ibal-pî-el. Two courses are preserved but there may have been more. It may be assigned to period IV (see fig. 14). In the extreme north end of the room is a thin screen wall with a narrow door which partitions off a narrow strip from the room. It is earlier than the clay foundations and may represent period II-B. A terracotta animal and rider plaque (Ish. 34:85, OIC 20, fig. 73c and pl. 35k here) was found in the robber dump from 3-T.31.

5-T.30, Almost square room. A conjectured door is shown in the south wall to 3-T.31. The floor was paved in period I-A (see fig. 3) around a vertical pottery drain with baked bricks measuring 36 × 36 × 8 centimeters. A conically-shaped gray stone bowl (Ish. 35:76), measuring 21 × 22.10 centimeters, with a flat-topped rim was found on the period I-A floor. A lapis lazuli cylinder seal (Ish. 35:72, OIP 72, pl. 86:913) was found above the period III floor.

1-U.30, Small rectangular room (see fig. 13). A conjectured door is restored in the north wall to 2-U.30. There are no special features. A hematite cylinder seal (Ish. 35:74, OIP 72, pl. 87:920) was found on the floor of period IV.

2-U.30, Large rectangular room. Two conjectured doors are restored in the south wall to 1-U.30 and in the west wall to 3-T.30; a door in the north wall to 1-T.29 is indicated by a pivotstone box of baked brick in the northeast corner during period I-A (see fig. 3). Remnants of baked brick pavements in the south part of the room also belong to I-A. A terracotta clay plaque showing a dog (Ish. 34:67, pl. 38h) came from the floor of period IV.

3-T.30, Rectangular room. A conjectured door is shown in the east wall to 2-U.30. At level 37.15 meters were remnants of a pavement belonging to period I-A (see fig. 3). A hematite cylinder seal (Ish. 34:129, OIC 20, fig. 68 and OIP 72, pl. 86:907) was found on the floor of period II-A. The walls are all mudbrick foundations of period IV which rest on clay foundations of period III. These latter foundations cut through a storage pot sunk below the floor of period II-B (see pl. 8b).

2-T.31, Small Rectangular Room. A conjectured door is restored in the plan (see fig. 3) of period I-A in the south end of the east wall to room 2-U.31. A terracotta god plaque fragment (Ish. 34:96, pl. 33h) was found in the top level of period IV.

F. THE PLACE OF THE KITÎTUM COMPLEX IN THE
HISTORY OF TEMPLE PLANS

Consideration of the place that the Kitîtum plan occupies in the history of ancient Mesopotamian temple plans may conveniently begin with a comparison of it with that of the nearby, but considerably older, Early Dynastic Oval at Khafājah. As shown on figure 18, which places the two plans side by side, the similarity between them is striking.[40]

In both plans steps ascend to a low first platform on which the complex stands. The entrance is in the short end wall and is placed off-center to the right. Through a gateroom with nonaligned doors one then entered a main rectangular court which contained one or more wells for water. Rows of rooms line this court on all sides. At the far end of the court, as one entered it, was situated a second upper platform to which a flight of stairs led. In the case of the Oval most of this platform and all of the sanctuary on top of it are gone and have to be restored. The height of the platform can, however, be gauged from the preserved lowest steps and their distance from the platform's front wall.[41] As for the sanctuary on top, the fact that all other known Early Dynastic temples in the Diyala region run to a single type, that of the so-called *Herdhaus*, allows one to reconstruct it on those lines with a fair degree of confidence. Delougaz, who excavated the Oval, chose the simplest possible such form, the single *Herdhaus*[42] cella consisting of a rectangular room entered by a door in the long side wall near the corner, having a hearth in the middle of the room, and a dais at the end wall farthest from the door. However, as pointed out by Heinrich, this simplest form represents, where it occurs historically, most often a reduction and impoverishment of the more full type of plan identified by him as *Mittelsaalhaus* and, independently, by H. Hill as single-, double-, or full-flanked main room house.[43] Since the Oval undoubtedly was planned as an edifice of great moment and consequence we have therefore here chosen rather to be guided by the contemporary plan of the Sîn temple X in Khafājah, the one dating to Early Dynastic III, restoring it from the better preserved older versions of Early Dynastic II.[44] We have also restored a double

40. The plan of the Oval shown is that of the third building period, the "squared oval" as reconstructed in Delougaz 1940, p. 112, fig. 103 and p. 116. We reconstructed the building on top of the platform differently, as indicated below. The plan of the Kitîtum complex is that of period I-A.

41. See Delougaz 1940, p. 69 and section B on pl. VI.

42. This term was coined by Andrae. It is widely used and widely understood so we use it here, but with the caveat that we understand by it a unit that can occur alone, but which in origin formed the core of a larger structure. Hill's term "Mainroom," or Heinrich's *Mittelsaal*, would be more precise but might not be so readily understood.

43. Heinrich 1982, p. 7 with note 15 and Hill in Delougaz, Hill, and Lloyd 1967, pp. 143ff. For the simple form as representing an impoverishment, an end product historically, rather than a beginning, see Heinrich 1982, p. 15.

44. See Delougaz and Lloyd 1942, pls. 12, 11, and 10. The platform in the Oval was at the base 30 meters wide by 25 meters deep (see Delougaz 1940, p. 42) which, allowing one meter for batter, would leave 29 × 24 meters for the top which is ample for a building like Sîn temple X, which was 21 meters wide to 17 meters deep. We see no compelling reason to assume that the side room added for the ED III version of Sîn temple X was an additional cella.

row of low mudbrick pillars in front of the dais such as is found in the sanctuary 18-R.42 in Sîn temple X,[45] in the cella of the Shara temple at Tell Aḡrab,[46] and—single row only—in Shrine II of the square Abu temple at Tell Asmar.[47] These pillars are traditionally called "offering tables," but as their tops are often rounded rather than flat they can hardly have been designed for that purpose. The only viable explanation that occurs to us is that they were anchors for curtains[48] hung from the ceiling and weighted at their lower edges with rods of wood or metal. The rods would swing against the pillars as anchors, so that no blast of wind or draft would lift the curtains and expose the deity on the dais behind them to profane gazes.

After mounting the stairs from the courtyard one had, in both the Oval and the Kitîtum plans, a choice of two entrances. In the Oval both led into a common vestibule from which one entered the *Herdhaus* cella by a single door only. In the Kitîtum complex the two entrances had separate vestibules from which to enter the *"Herdhaus"* cella which here, as will be seen, appears in an immensely enlarged version. This enlargement has made it so wide that roofing has become impossible so that most of the room now appears as an open courtyard. Only at the end, where the dais with the image of the deity was located, was it imperative to preserve the protection of a roof, and the solution chosen was the obvious one of replacing the hangings with more solid walls that would support rafters. Thus two "broadrooms" were created, cella and antecella, narrow enough to be comfortably roofed.[49]

45. See Delougaz and Lloyd 1942, p. 74 and cf. p. 76, figs. 68, 69, and pl. 12.

46. See Delougaz and Lloyd 1942, pp. 236f., and p. 230, figs. 176 and 177 as well as pl. 26, cella in M. 14.

47. See Delougaz and Lloyd 1942, p. 187 with fig. 148 and p. 176, fig. 133, Shrine II.

48. Such curtains are mentioned in late ritual texts as a means to shield divine statues from profane gazes. See *CAD* B, p. 254 b 6´ *birīt šiddī* and *AHw*, p. 230 *šiddu(m)* C. In the domestic chapels of the Isin / Larsa period in Ur, Woolley found evidence indicating that the cult images would normally have been so shielded. He writes: "In the corner of the room, either by the side of the altar or rising from the same base as it, there is a pedestal or table built of burnt bricks below and crude bricks above, about 0.60 meters square and a meter high, covered with a mud plaster which was moulded into a pattern, usually of panels imitating woodwork, and whitewashed. The pedestal stands on a projecting base and in one case (No. 4 Paternoster Row, Room 5 q.v.) there was at the corners of the base bitumen rings to hold horizontal rods fixed a centimeter or two above the brickwork which can only be explained as rods holding down the lower ends of curtains which could be drawn across the table to conceal it from view (v. pl. 44b) . . . The fact that the 'tables' were veiled would seem to imply that there was set upon them something which was only to be seen at certain times—presumably when a religious service was being conducted in the building—and such could scarcely be other than the representation of the household gods, whether that took the form of picture, statue or relief." (Woolley and Mallowan 1976, pp. 29f.).

49. The new temple form created by this excessive enlargement of the original "Herdhaus" unit seems to have achieved the status of a standard form, to be used also for small temples which could easily have been completely roofed over. See Woolley's description of the public chapels of Isin/Larsa date in Ur. "The essential elements of a public chapel are an open court and a covered sanctuary in the back wall of which, facing the door, is a recess for the cult statue" (Woolley and Mallowan 1976, p. 31) and his statement about the domestic chapels found in every house of any size. "It was nearly always a long and narrow room, the door being toward one end of one of the longer sides and in area it was the most considerable room in the house. There was no room above it; in fact, about half of it was open to the sky and only the end furthest from the entrance was covered in, roofed with a penthouse roof . . . The chapel was brick-paved throughout. At the far end from the door, under the roof, there was built against the wall a low altar of burnt brick overlaid with mud plaster, generally as long as the wall, about 1 meter wide and 0.35 meter high" (Woolley and Mallowan 1976, pp. 19f.).

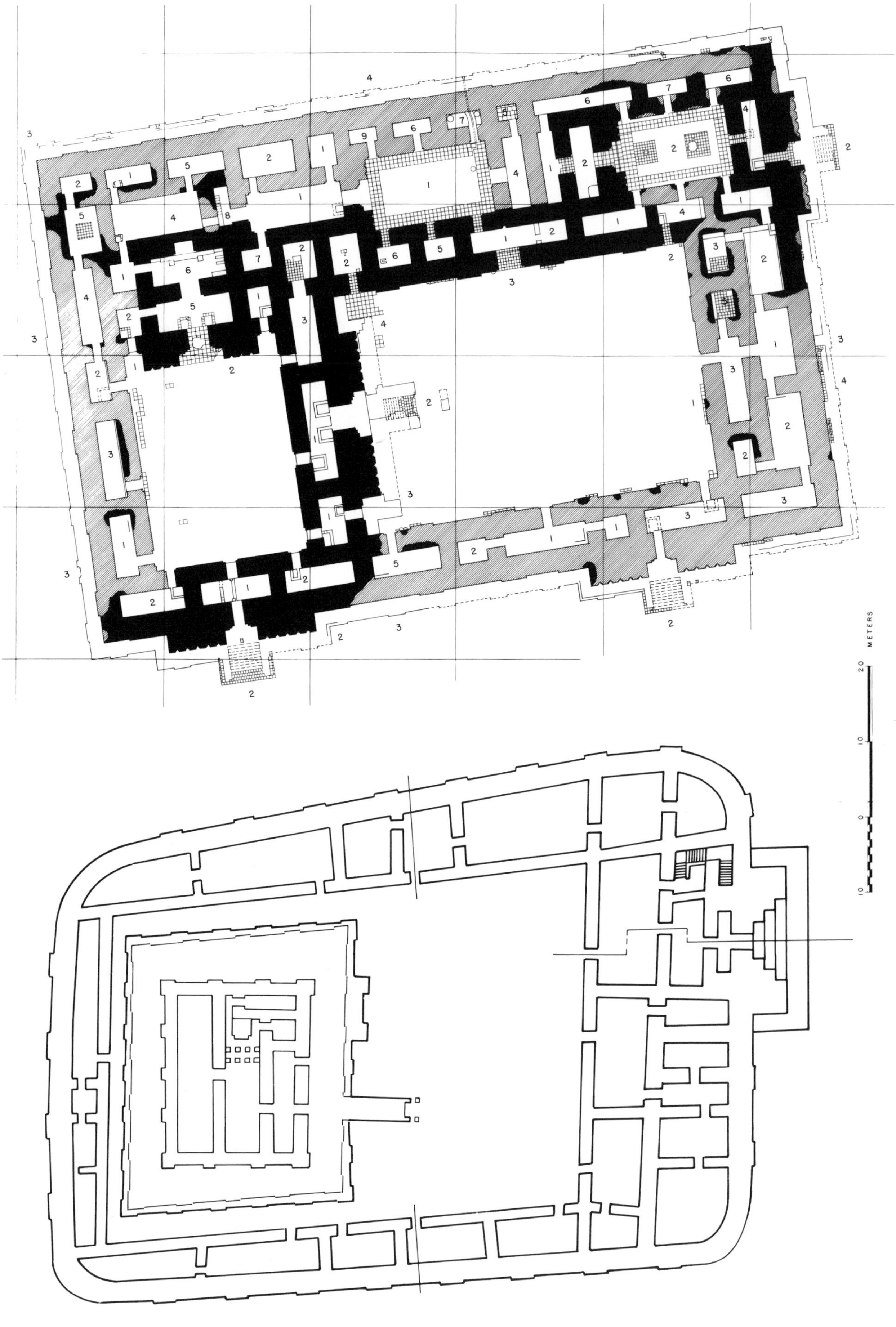

Figure 18. Comparative Plans of the Oval at Khafājah (after Delougaz 1940, fig. 103) and the Kitītum Temple at Ishchali.

The new entrance in the long axis of the Kitîtum structure opposite the gates of the antecella and cella (1-Q.32) is undoubtedly due to the innate human desire for symmetry, which led, at the last rebuilding of the Kitîtum complex, also to the opening of a similar median gate in through the east wing of the complex.[50] In Assyria, it may even, in much the same manner, have caused the replacement of the door of the old *Herdhaus* with a new one in the middle of the end wall facing the dais and cult niche, thus creating the characteristic Assyrian *Langraum* cella.

The view that the typical Babylonian temple with its rectangular court—entrance at one end and "broadroom" cella (or antecella and cella) at the other, represented historically but a vastly enlarged version of the traditional *Herdhaus* plan—differs, of course, from currently accepted opinion. Following Koldewey's study[51] it is generally thought that the *Breitraum* originated as a room built along the enclosure wall of a court or pen. As the court became lined with such rooms it turned into a *Hofhaus* and Koldewey distinguished between an *injunktiver*, a *conjunktiver*, and a *disjunktiver* type. The only dissenting voice that we know of was Frankfort's. Frankfort pointed out that historically in the Sîn temple in Khafājah, the sanctuary was primary, the court secondary, and not the other way around as Koldewey's hypothesis assumed;[52] but his objection does not seem to have had much effect. Of the two latest and major treatments of the history of ancient Mesopotamian temple plans, Lenzen's[53] still operates with Koldewey's *injunktiver Hofhaus Typus* and Heinrich's[54] similarly still sees the plan with *Breitraum* cella as firmly bound up with Koldewey's *injunktiver Hofhaus* or *Hürdenhaus* as Andrae renamed it.[55] Frankfort had argued that originally the open space in front of the temple was a logical place to carry out practical and menial tasks connected with the temple such as e.g., baking of bread and preparation of food, and that in time this open space was walled in for greater privacy, a concept which Heinrich accepted, calling it a "fronting court" (*der vorgelegte Hof*) but which he sees as a parallel feature different from the court of the *injunktiver Hofhaus*.

In the plan of the Sîn temple IV (see fig. 19), it will be seen, the temple proper is placed on a low platform to which steps lead up from the court. This platform was formed by the building of a set of substructure walls, the spaces between them were filled solid with clay and the actual walls of the temple were then built on them. Delougaz mentions that the construction was the same as the one used for the platform on which stood the Oval and he comments that since the Oval was a new temple its platform was laid on a bed of clean sand to insure ritual purity, while in the Sîn temple no such precautions were necessary since there the platform was built on the sacred remains of an earlier temple below.[56] We may now add the Kitîtum complex as a further example. There an imagined earlier temple was artificially duplicated in the substructure which was then filled with

50. The earliest examples of the plan with *Breitraum* cellas and gates aligned along the median axis of the structure known to us are the Agruna of Ningal in the Giparu in Ur which may be ascribed to Ur-Namma (see Weadock 1975, pp. 106f.), the Enki temple of Amar-Suen at Ur, and the Shu-Suen temple at Tell Asmar. It could well have its roots back in the Akkadē period, however.

51. Koldewey 1911, pp. 14f.

52. See Frankfort in Delougaz and Lloyd 1942, p. 311, n. 23.

53. Lenzen 1955, pp. 1-36.

54. Heinrich 1982, pp. 19f.

55. Andrae 1927, cols. 1033ff.

56. Delougaz and Lloyd 1942, p. 21.

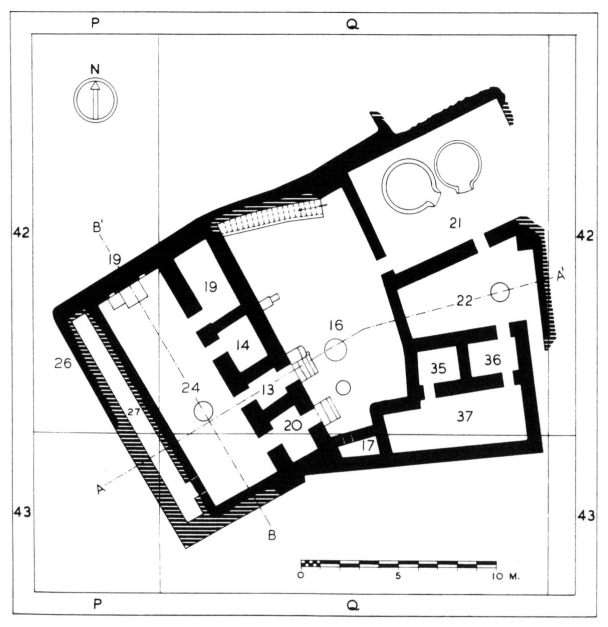

Figure 19. Plan of the Khafājah Sîn Temple IV (after Delougaz and Lloyd 1942, pl. 4B).

clean earth and had the actual temple built upon it.[57] The practice continued into Neo-Babylonian times when it is again exemplified in the substructure of the Harbour temple at Ur.[58]

The purpose of these substructure platforms, Frankfort convincingly argues, was to mark out the sacred site from the profane soil around it.[59] We would even recognize degrees: a lower platform to lift a temple complex out of its profane surroundings, and a second, upper, platform to set the structures devoted to the higher tasks of ritual and

57. Also, of course, other known cases of substructure such as those listed above in n. 14.

58. See n. 14 above (ch. 2).

59. Delougaz and Lloyd 1942, p. 311. We do not see any need to separate the substructure of Sîn temple IV from other late occurrences of this feature.

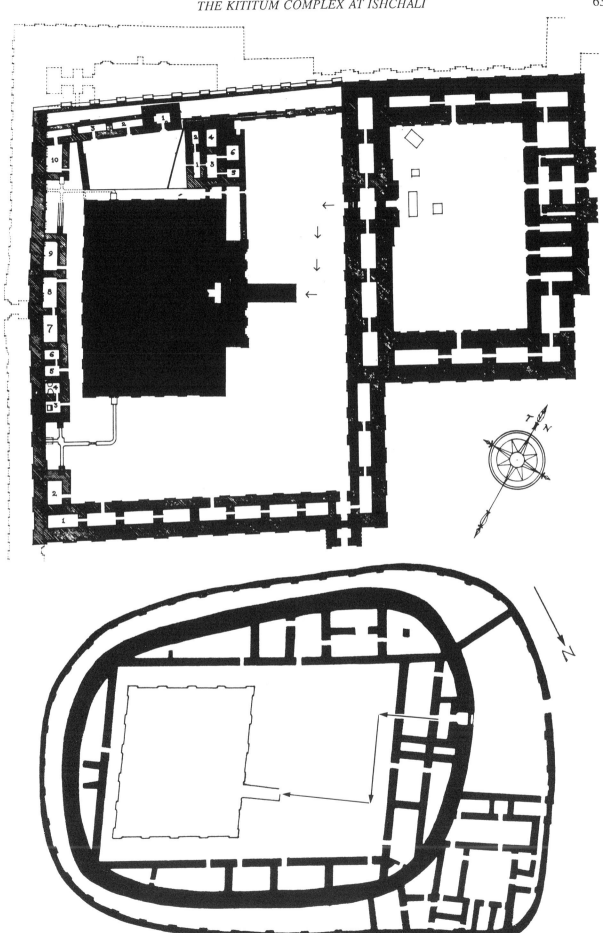

Figure 20. Comparative Plans of the Oval at Khafājah (after Delougaz 1940, pl. 11) and the Nanna Temple at Ur (after Woolley 1939, pl. 68).

administration apart from those serving mere practical and menial purposes: stores, craftsmen's shops, kitchens, et cetera, which were grouped around the main court on the lower level.[60]

There remains one major point to be considered, that of historical continuity. The Khafājah Oval and the Kitītum complex are easily half a millennium apart in time. The squared Oval dates from late Early Dynastic III, say between 2300 and 2400 B.C. while the Kitītum complex is Old Babylonian, around 1850 B.C. only. If, therefore, the close similarity between them is due, as suggested, to an abiding continuation of tradition governing for sacred architecture, rather than to mere accident, it should be possible also to find evidence of that tradition elsewhere and dating to the intervening centuries. Such is in fact the case.

As an earliest example one may mention the temple Eninnu built by Gudea for Ningirsu. It had, according to Gudea's cylinders, a main court with gates and stelae. From it a flight of stairs, Š u - g a l a m, led up to a gate on the top of d u b - l á, an upper platform, on which stood the upper temple with the god's bedroom with his bed and facilities for bathing and anointing.[61]

Next one may list the temple of Nanna in Ur built by Ur-Namma of the Third Dynasty of Ur around 2100 B.C. Its plan is shown in figure 20b next to that of the Oval of the first and original period (see fig. 20a). As will be seen, one enters the temple at Ur through a forecourt known from elsewhere as the "northern court" (k i s a l - s a g̃ - a n - n a)[62] and in Khafājah similarly through the forecourt of the outer Oval, to a main gate with stairs leading up to a court on a low platform, which in both plans has the temple well of fresh water. The gate is, like the one in the inner Oval in Khafājah, off center to the right. In front of one, as one enters, and well to the left is then—both in Ur and Khafājah—a stairway to an upper platform which in Ur takes the new imposing form of a ziqqurat.[63] On top of the ziqqurat was, as we know from inscriptions, Nanna's bedroom with his bed and vessels for bathing.[64]

In passing, it may be mentioned that the structures to the right of the ziqqurat as one faces it was the temple kitchen and dining hall, as we know from an inscription of Nur-Adad found in them.[65]

Not only the temple of Nanna in Ur, but also the temple of Enlil in Nippur (see fig. 21), was rebuilt by Ur-Namma. Here too the same basic plan is in evidence. One entered through a forecourt, here called K i - ù r "leveled ground," which contained the temple of Enlil's spouse Ninlil, É - g̃iš š ú - a. From the K i - ù r steps led through a main gate,

---

60. See the discussion of the function of the lower temple below pp. 69f.

61. Thureau-Dangin 1925, Gudea Cyl. A xxii. 20-xxv 19. See Jacobsen 1987, pp. 417-20.

62. Legrain 1926, 270, obv. ii.5 and iii.2; cf. Levine and Hallo 1967, p. 55. The notation [g̃]ú - e n - n a in obv. ii.4 "The totality of ê n s" (i.e., productive managers) probably refers to the group of throne daises in the west corner of the k i s a l - a n - n a, so no k i s a l "court" should be restored before it. The courtyard around the ziqqurat was known as "the main court" k i s a l - m a h.

63. This variant form of spelling for the word "ziggurat" is used here at the specific request of Th. Jacobsen on the basis of linguistic transliteration—*Gen. ed.*

64. Gadd and Kramer 1966, 133, obv. 25-27. Translation by S. N. Kramer, in Pritchard 1955, pp. 618f.

65. See n. 84 below (ch. 2).

Figure 21. Reconstructed Plan of the Temple of Enlil at Nippur (after Hilprecht 1903, p. 552).

A b u l - k i - k ù, to a low terrace with the main court, k i s a l - m a h.[66] Here was the temple well known as "the honey well" (p ú - l à l).[67] The gate is as in Khafājah, Ur, and Ishchali off center so that when one enters the main court the stairway to the upper platform— here a ziqqurat—is before one to the left. To the right of the ziqqurat is the kitchen excavated by Haines and McCown,[68] and on top of the ziqqurat were, as we know from

66. See Zimmern 1912, SK 9 and duplicates. It lists the parts of the temple in order from the top of the ziqqurat down to the main court and out.

67. Legrain 1926, no. 69.

68. McCown, Haines, and Hansen 1967, pp. 32-33.

the texts, Enlil's private quarters, the house that knows no daylight as well as the utensils for the god's bath.[69]

In essentials, thus, the same general plan can be seen to underlie a series of major Mesopotamian temples, which extends from the Early Dynastic down to the Old Babylonian periods, and is clear testimony to the existence of the normative architectural tradition such as we have suggested.[70]

G. THE FUNCTION OF THE KITÎTUM COMPLEX PLAN

As suggested by Frankfort, the function[71] of the temple's[72] lower, main platform (t e m e n)[73] was to lift the sacred observances of the temple out of a profane, every

---

69. Zimmern 1912, SK 9 and duplicates.

70. For earlier developments see Heinrich 1982.

71. While the intended function of an architectural plan and the elements that compose it will often be immediately clear, there are also cases in which textual evidence can help to specify it further, and sometimes textual evidence alone can tell what went on in a room or open space. We have therefore here given a measure of attention—mostly in the footnotes—to ancient terms for words that bear on the ancient temple and the function of it and its past.

72. Actually Sumerian had no special term for temple, the temple was the "house" (é) of a deity just as a private dwelling was the "house" (é) of its human owner. In Akkadian the word for house, *bîtum*, served in the same manner also for "temple" until about the middle of the second millennium B.C. when the name of Enlil's temple in Nippur, É - k u r, was generalized giving rise to the term *ekurru* "temple."

    This consistent designation of the temple as the "house" of a deity, not merely as a place of worship, is of course of prime importance for the interpretation of the temple plan. It must be seen basically as the plan of a dwelling intended to respond to the needs and functions of a dwelling. A dwelling can, of course, be simple or elaborate, a manor providing space not only for living quarters for the owner but space for a variety of activities to maintain him. The terms for such an elaborate complex seem to have è š or u n u, the latter written with the same sign as for the one for è š but with the addition of a number of sharply bent lines in its lower part. If, as seems likely, the sign was originally a picture of a temple on a platform, the lines in the u n u version may have been intended to represent bricks in herringbone pattern. The difference in meaning between è š and u n u is not clear—è š is rendered simply as *bîtum*, u n u as *šubtum* "seat," "dwelling." The area occupied by a temple complex was called u s g a, Akkadian *i/ešertum*, written with signs indicating "bounds (of) a god." It appears to be a variant of u s u g "taboo" and it should not be confused with another term written u s - g a (for u s - g â < u s - g u · a) that means "goat fattening (pen)"; apparently there were subtle differences of pronunciation not rendered by the script. A characteristic passage occurs in Thureau-Dangin 1925, Gudea Cyl. A xx.14 u s - g a - k ù - g e è š m u - ğ á - ğ á "he began placing the temple complex on the pure sacred premises." The phrase describes the beginning of the actual building and must refer to the temple to be built as a whole.

73. The first terrace called t e m e n was constructed, as noted above, by filling in the substructure. The Sumerian term for this was "to fill" (s i g) the temen as in Thureau-Dangin 1925, Gudea Cyl. A xi.18 u d t e m e n - ğ u₁₀ m a - s i - g e - n a "When you are filling my t e m e n for me." Since t e m e n serves as direct object of s i g to denote the thing filled, it apparently refers basically to the substructure alone, even though it is most often used *pars pro toto* for the filled in substructure, the platform as a whole, the terrace. From Old Babylonian times on, a further meaning of t e m e n is attested, that of "foundation document." In that meaning, however, it was construed with the verb ğ a r "to place" rather than with s i g in Sumerian (see Thureau-Dangin 1907, p. 218.d. 13-14). For the use in Akkadian see *AHw* s.v. *timmenu*.

    As substructure the t e m e n rested upon the foundation called in Sumerian u š from which Akkadian borrowed its term *uššu*. Besides u š Sumerian also has the term u r u₄ which Akkadian does not differentiate from u š, rendering both as *uššu*. Since u r u₄ is written with the sign for plow and plow furrow, it seems likely that the basic meaning of u r u₄ was foundation "trench" and that secondarily it was used also for the filled in trench, much as was the case with t e m e n.

day environment and provide for them pure hallowed ground.[74] One entered traditionally[75] by the stairs[76] near the northeast corner of the complex which led to the gate into the gateroom 4-T.29 which, as other gaterooms in the temple complex, has an outer and inner nonaligned[77] doorway, both with door leaves opening inward into the room. The outer door when closed will thus have barred entry from outside, while the inner door, opening upon the complex, would bar anybody from leaving it when closed. At the south end of the room there was a narrow screen wall partitioning off a small cubicle. A similar arrangement is found in other gaterooms of the complex; presumably these cubicles were places for the gate keeper to sleep when not engaged in opening doors or seeing to it that only authorized persons passed in or out.[78]

74. The holiness with which the ancient Mesopotamian temple was imbued demanded absolute and immaculate cleanliness. Terms for "pure" and "clean," k u g and s i k i l in Sumerian, *ellu* and *ebbu* in Akkadian, are standard attributes of temples and parts of temples in the texts. The very plot on which it stood and the area it occupied was sacred, taboo to the uninitiated like the Islamic *ḥarām*, a notion inherent in the term u s g a mentioned above (note 72, ch. 2). Architecturally this demand for purity found expression in the care taken to provide clean soil on which to build. The Oval in Khafājah was founded on a bed of clean sand. Ur-Baba tells in his inscription (Thureau-Dangin 1907, p. 60 ii.7-8) that he purified with fire the debris into which he was to cut the foundation trenches for his version of the temple Eninnu. Gudea likewise used purification with fire. In other cases purely ritual means of purification may have been preferred. At the few points where we descended to strata underlying the Kitîtum complex we noted no traces of fire.

75. See the comparison between the plan of the Kitîtum complex and that of the Oval in the previous chapter.

76. The Akkadian term for these and other stairs was *simmiltu*. In Sumerian k u n - s a g̃ was similarly used generally for any stairs in a temple. It refers to the stairs leading up to the outer gate of Ekur in the myth of Nanna's journey to Nippur line 258 (Ferrara 1973, p. 66) and it could apparently also be used of the inside stairs leading up to a higher platform with the upper temple, for the lexical text, Nabnîtu VII (= E) 287 (Finkel 1982, p. 113), explains it as *3 (= si-mil-tu) ša gi-gu-né-e* "stairs of (i.e., "to") an upper temple area."

77. The purpose of having the doors of a gateroom nonaligned may well be a desire for privacy, to prevent outsiders from looking in when the doors were opened, as suggested above by Mr. Hill (pp. 11 and 19). There is, however, also a tactical advantage. It makes it more difficult for an attacker to push through.

78. The inferences to be drawn from the plan are borne out by what we know from the texts. The gate to a temple or major estate would be guarded by a gatekeeper who would be on duty night and day, and would admit only persons he knew should have access to the building. In the case of strangers arriving at his fate he would keep them waiting until he had obtained instructions from the owner of the house, either directly or by alerting the chief servant, the s u k k a l, who would then consult the owner.

Thus, when Enlil's oldest son, the Moongod Nanna, arrives at Enlil's temple Ekur with a boat full of gifts for his father, the gatekeeper Kalkal knows him well enough so that when Nanna has identified himself and stated the purpose of his visit, Kalkal happily lets him in on his own responsibility (Ferrara 1973, pp. 66f., lines 254-314).

Similarly Inanna takes pride in the fact that she has entree to Ekur and her father Enlil in her self-praise (Zimmern 1913, SK 199.iii. 25-26) "when I am about to enter Ekur, Enlil's house the gatekeeper does not repulse me, the (chief) servant does not say to me 'stay behind'(?)." Cf. Poebel 1924, p. 54, presumably telling her to get in line with the other applicants for entry.

The gatekeeper—particularly if he is asleep in his cubicle—may, however, at times be slow to respond to a call from outside. In the lament, Reisner 1896, no. 43 Obv. ii, Inanna has to hammer on the gate until her hands are sore before she gets attention, while in the myth about her descent to the Nether World, she less politely throws lumps of clay at the gate to be noticed. Here, unlike Ekur, she is not known and so has to tell who she is and what is the purpose of her visit before the gatekeeper is willing to lay the matter before his mistress. From the Atrahasīs story one gathers that the gatekeeper would normally be asleep at night—presumably in his cubicle—for Kalkal is aroused by the noise made by the rioting younger gods. He does not report directly but alerts the s u k k a l, Nusku, who then informs Enlil. The presence of a cubicle to provide a sleeping place and privacy for the gatekeeper as a standard feature of gateroom plans helps one to understand better the passages in the "Myth of Enlil and Ninlil" in which Enlil hides

From the gateroom one passed into the courtyard of the small temple of Ninshubura who, as a servant deity, s u k k a l,[79] would suitably have the lower platform devoted to menial tasks as her domain. The cella in the west wing is a single cella as befits a minor deity like Ninshubura. Originally, as suggested above on pp. 28f., the small temple may have belonged to a different major deity and may have had both cella and antecella. The rooms behind and north of the cella seem in period IV to have been used by scribes recording the issuance of agricultural tools to workers, otherwise the badly eroded rooms around the court gave little indication of what their use may have been, though presumably some of them may have served as stores for the tools mentioned in the tablets.[80]

---

himself in the gate and then sleeps with Ninlil pretending he is the gatekeeper. In the dim light of a small cubicle he would have been hard to recognize.

A problem is raised by the existence of a second door in the gateroom which would prevent people from leaving the temple complex. That such measures were appropriate at city gates is clear. They served to prevent slaves and debtors from absconding (cf. Bergmann 1953, CH § 15 and Goetze 1956, CEšn §§ 51 and 52). Similarly the gates of the Nether World—envisioned as a city—have as primary duty to keep the ghosts in, so they will not return to plague the living. Even Nergal—when he wanted to leave the Nether World—in the myth of Nergal and Ereshkigal, had to convince the gatekeeper that he was a messenger dispatched by Ereshkigal. Also in temples, however, such measures may have been indicated, if only to know who was absent from the temple complex and for what reasons. That the temple personnel would normally sleep within the temple is suggested by the Nanshe Hymn line 115 which lists, as a misdemeanor, to burn and roast in the night within the temple. A difficulty is presented by the total absence of toilet facilities in the temple area. It agrees well with the sacred purity demanded for it, but if the personnel spent the night in the temple, they would clearly have had to be let out by the gatekeepers for calls of nature.

79. Ninshubura occurs in the Sumerian pantheon only as servant of another deity. The element š u b u r in her name is the Sumerian form of the name Š u b a r which designates the northern region later called Assyria. Since slaves were frequently recruited from there the term š u b u r became in time a designation for "slave," much the same way that the ethnic term Slav developed the meaning "slave" in Greek sklabos, Latin sclavus, slavus. The name Nin-šubura(k) "Queen of Subartu" could thus well have suggested an enslaved queen in a servile position. Her Akkadian name *Il-abrat* means "(tutelary) deity of the (simple) people."

As for her office, English has no term that would satisfactorily render s u k k a l. Closest is perhaps "secretary" if used in its original sense of "confidant," "confidential clerk," and sometimes with implications of "administrative secretary." The s u k k a l discusses proposed action with his master and advises him. He also serves as messenger to convey his master's decisions or to seek help for him, as well as to perform any other errand for him. He is also in charge of screening applications for audiences with his master and for ushering in those he finds acceptable. He is thus the natural person for the gatekeeper to consult about whether to admit or not admit a stranger and convenient—whether originally so planned or not—to have the s u k k a l of Inanna Kitîtum, Ninshubura, located immediately behind the gate. In the myth of Inanna and Enki the latter orders his s u k k a l, Isimud, to ready the meal, with which travelers were traditionally welcomed, for Inanna. The meal is served in the gate of Enki's temple I g i p i r i ĝ a after Inanna has entered. If a similar procedure for receiving guests was followed at the Kitîtum complex it would again be convenient to have Ninshubura's temple next to the gate to accommodate the visitor and his or her retinue. It could almost be considered an extension of the gate.

It should be added that the above considerations presuppose that the gates in the south wall were kept locked and unattended except at ceremonial occasions. The period IV gate cut at the center of the east wing can be disregarded as late and secondary.

80. The tablets are Ish. 34-T.76, 78, 80, 83, 85, and Ish. 34-T.96 plus 97 from 1-S.29 top; Ish. 34-T.119-125, 127-133 from 4-S.29 top, and Ish. 34-T.99-103 from 2-T.29. (Note that in Greengus 1979, pp. 56-57, the findspot 3-S.29 for Ish. 34-T.99, 100, 101, and 103 should now read 2-T.29.) The majority of the tablets have been published by Greengus (1979). See his discussion of them on p. 12 with its reference to a collection of bronze implements in The Oriental Institute Museum said to come from Ishchali by the dealer from whom they were bought in Baghdad in 1930. They may well have come from the area of the Ninshubura temple or the adjoining part of the east wing of the complex which communicated with it.

Through a gateroom 4-T.30 one passed from the court of the Ninshubura temple into the main courtyard of the complex. This gateroom too had nonaligned doorways with doorleaves and a cubicle for the gatekeeper. It thus could close off either of the two temple areas from the other though leaving both still accessible from the outside by the other entrances, the Ninshubura unit through 4-T.29, and the main court through the major gate in 3-T.32.[81] That there would be a need to close an inner unit like the Ninshubura temple off from the rest of the complex by a manned gate is surprising, but could conceivably be a precaution against theft. The goddess, as we know from the inventory found in her cella, owned much precious jewelry, a good deal of which would have been on display on her statue and constituted a very real temptation to a thief,[82] so it would be prudent to close off not only the cella itself, but the whole small temple when on festive occasions the main court (k i s a l - m a h) would be thronged with worshipers or in the daily routine open for deliveries from outside.

The rooms lining the main court on its east and south side are unfortunately badly preserved and yield little information about their original use, but it must seem reasonable to assume that they would have served normal domestic functions essential to the running of a temple estate. A list of such functions, which is given in Gudea's Cyl. A xxviii 3-13 (Thureau-Dangin 1925), enumerates "cowshed" (é - ĝ u d) for providing fresh milk, "kitchen" (g i r₄ - m a h, lit. "main oven"), "slaughterhouse" (ĝ í r - p a - n a, lit. "set of knives"), "Place of prebend deliveries" (é - k i - š u k u m), "libation place" (n e - s a ĝ) with store of wine, and "brewery" (é - s i r i š) for beer and strong drink.[83]

Of these various units only one seems clearly duplicated in the Kitîtum complex, the "kitchen," which can be recognized in the western unit of the north wing of the complex. Here cooking facilities, such as the two multiple fireplaces built against the north and south walls of room 1-Q.29, and in the courtyard 1-R.29, as well as the circular bread ovens in the adjoining rooms 2-Q.29 and 6-R.29, suggest a kitchen of institutional type, and the suggestion gains support from the fact that its position, to the right of the second platform, is precisely where, according to the history of the plan, the temple kitchen (g i r₄ - m a h),[84] it should be.

It may be added that both Enlil's temple in Nippur, Ekur, and Ninurta's temple there, Eshumesha, contained stores for adjuncts of ploughs, "handles," and "bags" (*bît a-he-e ù ta-ka-la-tum*, Bernhardt and Kramer 1975, pp. 97f., lines 5, 12, and 19).

81. In period IV there was also the secondary entrance through 1-U.30 and 3-T.31.

82. Ish. 35-T.99 (Greengus 1979, pl. 45:106) and Ish. 34-T.98 (Greengus 1979, pl. 44:104).

83. Cf. also the ancient plan, Thureau-Dangin 1903, Text no. 148, which has open space for a room of the weaver (é - u š - b a r), room of the donkeys (é - a n š e) and room of the perfect oxen (é - g u d - d u₇). The last item suggests the plan formed part of a temple. See also the plan published by Heinrich and Seidl 1967, p. 34, which has a shed for the weaver (é - u š - b a r), room of the *sukkallu* (é - s u k k a l), room of the cook (é - h a t i m), and store room ([é]-k i š ì b). This plan is probably also a temple plan if one may interpret the design at the end walls of three of the rooms as thrones set on throne daises and the rooms as cellas. A similar design showing the throne only appears on the plan held by Gudea in Statue B on the outside of the wall next to the stylus.

84. For temple kitchens at this position in the plan at Ur, Uruk, and Nippur, see McCown, Haines, and Hansen 1967, pp. 32f. In the Oval the corresponding room 1-2-N.45 was to the left of the platform. In the relevant structure at Ur copper cylinders with an inscription of Nûr-adad were found (Gadd and Legrain 1928, nos. 112 and 124, Figulla and Martin 1953, p. 58, Sollberger 1965, no. 67; cf. Landsberger 1931, pp. 115ff. and Kärki 1980, pp. 51-52). The sections dealing with the function of the structure reads u d - b i - a g i r i₄ -

The kitchen facilities found all belong to periods II-B, III, and IV; in period III two standard ovens or kitchen ranges replaced the multiple fireplaces in 1-Q.29, but there is no reason to assume that the function of the unit was different before then, even though such concrete evidence as could have shown it with certainty apparently was cleared out when the new clay floors of I-B and II-A were laid. Only heavy layers of ashes under them, ashes such as are met with on the upper floors, testify to sameness of usage with them.

Besides the temple kitchen, Gudea's list of facilities has a temple "slaughterhouse" (ǧír-pa-na) which will have had charge of killing and cutting up animals brought for sacrifice or for food at festive meals. If the Kitîtum temple also had such a facility—and offhand it must seem almost certain that it would—the most likely place to look for it would be at the east end of the main court near the well, since water would have been needed for rinsing off blood, and near the drain next to the well, which would be needed to carry the bloodied water outside the complex. Actually the puzzling square plinth of mudbrick at the head of the drain could very well have had a wooden top originally and served as a butcher's block. One will assume, in that case, that the recorded height of 1.50 meters actually represents the height of an original plinth some 70 to 80 centimeters above the floor level which was later raised another 70 to 80 centimeters to accommodate the new higher floor of period III.[85]

The observation just made, that a puzzling recorded height of a feature may have been the result of a heightening of a lower, earlier version, would seem to apply also to the curious masonry block in front of the main staircase at the west end of the courtyard. The height above the floor in the original building period, I-A, was some 50 centimeters which must be considered the norm. The rebuilt part above it is thus to be interpreted as containing stages adjusted to approximately this height above the successive later floors, the last of these an intermediate floor in period III. The importance of this plinth in front of the stairs is made clear by the fact that it was prefigured in the substructure and was

---

mah ú-sù-sù-ᵈEN-ZU-na-ka ninda-íl-e kìlib-dingir-re-ne-er du₈-mah unú-gal-ba mí-zi-dè-eš du₁₁-ga kin-sig kin-nim-ma gù nun-bi di-dam nam-ti-la-ni-šè mu-na-dù "At that time he built for him (i.e., Nanna/Suen) for his life the main oven, carrier of bread for all the gods at Suen's repasts, carefully tended for the superb pastry of their meals, that it seethe loudly at the evening and morning meals." Of other references to a gir₄, oven in the texts, one may cite the Hymn to Enki's temple in Eridu (Sjöberg and Bergmann 1969, 17-19) gir₄ ninda-íl ú-sù-sù-za U₆-nir èš-mah an-né-ús-sa-za gir₄-gal unú-gal-da sá-a-za "In (view of) your oven, carrier of bread of your repasts, in (view of) your ziqqurat, the august manor abutting heaven, in (view of) your great oven keeping pace with great meals," the Nanshe Hymn 57 with the almost identical "her great oven keeping pace with great meals," and the "Lament for Ur and Sumer" 314 (Gadd and Kramer 1966, 131 Obv. 18) gir₄-mah gira_x(U+MAŠ) gud udu nu-ak-e ir nu mu-un-ur₅-[ur₅]-e "The . . . main oven is no longer roasting oxen and sheep, no longer giving off aroma" which shows that the gir₄ could be used for meat as well as for breads. In view of the impressive dimensions of room 1-Q.21 and its stately towered gate, one might be inclined to think that the planner had intended it for a more formal use than as a kitchen, perhaps as a dining hall with the kitchen activities limited to the court and its surrounding rooms. However, other plans of such kitchens suggest that the food was carried up to the deities' private quarters in the upper temples. See McCown, Haines, and Hansen 1967, p. 33. Here the stairs in 8-Q.30 would have served. Note also that Gudea Cyl. A. XXV.14 (Thureau-Dangin 1925) mentions the evening meal (kin-<sig>-gi unù-gal) in connection with the structures on top of the platform.

85. See above pp. 30 and 36.

carried up from there as an irregular supporting pillar, and since its height and shape suggest an offering table,[86] it may very well be that we have in it an example of the one known as the "royal stand" (ki-lugal-gub) such as is known from the texts as an important feature in temple courtyards.[87]

It is not to be expected that the many and various uses to which the main courtyard of the Kitîtum temple will have been put will have left recognizable traces on the ground, or may be conjectured from textual references to standard functions of temple courtyards elsewhere.[88] Thus, while the main courtyard would seem an ideal setting for ritual acts at the annual festivals of a temple there is no firm evidence of such use, and one can only guess that perhaps some of the rites connected with Inanna's marriage to Dumuzi and the laments over his early death may have been enacted in the main courtyard of the Inanna Kitîtum temple at the times of year with which they were associated.

86. A remarkably close parallel is furnished by the Harbour temple at Ur, which had tables and altars of baked bricks similar to this masonry block of sun baked bricks, even to the irregularity of the masonry that carried up through the substructure filling. Woolley describes them thus: "But the strangest thing concerned the furnishing, the altar, the tables, and the statue base were built up to the height usual for such (the tables 18 inches, the altar 3 feet) with bricks carefully laid, but above this there was more brickwork, very irregularly laid rising to the full height of the surrounding walls, thus the table in the outer court, which was of the normal long and narrow shape, took on the effect of a brick screen and the altar in the inner court became a brick column; no one could have placed offerings or done sacrifice on them . . ."; and speaking of the sand used there for the filling: "As the sand was poured in from above, workmen laid bricks on the altar and tables, keeping pace with the rise of the sand (the fact that they were working from above would account for the irregular bricklaying) until . . . , et cetera." Woolley in Moorey 1982, pp. 245f.

87. The main court of a temple was apparently a favored place for the king to present offerings to the deity owning the temple and to make obeisance. The most common such offerings were bread and water offered up., e.g., by Gudea when he visited the temple of Nanshe: ensi-ke₄ kisal Sirat(r)^{ki}-ta-ka saĝ an-šè mi-ni-íl ninda ĝiš bí-tag a še$_x$ ì-dé (Thureau-Dangin 1925, Cyl. A. iv. 5-6) "The ruler lifted up the head in Siratr's courtyard, offered bread and libated cold water." Correspondingly the great Enlil Hymn says of the king that kisal-mah-e nidba si bí-in-sá "he directs shewbreads unto the main court" (i.e., of Ekur) and SK 4, rev. i.30-31 (Zimmern 1912, cf. Sjöberg 1960, no. 9) has: ^{d}Nanna ki-sa-al-ma-he ninda-ba ĝar-ra-zu "unto the main court unto your arrayed shewbreads." The place in the main court of a temple in which these royal offerings were presented is suggested by the Ninurta Hymn, Radau 1911, no. i.i. 9-11: É-šu-me-ša₄ ki-tuš-kù igi-šu-galam[-ma-ke₄] kisal-mah-zu gud-gal udu-gal-e si [ha-ra-ni-ib-sá]ki-lugal-gub-kù-zu šu ha-ra-ni-in-mú-[mú] "May he (i.e., Shu-Sin) direct a large ox and a large sheep into the holy dwelling Eshumesha at your main court at the front of the Shu-galam (stairs), may he make obeisance to you from your royal stand." The mention of the šu-galam stairs suggests a point in the courtyard in front of the stairs leading up to the upper temple, and the mention of the royal stand suggests that this was the name of it. It would therefore seem likely that the offering table in front of the stairs leading from the main courtyard of the Kitîtum complex up to the upper temple, as well as the similar such tables elsewhere represent "royal stands" from which the king would present his offerings as greeting gifts before his audience with the deity.

   Comparable such offering tables were found in Ekishnugal in Ur in the northern courtyard in front of the stairs to the ziqqurat terrace and—without stairs—in the courtyard before the gate to the antecella in the Harbour temple and the Nin-ezen temple at Ur. Compare the Ningal temple of Kurigalzu, the Shu-Sin temple at Tell Asmar, the Ningal temple at the *giparu* in Ur, and elsewhere.

88. One function which is regularly assigned to temple and palace courtyards is that of an arena for athletic games called ĝešpú lirum in Sumerian, *umāšu ù abāru* in Akkadian. They are generally thought to denote a form of wrestling, but their regular construction with the verb ra in Sumerian, *mahāṣu* in Akkadian, suggests that striking was also involved. Passages placing these games in main courts are: "The Cursing of Akkad'" lines 102-103 (Cooper 1983), Shulgi C lines 129-131 (Castellino 1972), SK 197 Obv. ii.10 (Zimmern 1913), and "The Wooing of Marduk" (Chiera 1934a, text no. 52) lines 69-75. There is no telling whether such contests were held in the Kitîtum temple or not.

The offering table just discussed stands in front of the stairs that lead up from the main court to the upper platform (d u b - l á).[89] The front of that platform consisted of a terrace of baked bricks, a rather unusual feature since baked bricks were a luxury in a country short of wood for fuel, and so were generally used sparingly and restricted to points where it was necessary to protect mudbricks against damage from water. The lavish use of them here would thus suggest that water was somehow involved. The explanation may be furnished by the texts, which speak of the upper levels of temples as g i g u n u s[90] and describe them as adorned with plantations of cedar. If, therefore, as seems reasonable, we may assume that the upper platform of the Kitîtum temple had such a plantation of cedars—presumably trees growing in barrels—the need to water them would demand waterproofing of the ground under them. Thus, the construction of the terrace with baked bricks laid in bitumen and, in a way, the easy accessibility of the well in the courtyard would make good planning sense.

From the terrace two separate doors led into the upper Kitîtum temple. This redundancy of entrances can be traced back historically to the phase of the temple plan represented by the Sîn temple where it occurs in its most puzzling form. Two separate doors lead into a gate room from which, however, only a single one leads on into the cella. The need for two outer doors rather than one seems hard to justify. The correct explanation was probably given by Hill when he suggested that the major one of the two entrances would normally be kept closed and opened only on ceremonial occasions. His suggestion gains textual support from the description of the structure on top of the upper platform of the temple of Ningirsu in Gudea's Cylinder A. It mentions "the gate by which the king enters,"[91] a term that clearly suggests that there were other, less grand, and festive ways into the building.

As for the structures that stood on the top of the upper platform of the Kitîtum complex, they proved to be sufficiently well preserved for the complete plan to be recovered. This was an extraordinary and unexpected stroke of luck, for a building thus highly placed is naturally greatly exposed to weathering and erosion. Actually, the Ishchali temple is the only such temple—*Hochtempel*, to use Andrae's term—that is known from any historical period in Mesopotamia whatever. It is thus of exceptional interest.

89. For the meaning "foundation platform" see *CAD* D, p. 163 s.v. *dublu* and Sjöberg and Bergmann 1969, p. 57 to line 321 as also Sjöberg 1973, p. 38 note 6. The d u b - l á is specifically an upper platform resting on a lower platform, the t e m e n. To the passages quoted by Sjöberg and Bergmann add Langdon 1912, p. 76 lines 26 and 34 *tu-ba-lu* and *tu-ba-lu-ù* with anaptyctic *a*. The final l of the word was probably vocalic, /l/ rendered variously as / l /, / l á /, or / l a l /.

90. See *CAD* G, pp. 67-70 s.v. *gigunû*, especially Gudea Statue B. v. 18 (Thureau-Dangin 1907) š à - b a g i - g u n u₂ ki-á g a-ni š i m - ğ i š - e r i n - n a m u - n a - n i - d ù "within it I built for him his beloved g i g u n u out of aromatic cedar" and SK 8 i.13 (Zimmern 1912) and dupl. 8.1.13 (Myhrman 1911) g i - g u n₄ - n a ᵍⁱˢt i r - š i m -ᵍⁱˢe r i n - n a - t a "from the Gigunu, the grove of aromatic cedars." For the stairs leading up from the court see above note 76 and the quote from Nabnîtu VII 287 (Finkel 1982) explaining k u n - s a ğ as "stairs of (i.e., leading up to) a g i g u n u."

91. Gudea Cyl. A. xxv.5 (Thureau-Dangin 1925) k á - k i - l u g a l - k u₄ - b i - t a "from its gate where the king enters." Reference could conceivably be to a rite such as the l u g a l - k u₄ - r a "entry of the king" of the Ur III texts (see Schneider 1924-30, pp. 59-61). More likely though, reference is to Ningirsu and l u g a l might be better rendered as "owner" than as "king." The entry of the god into his house could refer to a ceremonial bringing his statue back after its annual journey to Eridu.

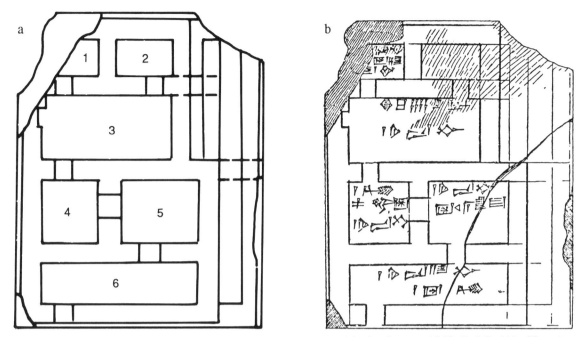

Figure 22. Drawing of Building on Clay Tablet from Tello: (*a*) after Lenzen 1955, Taf. 3, Abb. 33 and (*b*) after Thureau-Dangin 1898, p. 23.

At a first glance, though, as one looks at the plan, it will not seem much different from other well-known and familiar plans of temples built at ground level or on a single platform only; it has the familiar rectangular central courtyard surrounded on three sides by single rows of rooms. It has two entrances from the east and one from the south. At the north end of the court is a towered entrance to an antecella, and behind this is the cella with dais and cult niche—both are *Breitraums*. On either side of the dais is a square column of mudbrick which, we conjecture, once held a stone slab with a hole for a wooden canopy pole. In front of the dais stood probably a two-tiered offering table such as is shown on a relief from Tello of the time of Gudea,[92] as a fragment that probably came from such a pottery table was found in 2-R.30. It shows the body of a musician playing the lyre;[93] a statue of the goddess standing or seated, would have occupied the dais. The plaques found showing a goddess (i.e., Ish. 34:124, pl. 34a) may, as suggested by Frankfort in the preliminary report,[94] represent the cult image but this cannot be known with certainty.

Actually, only the very private and secluded unit of rooms behind the cella is unusual in the plan. Access to the unit is from the cella through a door in its short west wall. Help to interpret this unit comes from a drawing of a building on a tablet of the Akkadē period found at Tello[95] which apparently represents a private house (see fig. 22). It shows a small court marked k i s a l (room 5) from which a reception room, p a - p a h (room 4), leads into a large sitting room, k i - d ú r (room 3), from which again doors lead into two small rooms, one marked "innermost room," é - š à (room 1), and the other was probably marked "bedroom," é - n á (room 2), the surface is damaged here and no signs remain.

92. Cros 1910-14, p. 294; cf. also Frankfort 1955, pl. XXIV:f.

93. Ish. 34:79 found at 2-R.30 (floor of period III). (See Frankfort 1936, fig. 74 and pl. 39 here.)

94. See Frankfort 1936, p. 85, and fig. 67 on p. 89.

95. Thureau-Dangin 1903, Text no. 145. See also Lenzen 1955, Tafel 3, Abb. 33a for a redrawing according to the measurements given on the tablet.

Comparison with the Kitîtum unit shows the same arrangement of the sitting room and the two small rooms at the back, but the small room south of the sitting room here merely leads into the p a - p a h, for that term belongs, as we know from the texts, to the cella,[96] and there is an antecella between it and the court, k i s a l. These elaborations in the grander Kitîtum plan are only to be expected and do not affect the key point, which is that we are dealing in both cases with the plan of actual living quarters, the private rooms, the *harīm* of the goddess.

These private quarters of a deity on top of a ziqqurat or a high platform we know about from the texts. They contained the deity's bed and vessels for bathing and anointing him or her, presumably, that is, washing and oiling the wooden cult statue. They were the most sacred part of the temple, "the house of darkness" (é-itima = *simakkum*, *kiṣṣum*), and "the house that knows no daylight" (é-ud-nu-zu) shrouded in mysterious obscurity.[97] Correspondingly, the plan shows that no daylight reached these rooms. To make the goddess' bed, to bathe and anoint her, the priests must have used lamps, and actually we found in the room next to the antecella (2-P.30) remnants of two bronze lamps (pl. 30a-d). Their shape, that of the goddess' sacred animal, the lion, suggests that they served cultic purposes.

In 1-P.29, the room corresponding to "the innermost room" on the Akkadē plan, two accounts of gold and precious stones were found as well as various cylinder seals. The room, which had a door that could be locked, may thus well have been where the goddess kept her jewelry and other treasures. In the cella itself a cylinder seal dedicated to Inanna

---

96. See *AHw*, p. 823 s.v. *papahu(m)* for passages where the term is used for cella. In Section 2b we should prefer "reception room" to *Hauskapelle*.

97. For é-itima (ĜÁ×MI): *kiṣṣu* see Sjöberg and Bergmann 1969, p. 57 to line 29 and dictionaries (*CAD* and *AHw*) s.v. *kiṣṣu*. The name means "house of darkness" and ended in a genitive element -ak as shown by "Enmerkar and the lord of Aratta" line 391 nam-bi-šé itima-a-ka ba-an-ku₄ "because of this he went in to the dark chamber" (and by the loanword *simakku* derived from e₂-itimāk by elision of a contracted e-i and aspiration of t). For itima (UD×MI) *eṭûtu* "darkness" see *CAD* E, p. 413. The characteristic darkness of the é-itima is stressed by its epithet ud-nu-zu "knowing not daylight" in "The Cursing of Akkadē," line 129 (Cooper 1983), and the Eridu Lament (Green 1978, p. 138) ki-r u g a (place for antiphon) 6.12′ or i-bí nu-bar "not to be seen," SK 8 (Zimmern 1912) and dupl. It was used as a place of rest as shown by the great Enlil Hymn 1.76 kur-sig itima-kù ki ní-te-en-te-en-zu, "the mountain top (lit. 'narrow mountain') the holy itima your place of calming down," and as a place of retreat for coping with an emotional crisis as in the quotation from "Enmerkar and the Lord of Aratta" mentioned above.

In the itima the sacred ewers used to shower the gods' images at their ritual bath were apparently kept, to judge from "The Cursing of Akkadē," lines 129-130 (Cooper 1983), itima-é ud-nu-zu-ba kalam-e igi i-ni-in-bar ᵘʳᵘᵈᵘšen-kù-dingir-re-e-ne-ke₄ Uriᵏⁱ igi i-ni-in-bar, "Upon the itima, the house knowing not daylight the country laid eyes upon the holy copper ewer of the gods the Akkadians laid eyes." This sacred ewer is also mentioned in similar context in "The Lament for Ur and Sumer," lines 443-444 (Gadd and Kramer 1966, 133 obv. 25-26, 134 obv. 3′-4′), á-ná-da-kù⌐ ᵈNanna-ka ĝìr ki mu-u[n-su₈]-⌐ge-NE⌐ ᵘʳᵘᵈᵘšen-kù lú igi nu⌐-bar-re-dam erín-e igi ì-ni-[in-bar] "into Nanna's bed chamber they were stomping, the enemy saw the holy copper ewer not to be seen by man" but here it is seen, it seems, in Nanna's bed chamber. It may therefore well be that the two are identical, itima "house of darkness" being perhaps a more poetic term than á-ná-da "house in which one lies down." That the god was washed and anointed each night in preparation for his going to bed is indicated in Gudea Cyl. B. ix 6-9 (Thureau-Dangin 1925) which lists as duties of Ningirsu's valet de chambre, Kinda-zi: "to cleanse with water, clean with soap, and with oil of the shiny stone jar, and soap of the bowl, induce him (i.e., Ningirsu) to sweet sleep on his bed spread with clean hay." Whether this represented an actual daily cleaning of Ningirsu's statue or was supposed to take place invisibly in the world of the gods only, we have no means to decide.

Kitîtum was discovered (Ish. 34:45, OIC 20, fig. 68 and OIP 72, pl. 87:917). It was one of the first pieces of evidence that showed that the mistress of the temple was Inanna Kitîtum.

A word should perhaps be said about the term for cella, p a - p a h = *papahum*. As will be seen from the house plan from Tello and the position of the cella in the Kitîtum temple, the p a - p a h is the room that connects the private part of the house, the domain of the women and children, with the outer world. Therefore too, in the Sumerian tale of the fowler and his wife, it is from the door of the p a - p a h, from her domain behind it, that she abuses her husband.[98] This throws light on the function of the cella. It is the place where the owner of the temple deals with the outside, the non-private world. Here he gives orders, makes judgments, and hears petitions. It is his reception room and his office. In terms of Islamic architecture the cella is god's *iwan*, the living quarters of his *harīm*.

---

98. Copenhagen Nat. Mus. 10068 no. 9: d a m - a - n i ì n i m p a - p a h - a g ù i m - m a - n a - d [é - e] "his wife shouted a word to him from the *papahu*." For a variant version of the tale see Alster 1980, pp. 43-48.

CHAPTER 3

THE ISHCHALI CITY WALL AND THE CITY GATE
by Th. Jacobsen

Extending our excavations eastward along the street that ran east-west south of the Kitîtum complex we came upon a city gate and the city wall (see fig. 23). This latter was built of mudbrick and varied in width from seven to eight meters. Eight meters seemed to be the norm, the narrowing to seven meters was at the southeast corner of grid square W.31. To judge from the plan the builders first left untouched a small temple which lay in their path and merely strengthened its outer wall with a retaining wall of mudbrick built up against it. Eventually however, that must have seemed unsatisfactory, so the whole of the temple's east wing was filled in solid to make the city wall the same width throughout. In the section investigated, the wall was plain without buttresses and towers. A double drain pierced through it just north of the temple and emptied in a narrow groove in the revetment in front of it.

The city gate itself was set into the wall at an angle of slightly less than ninety degrees, its northern jamb projecting to bring the end of it on a line with the face of the city wall south of the gate. It had a single deep rabbet balancing a double rabbet in the southern jamb. The outer doorway led into a slightly skewed rectangular gateroom and was aligned with the inner doorway to the city. In the northwest corner of the gateroom was a bench-like later construction of mudbrick, the purpose of which is not clear. Possibly it was remnants of a cubicle for a watchman. In the gateroom two tablets were found, Ish. 34-T.149[1] and Ish. 34-T.153.[2] The first of these is a list of measures of areas, the second names overseers of detachments of workers or soldiers from the town of [ ]-⌈x⌉-am-ha-tum⌈ki⌉ and mentions a city gate. Unfortunately the lines, explaining what the connection of these detachments with the city gate in question was, are badly broken. Nor is it clear whether that gate is the one in which the document was found, although that seems likely.

Finds from the top level of the city gate include three terracotta plaque fragments (Ish. 34:92, 103, and 110, pls. 33n and 34c) as well as a number of bone pin fragments (see app. 4). An oblong-shaped bronze piece, 2.10 × 2.30 centimeters, is dated to Period II. A female terracotta plaque (Ish. 34:206, pl. 34m) was in a group of other finds, the period of which could not be determined.

---

1. Greengus 1979, pl. 98:292 and OBTIV 292 in Greengus 1986, pp. 88-91.
2. Greengus 1979, pl. 60:151. Tentatively one might suggest for rev. 13′ff. a reading ⌈naphar⌉ [x]+9 ERÍN LÚ[pl. l]a(?)-am-ha-dum^{ki} ša aš-šum ma-[ṣa-ar] abul-E[N!?-zu] . . . "Total x + 9 soldiers who for the guarding of the city gate of Sîn [were . . .]."

Figure 23. Ishchali—Plan of the City Wall, City Gate, and the Shamash "Gate" (Sîn) Temple.

CHAPTER 4

THE ISHCHALI "GATE" (SÎN) TEMPLE
by Th. Jacobsen

A. THE MAIN TEMPLE COMPLEX

Turning right immediately upon entering through the city gate one would have come upon the door to 1-W.32, an enclosed area with a thin walled compartment in its southeast corner, entered at the west end (see fig. 23). In this area were found two cylinder seals (Ish. 34:83 and 84, OIP 72, pl. 88:941 and 940). The area served as a forecourt to a small temple located at its north side, recognizable as such by its doubly rabbeted doorway flanked by simulated towers, each of which was decorated with five vertical T-shaped grooves. Apparently the ground level outside the temple had risen more quickly after its construction than had the one inside it, so in entering the temple one went down three steps of baked bricks set in the doorway. The gateroom, 1-W.31, was rectangular in shape and had aligned centered entry and exit doors. At the west end of the room a small cubicle had been partitioned off in the usual fashion. A terracotta god plaque fragment (Ish. 35:216, pl. 34g) was found in the top level of this room. The exit door led into a second vestibule, 2-W.31, through which one entered the central court, 3-V.31. The line of entry, whether by accident or design, was about a meter off to the east from the median axis of the court and the building generally, and thus not exactly on line with the entrance to antecella and cella either. The vestibule, 2-W.31, yielded a plaque fragment of a god holding weapons (Ish. 35:212, pl. 33l).

The court, 3-V.31, is rectangular and has a paved walk of baked bricks, three bricks wide on all sides. A drain of baked bricks takes rainwater outside the building through the room 6-W.31. In the top level of the court a cylinder seal (Ish. 35:31, OIP 72, pl. 88:939) was found and a terracotta god plaque (Ish. 35:79, pl. 35a) came from an undetermined period. The court is surrounded by rows of three mutually unconnected rooms. It has two parallel such rows at either end and single ones at the sides. The single rows carry all the way to the front of the building and severely limit the two middle rooms, the gaterooms. The doors to these various rooms from the court are evenly spaced, one in the middle and one at each end of the court's sides. They are all rabbeted, the door to the antecella, 2-V.30, is emphasized by being centered in the wall, being wider than the others, and double rabbeted. A pivotstone box behind its eastern jamb shows that it could be closed with a door. Inside the room the fragment of a limestone stela (Ish. 35:36, pl. 25),[1] and a jeweler's hematite weight in the shape of a lion's head (Ish. 35:37, pl. 46a) were found. From the antecella a second wide rabbeted door opens into the cella, 3-V.30, while a door in the east wall leads to the connected rooms 1- and 2-W.30. The cella has no niche and the brickwork in the north wall is unbroken and bonded. An interesting feature of the cella, 3-V.30, was a group of tablets found in it. It included two contracts, one of which (Ish. 35-T.28[2]) had the god Sîn heading the list of witnesses, and a considerable number of brief accounts of amounts of barley paid to people, most of whom were under the authority of an individual referred to only by his title *muškênum* "the client"; presumably he was a client of the temple who was in charge of some of its activities.[3] The cella also yielded a tablet, Ish. 35-T.62, dated to the year Ibal-pî-el died, four hematite date-shaped weights (Ish. 35:43-46; see pl. 45e for one example), two bronze nails (Ref. 35:60 and 70), a bronze pin (Ref. 35:71), and a terracotta leg model (Ref. 35:61).

In room 2-W.30 at the northeast corner of the building a cylinder seal (Ish. 35:95, OIP 72, pl. 88:938) was found. In 4-V.30 at the northwest corner of the building a copper lamp (Ish. 35:84, pl. 30f, g), three stone maceheads, and one fragment of a macehead were found (Ish. 35:80-83, pl. 41f-h). In this room also was the Ishchali Gilgamesh fragment (Ish. 35-T.117[4]).The room had a round bread oven (*tanoor*) against its north wall. Room 5-V.31 seems to have been used by a court scribe or notary. In it were three fragments of court records, Ish. 35-T.12,[5] 14,[6] and Ish. 34-T.22[7]; a fragment of a contract of sale or perhaps of the contesting of a sale, Ish. 35-T.17[8]; a fragment of an assignment of responsibility for grain in a storehouse, Ish. 35-T.21[9]; and a fragment of a guaranty document, Ish. 35-T.20[10]. It may be noted that in Ish. 35-T.14 the case is tried "in the gate of the god *Sîn-ša-kamānim*," and the same may have been the case in Ish. 35-T.12, but there the text is lost after the word for "gate." In Ish. 35-T.22 the oath is taken by Sîn and the ruler Sumu-abi-arim. Room 5-V.31 also had a fragment of a plaque (Ish. 35:87, pl. 35e) of a man carrying a gazelle.

1. The fragment remaining shows the lower parts of two figures facing each other. The one to the left is dressed in a long smooth robe and appears to represent the king. The one to the right places a foot on a square elevation and held, to judge from what remains, a coil of measuring line and a measuring stick in his right hand, a weapon in his left. See Frankfort 1943, pp. 21 and 34-35, no. 336 and pl. 75A. We should prefer to interpret the scene as showing the moongod Sîn handing to the ruler the builder's tools, symbols of peace and construction of temples, while holding back the weapon, symbol of war. An exact parallel would be the scene shown on the seal of Ilushu-ilia (Frankfort, Lloyd, and Jacobsen 1940, p. 215). Very similar is also the scene on the right side of the panel just below the top one on Ur-Namma's stela from Ur, except only that the moongod there is shown seated.

2. Greengus 1979, pl. 39:86 and OBTIV 86 in Greengus 1986, p. 40.

3. The tablets in question are Ish. 35-T.26, 28, 31-40, 50, 56-61, 63-66, and 77-86.

4. Greengus 1979, pl. 92:277 and cf. Bauer 1957, pp. 254-62.

5. Greengus 1979, pl. 14:28 and OBTIV 28 in Greengus 1986, pp. 25-26.

6. Greengus 1979, pl. 13:26 and OBTIV 26 in Greengus 1986, p. 24.

7. Greengus 1979, pl. 14:27 and OBTIV 27 in Greengus 1986, pp. 24-25.

8. Greengus 1979, pl. 21:38.

9. Greengus 1979, pl. 17:32.

10. Greengus 1979, pl. 38:83 and OBTIV 83 in Greengus 1986, p. 39.

In room 4-V.31 a cylinder seal (Ish. 35:77, OIP 72, pl. 88:942) was recovered. A long rectangular room, 2-V.31, contained five terracotta objects including a god plaque (Ish. 35:75, pl. 33e). At its south end the connecting small room, 1-V.32, had a list of twelve people described as LÚ *za-ra-nu-*[x] of the city gate of [d]S[în?] (Ish. 35-T.118[11]), and a tag with impression of the seal of a servant of Ipiq-Adad II and two lines of inscription referring to a captive (Ish. 35-T.120[12]).

The remaining rooms have few or no special features. The small room 5-W.31 was completely paved with baked brick, and a pavement was found in the southeast corner of 6-W.30. In the middle of the room was a box formed of four bricks set on edge in the floor. The drain from the court is mentioned above.

Attempts to date the Gate temple can be tentative only. From its latest occupation, the top layer, came tablets mentioning the so-called "local" rulers whom one would date to a time before the conquest of Ishchali and the region around it by Ipiq-Adad II of Eshnunna. They are Hadati and *Ṣí-la-n*[u?] (Ish. 35-T.26[13] and 35-T.33[14]), both from 3-V.30, as well as Sumu-abi-arim, mentioned in the oath formula of Ish. 34-T.22[15] found in 5-V.31. They would seem to have ruled fairly close to the conquest by Eshnunna in time, for from the same layer in 3-V.30 came a tablet dated to the year Ibal-pî-el died (Ish. 35-T.62), while 1-V.32 yielded a bulla ("label") with the seal impression of a servant of Ipiq-Adad (Ish. 35-T.120[16]). Since date formulas recording the death of a ruler usually record only the death of foreign rulers, the Ibal-pî-el in question is likely to be Ibal-pî-el I, who antedated the conquest, and the Ipiq-Adad of the seal impression, his son and successor Ipiq-Adad II, who accomplished it.

The city wall, which first avoided the temple, then took over its east wing, was earlier than the top stratum. It was built by one Ishme-bali according to a date formula[17] that reads mu Iš-me-ba-li lugal-[e] bàd-gal Ne-ri-ib-tum[ki] ba-dím-ma "year that king Ishme-bali built the great wall of Nêribtum." Nêribtum is the ancient name of Ishchali. Unfortunately, the time of Ishme-bali's reign cannot be established with any degree of certainty.

The gate temple itself was earlier than the city wall, but our only clue to its date is the one pointed to by Mr. Hill above, that the houses surrounding the gate temple can hardly antedate the original Kitîtum complex since they follow the line of the complex and recede to make way for the stairs at its northeast corner. As a pure guess therefore, and since Ipiq-Adad II dates to period II of the complex, the gate temple may belong to a period or so earlier, such as period I-A or I-B.

As mentioned, the tablet Ish. 35-T.14 found in the top stratum of 5-V.31 is the record of a lawsuit accepted for trial before the judges in "the gate of *Sîn-ša-Kamānim.*" In Ish.

11. Greengus 1979, pl. 89:270.
12. Greengus 1979, pl. 81:246.
13. Greengus 1979, pl. 26:50 and OBTIV 50 in Greengus 1986, p. 32.
14. Greengus 1979, pl. 89:271.
15. Greengus 1979, pl. 14:27 and OBTIV 27 in Greengus 1986, pp. 24-25.
16. Greengus 1979, pl. 81:246.
17. See Jacobsen in Harris 1955, p. 116, no. 94.2-4.

34-T.22, found in the same room and stratum, the oath is taken by the god Sîn and the ruler Sumu-abi-arim. In the cella of the temple, 3-V.30 (top stratum), was a contract of guaranty in which the god Sîn himself headed the list of witnesses implying that this contract had been concluded in front of the god, that is, in his cella. Taken together, these references strongly suggest that the god occurring in them, Sîn-ša-Kamānim, was the god of the Gate temple in which they were found. This form of the moongod is known from elsewhere to have been the city god of Nêribtum (Ishchali).[18]

B. THE OUTHOUSES

Built up against the Gate temple (see fig. 23) is a house comprised of rooms 6- and 5-V.30, 9-, 8-, and 6-V.31, south of which is an aggregate of flimsy sheds enclosed within the house by a fairly substantial wall. A terracotta god plaque (Ish. 35:91, pl. 34d) came from 9-V.31. Objects from the sheds (7-, 10-, and 11-V.31 and 2-, 4-, 7–12, and 16–18-V.32) included a female terracotta plaque (Ish. 35:62, pl. 34q) from 10-V.32 and a duck-shaped weight (Ish. 35:64, not illustrated) from 16-V.32. The wall enclosing the house and sheds forms the street wall facing the Kitîtum complex at its east end. A smaller house 3-, 13-, 14-, and 15-V.32 was built up against the temple at the west end of its southern facade[19] and west of this house were two unconnected rooms, 5- and 6-V.32.[20] In front of 3- and 6-V.32 two rectangular sheds were built out into the street. To the north of the temple are larger units, some of these such as 7-V.30 and 3-V.29 are perhaps courts. The walls here are fragmentary but show greater regularity and may belong to an official building.

The building built against the west side of the Gate temple poses a problem, particularly the flimsy structures at its south end, which can hardly be seen as a mere random accumulation of poor hovels since the substantial wall enclosing them implies both planning and resources. A possible explanation may be suggested by the two tablets found in 4-V.32 and 12-V.32, for the first of these, Ish. 35-T.105,[21] lists "250 baked bricks, in five days (bricks) of my stable" and the second, Ish. 35-T.106,[22] an account of barley which lists amounts for donkeys of the god Sîn as well as for people.[23] The sheds may thus represent stables and the building as a whole may have served as an inn or caravanserai for which its location, just inside the city gate, would be suitable.

---

18. Greengus 1979, pl. 112, no. 326, rev. 39-41 and p. 75. The name seems to mean "Sîn of the scone" and could conceivably be based on a comparison of the moon with a round barley cake.

19. A footed bronze cup (Ish. 35:60, pl. 30i) with handle was found in 3-V.32 and a cylindrical one (Ish. 35:135) without handle in 15-V.32, both in the top stratum. A fragment of a duck-shaped weight (Ish. 35:58) also came from the top stratum of 14-V.32.

20. Room 6-V.32 contained a terracotta lion plaque (Ish. 35:56, pl. 38d) from an undetermined period.

21. Greengus 1979, pl. 78:238.

22. Greengus 1979, pl. 64:167 and OBTIV 167 in Greengus 1986, pp. 66-67.

23. Greengus 1979, pl. 64:167. A clay cylinder seal (Ish. 35:65, OIP 72, pl. 89:949) also was found in room 12-V.32.

CHAPTER 5

THE "SERAI"
by Th. Jacobsen and T. A. Holland

A. THE PRIVATE HOUSES
(Th. Jacobsen)

The area in which we began excavations (fig. 24) puzzled us by the great number of interconnecting rooms it contained because there appeared to be too many rooms for a private house; so, to have a name for it, we tentatively called it the "Serai." Actually, however, there is no valid reason to consider it other than a private house, or rather, two neighboring private houses which had been joined together to accommodate a large household. The plan shows the northernmost house as consisting of rooms grouped around the small court 10-R.34 with its entrance from the street in the east wall of 1-R.33; the southern house has its center in the somewhat larger court, 4-R.34, and is entered by the door in the east wall of 5-R.34. The thick north wall of 2-Q.34 and 7-R.34 is apparently where the original two houses adjoined each other.

Comparison of the two plans shows the southern unit to be slightly more grand than the northern one. The rooms are larger and the plan has greater clarity. One might surmise, therefore, that this was where the family lived and that the northern unit represented servants' quarters, a suggestion that gains some support from the finding of bread ovens (*tanoors*) in 7-R.33 and 10-R.33.

B. THE TABLETS
(Th. Jacobsen)

A number of tablets were found in both the northern and southern part of the building, particularly in the paved room 13-R.34 in the southern part, which seems to have been used as a place to keep records. The tablets found there, apart from a school tablet Ish. 34-T.5,[1] fall into three groups. The first of these comprises two memoranda assigning

---

1. Greengus 1979, pl. 95:284. (NB. Room 13-R.34 had originally the designation 3-R.34. It was changed when the maps were readied for publication by Hill. Greengus quotes the original, not the final locus number.)

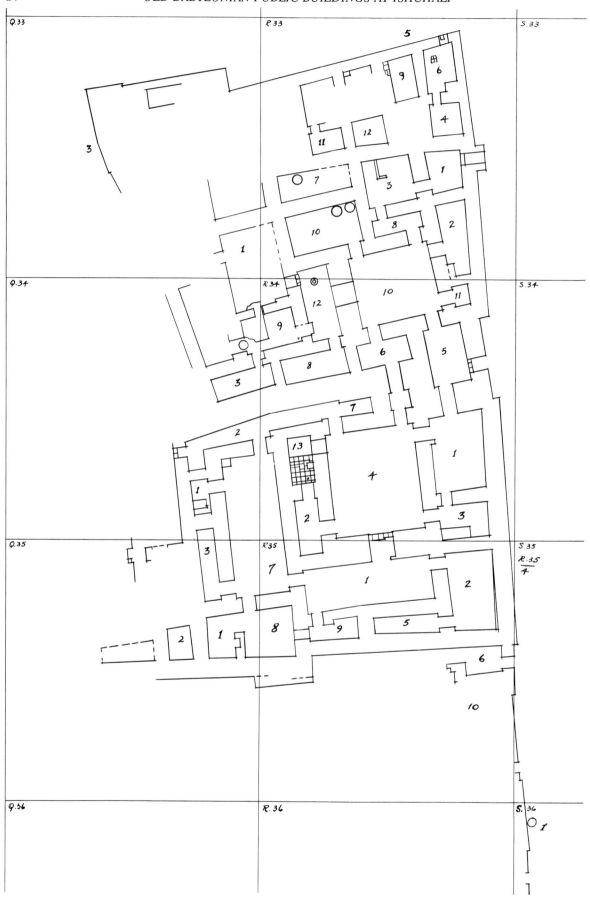

Figure 24. Ishchali—Plan of the "Serai."

responsibility: Ish. 34-T.25[2] lists three individuals as having to indemnify the government for the yield of illegally used land; Ish. 34-T.32[3] assigns responsibility for carrying out the responsibilities of the three individuals to one of them. The nature of the responsibilities is not stated. With these may be mentioned Ish. 34-T.23[4] found in the neighboring room 2-R.34. It records a loan of grain at interest to be repaid at harvest time. A second group consists of records of grain paid out to individuals, usually with mention of the owner of the field from which the grain came; it comprises Ish. 34-T.2, 4, 6, and 7.[5] The third group consists of tags from consignments of birds. The birds were requisitioned from the purveyor Ili-abushu by a certain Itur-Mardu whose seal is impressed on the tags, and who may well have been head of the household in the "Serai." His title, incompletely preserved on the seal impressions may be restored as [K]A-P[IRIG̃], that is "incantation priest" (*ašipu*). The recipients of the birds are mostly women, apparently members of the household for one of them. Tulīnum, who received a bird in Ish. 34-T.15,[6] is named owner of the field from which grain is paid out in Ish. 34-T.2. The birds will have been a welcome delicacy, not only for humans but also for the gods. The text Ish. 34-T.35[7] lists, instead of women, the gods Adad, Sîn, and Shamash as recipients.

In the northern part of the building tablets dealing with typical household accounts were found in room 10-R.33. Ish. 34-T.52[8] and 34-T.54[9] were accounts of wool rations for garments issued to the household; Ish. 34-T.51[10] is a receipt for a quantity of oil received and issued as rations by a woman named Iatum-marṣa, who occurs also in Ish. 34-T.54 as a recipient of a grain ration. This latter text, unfortunately in a bad state of preservation, accounts for expenditures of grain; the first item is a loan without interest, then follows payments for a boatman who brought and stored sesame, fodder for oxen, rations for individuals, among them a woman, Kalumi, who received wool in Ish. 34-T.54, and Iatum-marṣa who was in charge of the oil rations in Ish. 34-T.51. Then come payments to an ox driver, food ration for the wet nurse, et cetera. The tablets not only help to give an idea of the nature and function of the building as a major but private establishment, they also serve to date the level excavated. The date formulas recovered belong to the reign of Ibal-pî-el II and cover most of the latter's early years down to and including the eighth. The only ones missing are the ones for his second and fourth year.[11] Surprising is only the occurrence with the others of the date formula "*Šanat* d*Šul-gi-*dNanna *in-na-aq-ru* (Ish. 34-T.28)[12] "The year that Shulgi-nanna was gutted" and MU-ÚS-SA d*Šul-gi-na-na*ki (Ish. 34-

2. Greengus 1979, pl. 39:87.

3. Greengus 1979, pl. 40:88.

4. Greengus 1979, pl. 28:56.

5. Greengus 1979, pls. 65:170 and 66:178, 180.

6. Greengus 1979, pl. 49:118.

7. Greengus 1979, pl. 51:124 and OBTIV 124 in Greengus 1986, p. 56.

8. Greengus 1979, pl. 44:103 and OBTIV 103 in Greengus 1986, p. 46.

9. Greengus 1979, pl. 64:169 and OBTIV 169 in Greengus 1986, p. 68.

10. Greengus 1979, pl. 72:215.

11. For the formulas see ch. 6, *Year Dates Et Cetera*, nos. 12-16 and 21.

12. Greengus 1979, pl. 82:249 (NB. findspot 1-S.29 on p. 56 should read 3-R.34).

T.41) "The year after Shulgi-nanna." The former was found with a group of tablets in 3-R.34, the latter in the robber dumps at 3-Q.35. Usually this formula is considered as a formula belonging to Sîn-abushu who would appear to have reigned considerably earlier than Ibal-pî-el II. In view of the remarkable consistency and concentration of the other date formulas, one would probably consider the possibility that the gutting of Shulgi-nanna may have happened more than once and been the subject of more than one date formula. If so, the most likely place for the later one of these would seem to be the last year of Dadusha.

C. THE SMALL FINDS
(T. A. Holland)

1. NORTHERN UNIT

Two terracotta male figurine fragments (Ish. 34:6 and 7, pls. 33k and 35c) were found in room 1-R.33, and a terracotta lion figurine fragment (Ish. 34:115, pl. 38k) in room 8-R.34. Two steatite cylinder seals (Ish. 34:16 and 20) also were found in room 8-R.34 (OIP 72, pl. 89:947 and 948) as well as twelve hematite weights (Ish. 34:22, not illustrated) and one duck-shaped weight (Ish. 34:21, pl. 44i). A mold for a terracotta god plaque (Ish. 34:125, pl. 34h) and a model chariot fragment (Ref. 34:356, not illustrated) came from the partially excavated area of 3-Q.33.

2. SOUTHERN UNIT

Three metal objects (a silver wire, Ref. 34:19; a bronze pin, Ref. 34:13, and a copper arrowhead, Ish. 34:200, none illustrated) were found in rooms 2- and 3-R.34 and 7-R.35 respectively. The two bronze statues (pls. 26-29) discovered by a shepherd just under the surface of the "Serai" were pinpointed to the southern half of the large rectangular room 7-R.35 (see chap. 7). A bone cylinder seal, Ish. 34:15, came from room 7-R.35 (OIP 72, pl. 89:946). Other objects included a conical stone weight, Ish. 34:17, from room 1-R.35, a model boat fragment, Ref. 34:15, in room 2-Q.35, a terracotta female plaque fragment, Ref. 34:36, in room 8-R.35, and a pottery bottle, Ref. 34:12, and a terracotta goddess plaque fragment, Ref. 34:34, both from room 6-R.35. None of these are illustrated here.

3. GRAVE (10-R.35)

A grave was excavated just south of room 6-R.35 below the southern unit. The presence of a number of weights (i.e., Ish. 34:8, pl. 44q) and metal pieces amongst the grave goods may indicate that this was the burial of a metal worker. The other objects found in the grave are listed in appendices 1 and 4. They are not illustrated here.

4. SOUTHERN WALL AREA (1-S.36)

A large cache of terracotta figurine and plaque fragments was found in the area marked 1-S.36 (see fig. 23) just to the east of the eastern enclosure wall of the "Serai." The cache comprises a male figurine (Ish. 34:5, pl. 33j), a 'below-the-knees' fragment of a human figurine (Ish. 34:59, OIC 20, fig. 69b and pl. 33q here), a female plaque, Ish. 34:93 (pl. 36d), and three plaque and figurine fragments (not illustrated), Ref. 34:48, 57, and 76.

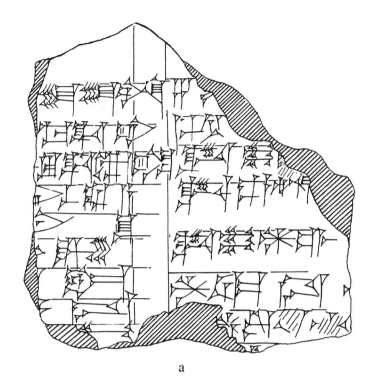

a

b

Figure 25. Ishchali—(*a*) Fragment of a Biconical Foundation Document (Ish. 35-T.1) from 2-P.31 and (*b*) Brick Inscription of Ipiq-Adad II (Found in Pavements at 2-Q.31, 4-R.30, and 2-T.30).

CHAPTER 6

EPIGRAPHIC MATERIAL FROM ISHCHALI
by Th. Jacobsen

A. INSCRIPTIONS

(1) ISH. 35-T.1 (Fig. 25a)

Fragment of the middle part of a biconical foundation document found at 2-P.31 in the mudbrick foundations of the Kitîtum complex. Columns i and iv of the inscription and parts of columns ii and iii are missing. The text reads:

] T u - t u - u	b^{ki}	5 d [a n n a
] m a - d a - b	i	1 1/2 n i n [d a n
⌈ù⌉ á - d a m -	b i - š è	á - d a h ᵈ[
i] n - b a r - r a - a		u s u u š u m - g [a l
b] i - š è		
g] i₄ - g i₄		á - d a h ᵈM a r - [
- n] e - n e		d i n g i r - s a g̃ - DU - g̃ [u₁₀
- u] n - g u b		[ù] ᵈI n a n n a - ⌈K i - t i⌉ [
] ⌈m u⌉		[n i n] - ⌈m è⌉ - [g̃ á
(lacuna)		(lacuna)

Any attempt at restoration must, of course, remain hypothetical but stressing its conjectural nature the following may be suggested. The measurement listed at the beginning of col. iii, "five double miles," that is to say 59.19 kilometers, and "one and one-half nindan," that is 8.91 meters are most easily understood as referring to the length and the width of a canal, the digging of which the inscription commemorates. As for who dug that canal, the only known canal builder at Ishchali was a certain Sîn-abushu, one of whose date formulas was found on a floor of the original Kitîtum complex. He could thus well have reigned when that complex was built and earlier, so that a fragment of an inscription of his commemorating an earlier work, the one mentioned in his date formula *šanat* ÍD *Sîn-a-bu-šu ih-ru-ú* "The year he dug the Sîn-abušu canal"[1] could have got into the foundations of the complex. That the fragment we have is not part of a foundation record of the complex in which it was found is clear from the fact that its lost fourth column

---

1. For this formula see Greengus 1979, p. 31, formula no. 38 and note 49. This particular formula is not duplicated among the excavated tablets.

would hardly have had enough space for such a record and that col. iii would hardly have listed Inanna Kitîtum in third place in a record of the building of a major temple complex for her. The circumstances of finding the fragment are also suggestive; the fragment was an isolated find and no other fragments were found although we searched the area diligently. Apparently the fragment had been imbedded in a mudbrick and it seems reasonable to assume that it had originally formed part of a deposit along the bank of the canal it commemorates, that this deposit became disturbed in the course of dredging, and that the mud dredged up containing this fragment was later used for brickmaking.

If, tentatively, we may ascribe the fragment to Sîn-abušu, the cities he is known to have controlled, among them Nêribtum, Šaduppum, Tutub, and Dûr-Rimuš,[2] suggest restoration for the broken off city names in the fragment. With due caution we would thus present as a possible restoration the following:

(i) ^{1}[Sîn-a-bu-šu] ^{2}[lugal] ^{3}[Dûr-Ri-mu/-uš^{ki}-me-en] ^{4}[ud ^{d}En-líl-/le] ^{5}[Ne-ri-ib-/tum^{ki}] (ii) ^{1}[ŠÀ-DUB^{ki}] Tu-tu-ub^{ki}/[ù] ma-da-bi ^{2}[uru-bi] ⌐ù⌐ á-dam-bi-šè ^{3}[igi zi i]n-bar-ra-a ^{4}[ki-b]i-šè ^{5}[bí-g]i$_4$-gi$_4$ ^{6}[UBARA-n]e-ne ^{7}[mu-u]n-gub ^{8}[íd] ⌐mu⌐/ [-pà-da/nam-lugal-la-ĝá] (iii) ^{15}d[anna gíd-bi] ^{2}1 1/2 nin[dan daĝal-bi] ^{3}á-dah ⌐d⌐[DN] ^{4}usu ušum-g[al-ĝu] ^{5}á-dah ^{d}Mar-[dú] ^{6}dingir saĝ-DU-ĝ[u$_{10}$] ^{7}⌐ù⌐ ^{d}Inanna-⌐Ki-ti⌐$^{[ki]}$ ^{8}[nin]-⌐mè⌐-[ĝá-ta] ^{9}[mu-ba-al] (iv) ^{1}[. . .

[I, Sîn-abušu, king of Dûr-Rimuš,[3]] did, [when Enlil] had looked with favor upon Nêribtum, Šaduppum, and Tutub as well as upon their territories, upon their cities as well as their settled tracts, restore them to their places and set up their protective emblems. A canal (called) by my royal name (a canal), the length of which is 5 double miles, the width of which is 1 1/2 nindan, I dug with the aid of DN my uniquely great strength, the aid of Mardu, my tutelary god, as well as of Inanna Kitîtum, mistress of my battle array . . .

(2) ISH. 34:45

Inscription on a cylinder seal[4] found in the cella of the upper temple, 6-Q.30, on the floor of period I-II.

---

2. See Greengus 1979, p. 14 note 70.

3. Dûr-Rimush is probably to be identified with the nearby mound known as Bismaya. Bismaya's rectangular shape fits a fortress (*dūrum*) of the Old Babylonian period—Dûr-Samsuiluna, Khafājah Mounds B+C, was so shaped (fig. 27)—and the issuing of a *mîšarum* decree from there, often referred to in the texts, shows that it was a royal city.

4. Cf. Frankfort 1955, p. 47 no. 917, p. 52, and pl. 87 no. 917.

Ma-at-ta-tum	Mattatum,
mārat U-bar-rum	daughter of Ubarrum,
a-na ba-la-ṭì-ša	for her recovery
a-na ᵈ*Ki-ti-tum*	to Kitîtum
i-qí-iš	presented (this seal)

This seal was, apparently, originally Mattatum's personal seal, which she had reinscribed in part to make it into a votive offering.

(3) BRICK INSCRIPTION OF IPIQ-ADAD II (Fig. 25b)

Inscription on baked bricks measuring $40 \times 40 \times 9$ centimeters found in pavements at 2-Q.31, 4-R.30, and 2-T.30 all belonging to period II. They also were used to build the period II drain at the east end of the main court and occurred in secondary use in the remnants of the stairway at 2-R.31 of period III. The bricks on which the inscription appeared were unfortunately of a texture more soft than usual and since in every case the inscription was on the upper, exposed surface, weathering and walking over it had destroyed the signs so that very few specimens retained traces of more than a few signs and the division lines, which were more deeply impressed than were the signs. The text as recovered is thus a composite based on the inspection of numerous specimens. It reads:

a-na ᵈ*Inanna Ki-ti-tum*	To Inanna Kitîtum
ᵈ*I-pí-iq-*ᵈ*Adad*	did Ipiq-Adad,
⸢*šarrum*⸣ [*d*]*a-an-núm*	the mighty king,
⸢*šarrum*⸣ *m*[*u-ra*]*-pí-*⸢*iš*⸣	the king who
Èš-⸢*nun*⸣ᵏⁱ*-*[*n*]*a*	enlarged Eshnunna,
re' ṣa-[*al*]*-ma-at*	shepherd of the dark
qá-qá-di-im	headed (people),
na-ra-am ᵈ⸢*Tišpak*⸣	beloved of Tišpak,
mār I-ba-aḷ-pi-el	son of Ibal-pî-el,
*Ne-ri-ib-tum*ᵏⁱ	grant
i-qí-si-im	Nêribtum

As will be noted the inscription does not refer to a building or rebuilding, but records a grant. It is thus likely to belong to the later part of period II, II-B, which is marked by reflooring only, rather than to II-A. The grant mentioned presumably consisted in assigning the income from taxes paid by Nêribtum to Inanna Kitîtum and her temple.

(4) BRICK INSCRIPTION OF IBAL-PÎ-EL II

Bricks with the stamp of Ibal-pî-el II measuring $32 \times 32 \times 8.50$ centimeters and $41 \times 41 \times 8.50$ centimeters were found, the larger size characteristic of paving bricks. Findspots in the Kitîtum complex were 3-T.31 in the sill of the west door (period III), 3-T.32 in the sill of the south door (period IV), 2-T.30 pavement (period IV), and 2-5.29

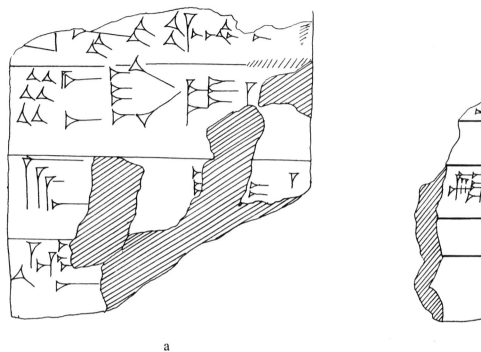

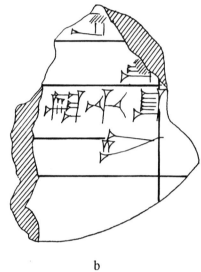

a   b

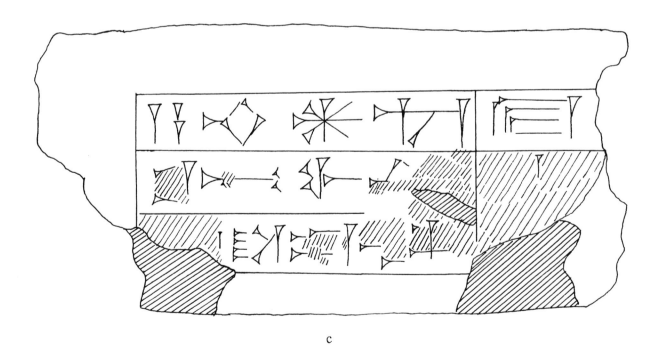

c

Figure 26. Ishchali—(*a*) Fragment of Brick Inscription (Ish. B.4) of Ibal-pî-el from the "Serai" (6-R.35),
(*b*) Fragment of an Inscribed Clay Nail (Ish. 34-T.1) from the City Wall, and (*c*) Fragment of a
Brick Inscription of Sumu-Amnanim (=Ish. 34-T.1) from the Surface of the Mound.

pivotstone box and sill of the east door (period IV). Another fragment also was found in the "Serai," 6-R.35 (see fig. 26a). The Ishchali brick inscriptions are identical in all particulars with the Ibal-pî-el II brick inscriptions found at Tell Asmar.[5] The Asmar inscriptions read:

I-ba-al-pi-el	Ibal-pî-el
šarrum da-an-nu-um	the mighty king
šàr Èš-nun-na[ki]	king of Eshnunna
na-ra-am [d]*Tišpak*	beloved of Tišpak
mār Da-du-ša	son of Daduša

5. ISH. 34-T. 1 (Fig. 26b)

Fragment of an inscribed clay nail found inside the city wall in the top stratum. It reads:

(lacuna)	
[ ] *si*(?) [?]	. . .
[ ]-*šu*	. . .
[*a-na ba*]-*la-ṭì-šu*	for his health
[*ib-*] *ni*	he built

The nail may have been inserted in the city wall. If so, it may have recorded the building of that wall by Ishme-bali who, according to a date formula of his, built the city wall of Nêribtum.[6]

(6) BRICK INSCRIPTIONS OF SUMU-AMNANIM (Figs. 26c and 27)

A few fragments (fig. 26c) of an inscription of Sumu-Amnanim and one reasonably complete specimen (fig. 27) were picked up on the surface of the mound at various points. Whether, as seems most probable, they come from a structure at Ishchali or were brought over from neighboring mounds is not clear. The inscription reads:

a-na [d]*Inanna*	For Inanna
Su-mu Aw$_x$(WA)-⌈*na*⌉(!?)-*num*	did Sumu-Amnānum,
šar Ša-at-la-aš [ki]	king of Shatlash,
É- GIBIL	construct
ù É- MÌN	the "new house"
i-pu-uš	as well as the "double house"

---

5. Frankfort, Lloyd, and Jacobsen 1940, p. 139, building inscription no. 15 and pl. 17:15.
6. See Jacobsen in Harris 1959, p. 116, no. 94.2-4 (see above p. 81).

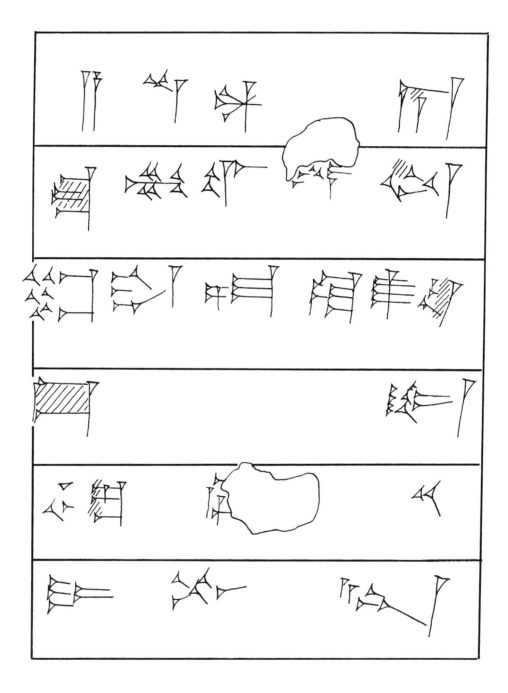

Figure 27. Ishchali—Brick Inscription of Sumu-Amnanim from the Surface of the Mound.

B. YEAR DATES ET CETERA

1. PERIODS I AND II

In the higher parts of the Kitîtum complex it was not possible to distinguish between the floor of period I and that of period II. Apparently the original floor was kept clean and was reused through period II. Dated tablets and seal impressions mentioning names of rulers found on it were:

1. [MU ᵈŠ]ul-gi-ᵈ⌈Nanna⌉ ⌈in⌉-na-aq-ru
    "Year when Shulgi-Nanna was gutted."
        Ish. 34-T.68 at 1-P.30 (on floor of I-II)

    MU ᵈŠul-gi-ᵈNanna in-na-aq-ru
        Ish. 34-T.28 at 3-R.34 (top)[7]
            This date belongs to the reign of Sîn-abušu. See Greengus 1979, p. 34 no. 60.

2. MU-ÚS-SA ᵈŠul-gi-na-naᵏⁱ
    "Year following Shulgi-Nanna (was gutted)."
        Ish. 34-T.41 at 3-Q.35 (in robber dump)[8]

3. ⌈MU⌉ Hu-ri-ib-šumᵏⁱ [mu]-⌈un⌉-dù
    "Year when he (re)built Huribšum."
        Ish. 34-T.66 at 1-P.30 (on floor of I-II)[9]

4. Seal impressions of servant of Ikūn-pî-Sîn
        Ish. 34-T.72 at 2-P.30 (on floor of I-II)
        Ish. 34-T.73 at 6-Q.30 (on floor of I-II)

5. [MU I]-qí-iš-ᵈTišpak [. . .] x Ia-ku-un-[   ]x-⌈har⌉-ra KÚR-u
    "Year when Iqīš-Tishpak wrecked (?). . .Yakun-[. . .] and [. . .]-harra."[10]
        Ish. 34-T.87 at 2-Q.31 (on floor of I-II)

6. MU ᵍⁱˢGU-ZA ⌈BÁRA⌉-M[AH ᵈEN-ZU ᵈI-pí-iq]-ᵈAdad [MU-DÍM]
    "Year when Ipiq-Adad fashioned the throne of Sîn's main throne dais."
        Ish. 34-T.90 at 1-P.29 (top)

---

7. These latter tablets may have come into the stratum in which they were found through construction work touching earlier layers or with fill brought from elsewhere.

8. See n. 7 (ch. 6) above.

9. Presumably this formula is to be kept separate from MU BÀD Hu-ri-ib-[šumᵏⁱ] occurring on Ish. 34-T.60 found at 1-Q.30 top, i.e., period III-IV.

10. The city names Iakunum and Karahar mentioned in date formulas from Trench B at Tell Asmar may conceivably be shortened forms of Iakun-[x] and [Kar]a-har-ra of this formula. See Frankfort, Lloyd, and Jacobsen 1940, p. 198.

7. MU *Ha-da-ti Maš*(?)-⌜*kán*⌝(?)-⌜*ba*⌝(?)[*-ar-mi*]
   "Year when Hadati . . . Maškan-B[armi](?)."
      Ish. 35-T.26 at 3-V.30 (top)

8. MU *Ṣí-la-n*[*u?*] [. . .]*a-na ki-di-im* x [. . .]
   "Year when . . ."
      Ish. 35-T.33 at 3-V.30 (top)

9. MU I-b a-a l-p i-e l ba-TIL
   "Year when Ibal-pî-el (I) died."
      Ish. 35-T.62 at 3-V.30

2. PERIODS III AND IV

10. MU N a - r a - a m - ᵈEN-ZU K a - k u - l a - t i m   i ṣ - b a - t u
    "Year when Naram-Sîn seized Kakulatim."
       Ish. 34-T.112 at 1-S.29 (top)

11. MU ᵍⁱˢGIGIR-GAL-NU-DI ᵈUTU
    "Year the . . . chariot of Shamash . . ."
       Ish. 34-T.111 at 6-Q.30 (in robber dump)
          This formula belongs to the reign of Daduša. See Greengus 1979, p. 29
          note 40.

12. MU ᵐI - b a - a l - p i - [e l   l u g a l]
    "Year when Ibal-pî-el [became king]."
       Ish. 34-T.54 at 10-R.33 (top)
          If correctly restored this formula marked Ibal-pî-el II's first year.

13. MU *abul Ki-kur I-ba-al-pi-el i-pu-šu*
    "Year when Ibal-pî-el made the gate of Kikurrum."
       Ish. 34-T.23 at 2-R.34 (top)
          Formula for Ibal-pî-el II's third year.

14. MU ᵈŠ a m š iˢⁱ- ᵈA d a d ba-TIL
    "Year when Šamši-Adad died."
       Ish. 34-T.49 at R.34-35 (dump)
          Formula for Ibal-pî-el II's fifth year.

15. MU Bît-*Eš₄-tár* BA-DÍM
    "Year when the Temple of Ishtar was constructed."
       Ish. 34-T.3 at 1-R.35 (top)
          Formula for Ibal-pî-el II's sixth year.

16. MU É-sá-ğar-ra-a-⌜ni é⌝ ᵈEn-líl(!?) ba-an-⌜x⌝

"Year when Esagarrani, the temple of Enlil was . . ."

   Ish. 35-T.53 at 2-S.29 (in pivotstone box built with bricks with Ibal-pî-el's stamp)

      Formula for Ibal-pî-el II's eighth year.[11]

   MU É-sá-ğ[ar-ra-n]i é ᵈEn-líl-lá m[u-un]-⌜na⌝-[dù]

"Year when he built Enlil's Temple Esagarrani for him."

   Ish. 34-T.146 at 2-R.30 (floor of IV)

   MU ⌜É-ᵈEn-líl(?) in-ne-ep-šu⌝

"Year when the temple of Enlil was constructed."

   Ish. 34-T.10 at 1-R.35 (top)

17. MU Ra-pí-qumᵏⁱ ba-gul

"Year when Rapiqum was demolished."

   Ish. 35-T.53 at 2-S.29 (in pivotstone box as no. 16 above)

      Formula for Ibal-pî-el II's ninth year.[12]

18. MU erin Su-bir₄ᵏⁱ ᵍⁱˢtukul ba-an-sìg

"Year when the host of Subartu was smit with weapons."

   Ish. 35-T.53 at 2-S.29 (in pivotstone box as no. 16 above)

      Formula for Ibal-pî-el II's tenth year.[13]

19. MU ᵍⁱˢnarkabat šēpi ša ᵈAdad

"Year, when the personal chariot of Adad (was . . .)."

   Ish. 34-T.109 at 6-Q.30 (in robber dump)

      The formula belongs to the reign of Ibal-pî-el II. See Greengus 1979, pp. 28-29 notes 33-39.

20. Seal impressions of servants of Ibal-pî-el II were: Ish. 35-T.25 at 2-S.29 between floor of III and floor of IV; Ish. 34-T.95 at 2-Q.31, floor of I or II, a letter to the *sangû* Abizum; and Ish. 34-T.74 at 6-Q.30, floor of III-IV, letter with seal impression of the *sangû* Abizum, servant of Ibal-pî-el.

---

11. The formulas listed as nos. 16, 17, and 18 occur in this order on tablet Ish. 35-T.53.

12. See n. 11 (ch. 6) above.

13. See n. 11 (ch. 6) above.

21. MU GUD-APIN KÙ-GI
    "Year when a golden (statue) of a plough ox . . ."
        Ish. 34-T.110 at 6-Q.30 (in robber dump)
        Ish. 34-T.70 at 5-Q.30 (top)
        Ish. 34-T.145 at 2-R.30 (uppermost floor)
        Ish. 34-T.154 at 5-R.32 (at east end of room, on floor 1.10 meters below
        surface)

    MU GUD ᵍⁱˢAPIN KÙ-GI
        Ish. 35-T.9 at 3-R.34 (in robber dump)
            The formula probably belongs late in Ibal-pî-el II's reign.

22. MU BÀD *Hu-ri-ib*-[*šum*ᵏⁱ]
    "Year when the city wall of Huribšum . . ."
        Ish. 34-T.60 at 1-Q.30 (top)[14]

---

14. Cf. formula no. 3 on p. 95 above.

CHAPTER 7

DESCRIPTION OF MAJOR FINDS FROM ISHCHALI
by Th. Jacobsen

A. BRONZE STATUES

The two bronze statues shown on plates 25-28[1] were found, as mentioned above, by a shepherd as he idly scratched the ground with his shepherd's crook. They were sold to a dealer from whom The Oriental Institute purchased them in Baghdad in 1919. They are now in The Oriental Institute Museum listed as A7119 and A7120.

The spot where they turned up was remembered by nearby villagers so when regular excavations began in 1934 it was pointed out to us and we were able to clean and uncover the clear imprint left by the round bronze basin in which they lay when found. The location of the imprint was the one to which we gave the locus number 7-R.35. It proved, when excavated, to be a large room in a private house of the period of Ibal-pî-el II.[2] The depositing of the bronze basin must have been later than that, however, for it was found directly under the surface. Apparently it had been hid with its contents for safekeeping under the floor of a house above the Ibal-pî-el II one, all traces of which had been eroded away.

Where the statues originally came from is thus a moot question. They could conceivably have stood in a domestic chapel like the ones excavated by Woolley in private houses of the same date at Ur,[3] perhaps even in such a chapel in the house eroded away, and could have been concealed for safety at a time of crisis. It is also possible, however, that they may represent loot taken on a campaign, or they could be stolen goods hidden by a thief. Offhand the first of these suggestions, that they come from a domestic chapel above the spot where they were found, seems the simplest assumption.

That the statues originally must have belonged to a chapel is indicated by the fact that they represent deities, are cult statues, and that they represent deities rather than humans is clear from the fact that they are given not one but four faces each, which places them firmly as supernatural beings. Their moderate size, further, seems appropriate for a chapel, less so for a major temple.

1. Also see Frankfort 1943, nos. 338-39, pp. 21 and 34-35, pls. 77-81.
2. See above pp. 83f. and 85f.
3. See Woolley and Mallowan 1976, pp. 19ff.

The largest of the statues is 17.30 centimeters high and shows a god in standing position, his right foot placed on the back of a reclining ram, his right hand holding a curved weapon, his left closed and held against his chest.[4] This stance is a traditional one for a victorious warrior. It is taken by a human king on the relief of Anu-banini,[5] who places his foot on a supine enemy, and it is frequently found on cylinder seals of Isin-Larsa and Old Babylonian times with representations of Inanna as goddess of war. She places her foot not on an enemy but on her emblem, the lion, and rather than placing an empty hand at her chest she holds out in it a multiple mace.[6]

The god is shown barefoot—Frankfort justly remarked on the sensitivity with which the feet are rendered[7]—and is dressed in a coat of sheepskin.[8] Under the coat he seems to wear a tight fitting long sleeved doublet with rolls of cloth at the wrists, but it is also possible that the artist intended the arms and right shoulder to be nude with double armlets at both wrists. On the head he wears a flat round cap with a short beak-like visor in front.[9] The exact nature of the weapon the god carries in his right hand is difficult to determine due to corrosion. Tentatively one may suggest that it was an axe with blade such as the one shown in Salonen 1966, Tafel IV.2.

As to who the god thus pictured might be, indications are not too clear and any attempt at identification must be offered with reservations as necessarily hypothetical only, and subject to revision should new data turn up to broaden our basis for judgment.

This said, we may suggest that only two features seem distinct enough to offer a possible clue; the ram under the god's foot and his plethora of faces. The curved weapon he carries is indistinct and even if our suggested restoration of it as an axe should be

---

4. The hand almost certainly originally held a bow which, made of fairly thin copper wire, was lost completely through oxidation. The bow is the weapon traditionally held in the left hand and in the traditional stance of the victor it is held at the chest. Cf. the figure of Naram-suen on the Victory Stele and on the rock relief at Darband-i-Gawr (Moortgat 1969, pls. 156a and 157) and the figure of Anu-banini in his rock relief (Porada 1962 p. 40, fig. 15).

   Mr. John A. Larson, Museum Archivist of the Oriental Institute kindly examined the hand closely for me and consulted Dr. Ray Tindel and Professor Helene Kantor. Mr. Larson writes (letter of July 9, 1986) "In its present condition the top of the clenched hand bears a tiny knob about the size of a straight-pin. At the bottom there is a circular opening which is encircled by the little finger and the palm and heel of the hand." Mr. Larson also consulted old photographs taken before cleaning and after a first electrolytic treatment. He writes "The old photographs show a bent-over upper projection . . . with a thicker diameter than the remaining trace would suggest, probably roughly comparable to the diameter of the hole at the bottom. This feature . . . is no longer present today."

   These findings are, I believe, compatible with the assumption that the hand held a bow, perhaps made in an upper and a lower section, now lost. The bow and arrow is a typical attribute of gods of thunderstorm and symbolizes lightning. Compare the god with the lion (thunder) and bow and arrows (lightning), presumably Nin-girsu, who is pictured on the Seal of Adda (Frankfort 1955, pl. 19a).

5. Porada 1965, p. 40, fig. 15. The hand Anu-banini places against his chest holds a bow and an arrow. The curved weapon in his other hand looks exceedingly odd as drawn. One is tempted to assume that the surface of the rock here was weathered, showing only the bare outline of an axe such as the one Inanna holds on the seals showing her in similar stance.

6. Cf., Frankfort 1939, pl. xxvi:1; Buchanan 1981, nos. 931-937; and other publications of cylinder seals.

7. Frankfort 1943, p. 21.

8. Or in material imitating sheepskin. Note that the coat of the ram is rendered in a manner identical with that of the god's cloak.

9. Since only the front of the cap is shown over each face it is not possible to say what its side and back may have been like.

correct, that would be of little help since such axes were carried by Inanna and various other gods in representations of them.[10]

Beginning, then, with the ram and considering its role in the composition one will notice that it occupies the same position as the subdued enemy in the Anu-banini relief and the lion in the standard representation of Inanna on the seals, which is to say, as vanquished foe or as emblem, two roles that curiously enough often merge in ancient Mesopotamian mythology.[11]

Asking next therefore, which known god has a ram as vanquished enemy or emblem, one is led to consider Ea, whose emblem is a ram's head on a pole or unnaturally long neck. It is pictured mounted on a stick on the cylinder seal (Frankfort 1939, pl. 27.i) and sculptured in the round; it was found in the Chapel of the Ram in Ur, where, similarly mounted, it apparently was the chief object of worship.[12] In later representations on boundary stones the stick carrying it is often broadened so that it looks like an unnaturally elongated neck. The name of this ram's head is given on the so-called Nazi-maruttash kudurru[13] as *Mu-um* which is a variant, also found elsewhere,[14] of the name Mummu familiar from *Enûma elish*. It appears, thus, that it represents the vizier of Apsû whom Ea vanquished on the same occasion on which he slew Apsû.

Interesting as this is, it does not though take us much further toward understanding what Mummu represents and why he is given form as a ram or ram's head, but fortunately a later passage in *Enûma elish* gives a clue. It deals with one of Marduk's many names, Addu, which identifies him, in one of his aspects, with the god of storms and rains, better known as Adad. The gods wish that (VII. 119-122):

> [d]*Ad-du lu-ú šùm-šú kiš-šat šame*[c] *le-rim-ma*
> *ṭa-a-bu rig-ma-šú eli erṣe-tim li-ir-ta-ṣì-in*
> *mu-um-mu er-pe-e-ti liš-tak-si-ba-am-ma*
> *šap-liš a-na nišē*[meš] *te-eʾ-ú-ta lid-din*

> "May he cover the whole of the sky,
> and his sonorous voice roar over the earth!
> Let Mummu of the clouds be trimmed
> so that he give food to the people below"[15]

---

10. See Moortgat 1969, pl. G.5 (Nergal) and G. 8 (Inanna). Compare the relief on pl. 13 which shows this type of axe held by a human soldier.

11. See Jacobsen 1970, pp. 4f.

12. See Woolley and Mallowan 1976, p. 31 and pl. 59a.

13. Scheil 1900, pl. 16-19, col. iv 5-6. *Mu-um su-hur-ma-šu a-ši-ir-tum rabîtum*(GAL) *šá* [d]*É-a*. "Ea's Mum, goatfish, (and) great sanctuary." The emblem described shows the ram's head on a long curved neck over a building out of which the goatfish protrudes. See Seidel 1968, pp. 33ff. and pp. 165ff. (Widderstab).

14. See Nougayrol 1947, p. 30 line 3 (var. *mu-um* Thureau-Dangin 1922, 6.47r) and Macmillan 1906, p. 664 line 15.

15. For *lirimma* and *lirtaṣin* see *CAD* A/2, p. 229 d.2´ and *AHw*, p. 959, *raṣānu* I. *ṭâbu* "sweet" when used of sound presumably denotes a pleasing quality so when, as here, it is used of the thunder "sonorous" seems a likely shade of meaning, *lištakṣibamma* we interpret as precative 3p.m.sg. Ventive III₂ with passive force of *kaṣābu* "to cut," "to trim." Compare *CAD* and *AHw* s.v. *kaṣābu*.

The reference here is clearly to the rain of the thundershower which sustains the crops and provides food for mankind, and light is thrown upon the trimming of Mummu by a passage in Gudea's Cylinder B, col. iv. 7-8 (Thureau-Dangin 1925) where we are told how, on the occasion of preparing the newly built temple for receiving its owner, the goddess Nanshe brought rains so that tamarisk and other plants needed for scouring the floors could grow forth. To that end she sang holy incantations and she:

> u_6-$\tilde{g}e_6$-ga umbin mi-ni-ib-gur$_{10}$
> im-ma-al an-na-ke$_4$
> ubur si ba-ni-íb-sá

> "sheared black ewes
> and set going properly
> the udders on the cows of heaven."

We know that the heavy rain clouds were often seen mythopoetically as the udders of heavenly cows from which flowed the rain, their milk, and the shearing of black ewes which is paralleled by another such image: the rain falling from a heavenly cloud-sheep like wool falling from a sheep at sheep shearing. "Mummu of the clouds" who is "trimmed" or "shorn" in the *Enûma elish* passage is thus a sheep or ram, the wool of which is the clouds and falls as rain when the ram is shorn. The image of the clouds as sheep or lambs is not difficult to accept, for clouds often have a woolly look and in the Danish language, for instance, fluffy white clouds are known as "lamb clouds" (*Lammeskyer*).

The interpretation of Mummu here suggested fits with what else we know about Mummu. In *Enûma elish* Ea, after his victory over Apsû, sat down on his body and "Mummu he seized, holding his *ṣerretu*." The word *ṣerretu* can mean "nose-rope" or denote a shepherd's crook for catching and holding sheep.[16] If this second meaning is intended here it might refer to the stick on which the ram's head was mounted when set up in a chapel or carried, interpreting the stick as a shepherd's crook for holding the ram Mummu. It does not seem to correspond to anything in nature.

Mummu's close connection with Apsû—apparently he was not only Apsû's vizier but also his son—likewise makes good sense if Mummu is seen as the rainclouds, for Apsû was the assumed subterranean fresh water sea that came to the surface in the marshes, and the Ancients were well aware that clouds originated as vapors rising from the marshes which thus "engendered" them.

Turning next to the question of the second distinctive trait of the figure of the god portrayed in the statue, his four faces, we confront a feature that is not only distinctive but, as far as we know, unique. No other known deity of the ancient Mesopotamian pantheon was thus imagined, so we must here try to infer the meaning of those four faces from the feature itself.

We mentioned that the passage in *Enûma elish* that referred to "Mummu of the clouds" dealt with a god of winds and weather, Marduk in his aspect of Addu, god of thunderstorms and rain. Now, the winds were in ancient Mesopotamia typically four, so

16. See CAD Ṣ, s.v. *ṣerretu* A, especially the discussion in the second column on page 136.

much so that they could be referred to as wind one, wind two, wind three, and wind four rather than as south, north, east, and west wind. A god of the winds might therefore well have been envisioned as facing in the directions in which these winds blew, they being the breath emitted from his mouth. Some such concept seems in fact to underlie the cuneiform sign with which one of Addu's names was written, for it consists of four separate signs for "wind facing outward from the center," that is, facing in the direction of the four winds. The reading of the sign is Mermer.[17]

If it is conceivable, then, that the god of winds might embody their fourfold nature, and that this might find mythopoetic expression by giving him four faces, there is still the question of actual identification of the four-faced god of the statue and putting a name to him.

The most logical candidate, considering the *Enûma elish* passage with "Mummu of the clouds," is presumably Marduk since the passage deals with him. Nor would it seem unnatural that a statue of Marduk should be found in Ishchali (ancient Nêribtum) for the region was under Babylonian control from the end of Hammurapi's reign and under his son and successor, Samsuiluna, who built Dur-Samsuiluna at nearby Khafājah. A difficulty here is, though, that Marduk was not given four faces. The passage in *Enûma elish* (I.92-98) that describes him is as follows:

> Tall he was, exceedingly, surpassing them in all things
> Subtle beyond conceit his measures were
> incomprehensible, perturbing to behold.
> Four were his eyes and four his ears.
> Fire blazed forth when he moved his lips.
> Large grew out the four ears
> and the eyes in the same way
> were scanning the All.

Here four eyes and four ears add up to only two normal faces.[18] One might therefore well rule out identification with Marduk altogether were it not for a very curious line in the seventh tablet of *Enûma elish* in the list of Marduk's names. The passage in question (VII.109-114) deals with Marduk's name É-siskur and says:

> May Esiskur sit on high in the House of Petition.
> May the gods bring in their greeting gifts before him.
> They will receive their work assignments and wages.
> No one can do anything that takes skill without him.
> In his build there are four (ordinary) people.
> No god whatever, other than he, can let them know
> the instructions for their days (work).

---

17. Deimel 1947, p. 722 no. 721n.

18. We do not consider an interpretation of line 95: 4 IGI-MIN-*šú* 4 GEŠTU-MIN-*šú* as "four were his pair of eyes, four his pair of ears" possible.

That Marduk's bodily build comprises four people does seem to fit in with the four faces on the Ishchali statue and presupposes some such idea about Marduk's bodily form even though the author of *Enûma elish* here clearly uses it to indicate that Marduk has the skill of four single persons.

The passage comes, as mentioned, from the list of Marduk's names and that list clearly builds on more and different traditions than the one embodied in the main body of the story. It seems, therefore, not impossible that the Esiskur passage may retain a different and perhaps older tradition about Marduk's form than that of tablet I, a tradition according to which, as god of winds and rainstorms he had a more logical four than two faces. It is therefore not altogether excluded that the Ishchali statuette is in fact meant to represent Marduk, but it seems definitely more preferable and cautious to identify it tentatively as a god of the winds but to leave it nameless.

The statue of the goddess measures 16.20 centimeters in height. It shows the goddess seated on a taboret and holding with both hands a flowing vase against her waist. Her dress is decorated with horizontal wavy lines spaced well apart. It covers both shoulders but leaves her arms free. Each arm wears a bracelet around the wrist. The head was broken off anciently and of the four faces now only one, the one at the back, remains intact. She wears a hat that has a high cylindrical crown with paneled decoration. The brim of the hat comes to points or vizors at each face much like the flat cap worn by the god. A somewhat similar headdress is worn by the two winged figures shown in Porada 1948, nos. 958 and 959 on pl. 145, but the similarity could be accidental.

Identification is even more difficult than with the god. The one distinctive feature is the flowing vase that she holds. It can stand for rivers or for rain.[19] Since she is presumably the consort of the god and shows like him four faces, the latter interpretation seems the more probable one, making her, tentatively, a goddess of rainstorms.

B. THE MOUFLON BOWL

Among the various objects found on the common floor of periods III-IV in 4-Q.30 was a fragment of a bowl (Ish. 34:117) made of bituminous stone (pl. 31). To judge from its shape the bowl of which it had formed part was shaped like an inverted frustum and was decorated on rim and sides with carvings of mouflons (*Ovis orientalis*).[20] The fragment preserves one such mouflon and the very tail end of another, and since the curve of the rim of the fragment forms roughly one-third of a complete circle the bowl of which it formed part will have had three mouflons as shown in the restoration on plate 32.

The mouflon on the fragment is shown lying down. Its side is rendered in relief, its head is turned ninety degrees to the left and is in the round. The hair[21] of the mouflon is represented by horizontal panels with hatching in herringbone pattern, the eyes are inlaid with shell, the large horns curve back in a wide arch on either side of the head. The total impression conveyed is of remarkable gracefulness and vitality.

---

19. It is held by the flying rain cloud goddesses on the water basin of Gudea. See Moortgat 1969, pl. 188.

20. Thus correctly Frankfort 1936, p. 85 and Frankfort 1956, p. 60. The identification as ibex is not tenable.

21. All wild sheep have hairs rather than wool.

The closest relation of the fragment is with a number of similar bowls of bituminous stone and decorated with mouflons found at Susa in Elam. It is therefore to be assumed that the Ishchali fragment represents an import from there rather than a local produce.[22]

C. THE MONKEY STATUETTE

An alabaster statuette of a seated monkey (Ish. 35:48, pl. 40e, f) was found on the period II-A floor of the room 2-S.29, which by then had been remodeled to serve as cella in the small Ninshubura temple in the east part of the north wing of the complex. The statuette is ably carved and renders the animal well. It has been discussed by Frankfort[23] who suggested that since it has a hole in the bottom so that it can be mounted on a slim pole, it may have served as an emblem to be carried in ritual processions and on other ceremonial occasions. This is a natural assumption since it was found in a cella of a temple and it may well be right.

It is not, however, altogether without difficulty, for the monkey is not native to Mesopotamia and so it is difficult to imagine how it could have become the emblem of a Mesopotamian deity. How exotic and extraordinary it seemed may be seen from the fact that Ibbi-Suen of the Third Dynasty of Ur found the acquisition of a monkey an event of sufficient importance to name one of his years of reign after.[24] It was probably this same monkey that inspired an amused scribe to compose a fictive letter from it to its mother complaining about not seeing anything of the famous cities Ur, in which it was, and nearby Eridu and about the sour mash it was fed. The letter reads:

> Voyager, voyager, when you talk with my mother this is what Monkey has to say: 'While Ur is Nanna's delightful city and Eridu Enki's abounding city, I am made to sit behind the door to the house of the chief musician and am fed sour mash. Lest I die of it, have a wayfarer deliver to me bread that is not sour and beer that is not sour. It is urgent! Hala-Dada, let not your mother make you let the day go toward even, it is urgent!'[25]

22. See Frankfort 1956, p. 60 and Porada 1962, pp. 52-54.

23. See Frankfort 1943, pp. 20f., no. 335.

24. mu ^{d}I-bí-^{d}EN-ZU lugal-Uri^{ki}-ma-ra uku$_y$ (UGÚ)^{ku}-bi-dugud kur-bi mu-na-e-ra-a, "Year when a noble monkey was brought to Ibbi-Suen, king of Ur from its mountains." Legrain 1947, 111, 112, and 863.

25. The text of the letter reads: ^{1}lú-di* lú-di* ama-g̃u$_{10}$-ra ^{2}ù-na-a*-dug$_4$ ^{3}*uku$_x$ (UGÚ)^{ku}-bi na-ab-bé-a ^{4}Urim^{ki} uru-kiri$_3$-zal-^{d}Nanna-kam ^{5}Eridug uru-hé-g̃ál-^{d}En-ki-ga-kam* ^{6}g̃á-e egir $^{g̃iš}$ig é*-nar-gal-la<-ka>** al-tuš-en ^{7}igi-tum$_4$-lá mu-gu$_7$-e* ^{8}nam-ba-da-úš-en ^{9}ninda ba-ra-bil-lá kaš ba-ra-bil-lá ^{10}lú-du-kaskal* šu tag$_4$-ma-ab ^{11}a-ma-ru-kam ^{12}Ha-la-Da-da ama-zu ud nam-bí-te-en-te-⌈en⌉* ^{13}a-ma-ru-kam

Sources: A=Lutz 1919 no. 92, B=Lutz 1919 no. 93, C=Chiera 1934b no. 8, D=Kramer 1944 no. 129, E=Kramer 1969 pl. 124 (66) Ni 5218. Textual notes: Line 1, *E: -di$_6$; Line 2, *B and probably E: om. -a-; Line 3, *D and E use the wedge for personal name; Line 5, *B: -ka, Line 6, *C: om. é-, **B: -ka; Line 7, *B: -en, C: ⌈e⌉-[en(?)]; Line 10: *B: + -e; Lines 12-13 * B: om., C has the beginning of an Akkadian translation: [a]-la-ak ⌈har⌉-r[a-nim].

The messenger, it will be noted, is addressed twice, first by the general term "voyager, traveler," then again specifically by name. This may be seen as an instance of the popular "particularizing stanza" (cf.

That a monkey—or possibly a statue of one—was considered a gift rare enough to be given to a god is indicated by two Old Babylonian cylinder seals which show an audience before a god who, to judge by the full and new moon emblem above him was Nanna-Suen.[26] That the seals represent a god is also indicated by the various mythological space fillers of the two seals. Yet, the central figure does not wear a horned crown but a simple cap and it holds out a small vase. Thus the central scene is exactly like the well-known one of Ibbi-Suen handing a vase containing an official seal to a newly appointed official.[27] The only difference is that there the king is beardless; in the Old Babylonian seals the corresponding figure wears a beard. The similarity, though striking, may of course be fortuitous, but then again, since the two seals clearly use a traditional design, that tradition could well have had its origin in an admired later version of the Ibbi-Suen scene in which the king was shown as a mature man with beard and with his popular monkey. Certainty is of course out of the question.

As for the Ishchali monkey, the fact that monkeys were not native to Mesopotamia, but rare and exotic creatures, implies that a monkey would make an unusual and highly valued gift; also, the generally secular and amused attitude toward it, exemplified in the case of Ibbi-Suen's monkey, makes it seem worthwhile as a possible alternative to consider a secular use for it rather than a ritual one. The statuette may have been given to Ninshubura merely for her presumed pleasure and amusement at its lifelikeness.

D. THE ALABASTER CUP

A fragment of a cylindrical cup or vase of alabaster (Ish. 34:30) was found on the common floor of periods I and II in the western half of 4-Q.30. It measured $10.10 \times 5.60 \times 0.80$ centimeters. The cup was decorated with a scene carved in bas relief, part of which is preserved on the fragment (pl. 25a). The preserved portion shows from left to right remnants of two figures approaching a gate held open by an attendant. Of the figure at the extreme left edge of the sherd only the front of a fringed robe is preserved. The fringe at the lower edge of this robe touches the ground, which suggests that the wearer was a

---

Jacobsen 1970, pp. 334f.). The second address seems to survive only in source A. Presumably the messenger named was an actual person well known to the author of the pretended letter and his friends, but of no interest to later copyists.

The suffixed verbal form -àm marks, when used as a particle after a clause accompanying circumstance, background, which can be causal, merely descriptive, or, as here, contrastive. A preferred Akkadian rendering of the Sumerian verbal prefix a l - is by permansive of the factitive D stem (cf. Poebel 1923, §581). So a translation of a l - t u š - e n in line 6 as "I am lodged" seems preferable to "I sit," since the lodgings are clearly not to its taste. The term i g i - t u m₄ - l á in line 7 denotes, as shown by the context, a kind of food, probably a sour kind since the monkey insists on bread and beer that is not sour. The word occurs in I z i XV ii (Civil 1971, p. 169) 17´-18´ and is translated as *imrum* "forage" but also as *imātu* which had, one may assume, a similar meaning. A sour variety i g i - t u m₄ - l á - b i l - l á - t i l₄ - e "seething(?) sour i g i - t u m₄ - l á" was according to line 20´ of the passage in I z i fed to donkeys. It is rendered as *i-ma-tú i-me-ri* "*imatu*-forage of donkeys." Our reading - b i l - l á - t i l₄ - e in line 20´ is based on the copy of the signs given in the footnote to the line in Civil (1971). For i g i₄ - t u m₄ - l á "sour mash" which is often used as a feed to fatten up equids and which may "seethe" when fermenting would thus seem a suitable meaning.

For a treatment of the text see Powell 1978, pp. 163-95.

26. Frankfort 1939, pl. XXVIe, and Frankfort 1955, pl. 89, no. 957.

27. Frankfort 1956, pl. 54(A).

woman. The ground is rendered by three or more horizontal lines of traditional mountain design. The figure farther to the right is preserved in the lower half. It also wears a fringed robe but its robe is shorter and has no bottom fringe, so that it leaves the calves free. An arm, presumably meant as the left one, is held out toward the door opening at an angle of 220°. The attendant wears a fringed skirt. His upper body is bare. The head is broken away but traces at the neck seem to be renderings of hair. The doorleaf is paneled. Its top panel is decorated with horizontal lines of V-shaped incisions, the other panels are plain and presumably render the boards of a wooden doorleaf divided by a series of horizontal bands of wood or metal.

In seeking to visualize the scene of which the preserved fragment formed a part, one is led by the doorleaf with its attendant and the mountain pattern, suggesting localization in the eastern mountains, to consider the traditional motifs of audience before the sun-god in which the god is shown either stepping through the gate of heaven and over the eastern mountains at sunrise, or seated in the gate, presumably to hold court (cf. Frankfort 1939, pl. XVIIIa and b). The two figures about to enter the gate may be a man and his wife approaching the god with their offerings. For a parallel cf. Frankfort 1939, pl. XXIIc and Porada 1947, p. 33, no 29.

APPENDIX 1

CATALOGUE OF ISHCHALI OBJECT REGISTER NUMBERS

Ish. No.	Object	Locus	Plate/Figure
1934 EXCAVATIONS			
Ish. 34:1	Cylinder Seal	Surface	OIP 72, pl. 89:957
Ish. 34:2	Duck Weight	NW side, Survey Hill	—
Ish. 34:3	Weights	0.33, Dig House	—
Ish. 34:4	Weight	W side, Survey Hill	45a
Ish. 34:5	Plaque	"Serai," 1-S.36 (Top)	33j (OIC 20, fig. 69a)
Ish. 34:6	Plaque	"Serai," 1-R.33 (Top)	35c
Ish. 34:7	Plaque	"Serai," 1-R.33 (Top)	33k
Ish. 34:8	Duck Weight	"Serai," 10-R.35 (Grave)	44q
Ish. 34:9	Duck Weight	"Serai," 10-R.35 (Grave)	—
Ish. 34:10	Weights	"Serai," 10-R.35 (Grave)	—
Ish. 34:11	Metal Pieces	"Serai," 10-R.35 (Grave)	—
Ish. 34:12	Stones	"Serai," 10-R.35 (Grave)	—
Ish. 34:13	Shell Pieces	"Serai," 10-R.35 (Grave)	—
Ish. 34:14	Weight	"Serai," 10-R.35 (Grave)	—
Ish. 34:15	Cylinder Seal	"Serai," 7-R.35	OIP 72, pl. 89:946
Ish. 34:16	Cylinder Seal	"Serai," 8-R.34 (Top)	OIP 72, pl. 89:948
Ish. 34:17	Weight	"Serai," 1-R.35 (Top)	46b
Ish. 34:18	Weight	Surface	—
Ish. 34:19	Weight	Surface	OIP 72, pl. 89:953
Ish. 34:20	Cylinder Seal	"Serai," 8-R.34 (Top)	OIP 72, pl. 89:947
Ish. 34:21	Duck Weight	"Serai," 8-R.34 (Top)	44i
Ish. 34:22	Weights	"Serai," 8-R.34 (Top)	—
Ish. 34:23	Duck Weight	"Serai," 6-R.33 (Top)	44h
Ish. 34:24	Cylinder Seal	N. of 2-Q.29	OIP 72, pl. 88:932
Ish. 34:25	Cylinder Seal	Surface	OIP 72, pl. 89:953
Ish. 34:26	Cylinder Seal	2-Q.30 (Top)	—
Ish. 34:27	Pot	"Serai," 7-R.33 (Top)	—
Ish. 34:28	Lid	2-R.30 (Top)	—
Ish. 34:29	Weight	2-R.30 (Top)	44d
Ish. 34:30	Cup(?)	4-Q.30 (W part)	—
Ish. 34:31	Shell	4-Q.30 (Top)	—
Ish. 34:32	Bowl Base	4-Q.30 (Top)	40g, h

Catalogue of Ishchali Object Register Numbers (*cont.*)

Ish. No.	Object	Locus	Plate/Figure
		1934 EXCAVATIONS (*cont.*)	
Ish. 34:33	Beads	4-Q.30 (Top)	43b
Ish. 34:34	Cylinder Seal	1-P.29 (Top)	OIP 72, pl. 86:915
Ish. 34:35	Cylinder Seal	1-P.29 (Top)	OIP 72, p. 60
Ish. 34:36	Cylinder Seal	1-P.29 (Top)	OIP 72, pl. 86:914
Ish. 34:37	Cylinder Seal	4-Q.30 (Top)	—
Ish. 34:38	Cylinder Seal	4-Q.30 (Top)	—
Ish. 34:39	Cylinder Seal	4-Q.30 (Top)	OIP 72, pl. 87:923
Ish. 34:40	Plaque	2-R.29	34b (OIC 20, fig. 71)
Ish. 34:41	Plaque	5-Q.30 (Top)	35b (OIC 20, fig. 73b)
Ish. 34:42	Amulet (Weight?)	6-Q.30	44a
Ish. 34:43	Amulet (Weight?)	6-Q.30	44b
Ish. 34:44	Bowl Fragment	4-Q.30	40d
Ish. 34:45	Cylinder Seal	6-Q.30	OIC 20, fig. 68; OIP 72, pl. 87: 917
Ish. 34:46	Cylinder Seal	5-Q.30	OIP 72, pl. 86:901
Ish. 34:47	Cylinder Seal	5-Q.30 (Top)	OIP 72, p. 61
Ish. 34:48	Cylinder Seal	4-Q.30 (Top)	OIP 72, pl. 87:922
Ish. 34:49	Cylinder Seal	4-Q.30 (Top)	OIP 72, pl. 87:925
Ish. 34:50	Cylinder Seal	4-Q.30 (Top)	OIP 72, p. 61
Ish. 34:51	Lamp	2-P.30 (SE corner)	30a, b (OIC 20, fig. 75)
Ish. 34:52	Lamp	2-P.30 (SE corner)	30c, d (OIC 20, fig. 76)
Ish. 34:53	Cylinder Seal	1-P.30	—
Ish. 34:54	Cylinder Seal	1-P.30	—
Ish. 34:55	Macehead	5-Q.30	—
Ish. 34:56	Stamp Seal	5-Q.30	42a
Ish. 34:57	Plaque	5-Q.30	38a (OIC 20, fig. 72d)
Ish. 34:58	Plaque	5-Q.30	38b
Ish. 34:59	Plaque	"Serai," 1-S.36 (Top)	33q (OIC 20, fig. 69b)
Ish. 34:60	Plaque	2-R.30 (Top)	38g
Ish. 34:61	Plaque	Dump	36a (OIC 20, fig. 73a)
Ish. 34:62	Duck Weight	2-S.30 (Top)	44m
Ish. 34:63	Weights	2-S.30 (Top)	—
Ish. 34:64	Cylinder Seal	5-R.29 (Top)	OIP 72, pl. 87:918
Ish. 34:65	Seal Impressions	7-R.29 (Top)	—
Ish. 34:66	Pendant(?)	7-R.29 (Top)	—
Ish. 34:67	Plaque	2-U.30 (Top)	38h
Ish. 34:68	Cylinder Seal	1-P.31	OIP 72, pl. 86:903
Ish. 34:69	Cylinder Seal	5-Q.30 (E pivotstone box)	OIP 72, pl. 86:912
Ish. 34:70	Bead	5-Q.30 (E pivotstone box)	—
Ish. 34:71	Necklace	5-Q.30 (E pivotstone box)	—
Ish. 34:72	Cylinder Seal	5-Q.30 (E pivotstone box)	OIP 72, pl. 86:911
Ish. 34:73	Stamp Seal	5-Q.30 (Beside pivotstone box)	42c

Catalogue of Ishchali Object Register Numbers (*cont.*)

Ish. No.	Object	Locus	Plate/Figure
Ish. No.	*Object*	*Locus*	*Plate/Figure*

1934 EXCAVATIONS (*cont.*)

Ish. 34:74	Cylinder Seal	4-S.29 (Top)	OIP 72, pl. 87:921
Ish. 34:75	Cylinder Seal	Kitîtum Temple dump	OIP 72, pl. 88:937
Ish. 34:76	Cylinder Seal	2-R.32 (Top)	OIP 72, pl. 87:928
Ish. 34:77	Pendant	2-T.30 (Top)	—
Ish. 34:78	Bead	1-T.30 (Top)	—
Ish. 34:79	Relief	2-R.30	39c (OIC 20, fig. 74)
Ish. 34:80	Figurine	3-T.32	41d
Ish. 34:81	Duck Weight	Surface	44e
Ish. 34:82	Cylinder Seal	4-R.32 (Top)	OIP 72, pl. 87:919
Ish. 34:83	Cylinder Seal	1-W.32	OIP 72, pl. 88:941
Ish. 34:84	Cylinder Seal	1-W.32	OIP 72, pl. 88:940
Ish. 34:85	Plaque	3-T.31 (Robber dump)	35k (OIC 20, fig. 73c)
Ish. 34:86	Cylinder Seal	4-Q.30 (Libn bench)	OIP 72, pl. 86:910
Ish. 34:87	Cylinder Seal	4-Q.30 (Top of wall)	OIP 72, pl. 87:924
Ish. 34:88	Model Bed	Dump	37c
Ish. 34:89	Model Bed	1-R.32 (Top)	37b
Ish. 34:90	Plaque	Dump	35m
Ish. 34:91	Plaque	2-S.29 (Top)	34l
Ish. 34:92	Plaque	City Gate (Top)	33n (OIC 20, fig. 70a)
Ish. 34:93	Plaque	"Serai," 1-S.36 (Top)	36d
Ish. 34:94	Plaque	Surface	33a (OIC 20, fig. 69c)
Ish. 34:95	Plaque	Surface	33o
Ish. 34:96	Plaque	2-T.31 (Top)	33h
Ish. 34:97	Plaque	3-P.32	35d (OIC 20, fig. 72c)
Ish. 34:98	Plaque	3-P.32	35d (OIC 20, fig. 72c)
Ish. 34:99	Plaque	4-T.29 (Top)	33c (OIC 20, fig. 69e)
Ish. 34:100	Plaque	5-T.29 (Top)	33g (OIC 20, fig. 70c)
Ish. 34:101	Plaque	6-R.29 (Top)	33f
Ish. 34:102	Plaque	Surface	33b (OIC 20, fig. 69d)
Ish. 34:103	Plaque	City Gate (Top)	34c (OIC 20, fig. 71)
Ish. 34:104	Plaque	3-S.30 (Top)	35g
Ish. 34:105	Plaque	Surface	33d (OIC 20, fig. 69f)
Ish. 34:106	Plaque	2-R.29	35n (OIC 20, fig. 70d)
Ish. 34:107	Plaque	2-S.30 (Top)	35m
Ish. 34:108	Plaque	1-Q.29 (Top)	35o
Ish. 34:109	Plaque	2-T.29 (Top)	35p
Ish. 34:110	Plaque	City Gate (Top)	34c (OIC 20, fig. 71)
Ish. 34:111	Plaque	Dump	35j (OIC 20, fig. 72b)
Ish. 34:112	Plaque	Dump	34k (OIC 20, fig. 72a)
Ish. 34:113	Plaque	2-P.31 (W wall)	33p
Ish. 34:114	Plaque	3-S.30 (Top)	34o (OIC 20, fig. 70b)
Ish. 34:115	Figurine	"Serai," 8-R.35 (Top)	38k

Catalogue of Ishchali Object Register Numbers (*cont.*)

Ish. No.	Object	Locus	Plate/Figure
1934 EXCAVATIONS (*cont.*)			
Ish. 34:116	Plaque	Surface	38f
Ish. 34:117	Bowl	4-Q.30	31, 32 (OIC 20, figs. 78, 79)
Ish. 34:118	Metal Fragment	City Gate (N side)	—
Ish. 34:119	Cylinder Seal	Surface (N of Kitîtum Temple)	OIP 72, pl. 88:933
Ish. 34:120	Cylinder Seal	Outside (N of Kitîtum wall and opposite 2-P.29)	OIP 72, pl. 88:931
Ish. 34:121	Cylinder Seal	1-P.30	OIP 72, pl. 87:916
Ish. 34:122	Duck Weight	Street (U.32)	44f
Ish. 34:123	Cylinder Seal	Street (T.28)	OIP 72, pl. 88:929
Ish. 34:124	Plaque	5-R.30	34a (OIC 20, fig. 67)
Ish. 34:125	Plaque Mold	"Serai," 3-Q.33 (Top)	34h
Ish. 34:126	Plaque Mold	Dump	34n
Ish. 34:127	Cylinder Seal	5-R.30	OIP 72, pl. 86:908
Ish. 34:128	Cylinder Seal	1-P.31	OIP 72, pl. 86:902
Ish. 34:129	Cylinder Seal	3-T.30	OIP 72, pl. 86:907
Ish. 34:130	Amulet	4-Q.30 (Top)	41e
Ish. 34:131	Bead Spacer	1-P.30	—
Ish. 34:132	Bead Spacer	1-P.30	—
Ish. 34:133	Stamp Seal	4-Q.30	42e
Ish. 34:134	Stamp Seal	4-Q.30	42d
Ish. 34:135	Stamp Seal	6-Q.30	42f
Ish. 34:136	Stamp Seal	4-Q.30	42g
Ish. 34:137	Stamp Seal	4-Q.30	42b
Ish. 34:138	Beads	1-P.30, 4- and 5-Q.30	43a
Ish. 34:139	Statuette Head	2-R.31	40a-c (OIC 20, fig. 77; OIP 60, pl. 73A-C)
Ish. 34:140-99	(nos. not used)		
Ish. 34:200	Arrowhead	7-R.35 (Top)	—
Ish. 34:201	Relief Fragment	4-Q.30	41a
Ish. 34:202	Stone Inlay	Temple dump	41c
Ish. 34:203	Arrowhead	4-R.29	30e
No Ish. no.	Metal Statuette	7-R.35	26, 27 (OIP 60, pls. 77-79)
No Ish. no.	Metal Statuette	7-R.35	28, 29 (OIP 60, pls. 79-81)
1935 EXCAVATIONS			
Ish. 35:1	Amulet(?)	Dump	—
Ish. 35:2	Stamp Seal	Surface	—
Ish. 35:3	Model Bed	Surface	37a
Ish. 35:4	Cylinder Seal	Surface	OIP 72, pl. 89:952
Ish. 35:5	Cylinder Seal	1-R.32 (Top of wall)	OIP 72, pl. 87:926

Catalogue of Ishchali Object Register Numbers (*cont.*)

Ish. No.	Object	Locus	Plate/Figure
1935 EXCAVATIONS (*cont.*)			
Ish. 35:6	Cylinder Seal	Street (2-T.32)	OIP 72, pl. 88:935
Ish. 35:7	Weight	Dump	44c
Ish. 35:8	Plaque	1-R.29	35l
Ish. 35:9	Duck Weight	Surface	44k
Ish. 35:10	Duck Weight	Surface	44l
Ish. 35:11	Bead	Surface	46c
Ish. 35:12	Duck Weight	Surface	44j
Ish. 35:13	Weight	Surface	—
Ish. 35:14	Weight	Surface	—
Ish. 35:15	Weight	Surface	45d
Ish. 35:16	Weight	Surface	45c
Ish. 35:17	Cylinder Seal	Surface (W of Tell)	OIP 72, pl. 89:950
Ish. 35:18	Weight	Dump	45f
Ish. 35:19	Weight	1-R.29	—
Ish. 35:20	Bead	2-T.32	—
Ish. 35:21	Shell	6-Q.30	46d
Ish. 35:22	Duck Weight	Surface	44n
Ish. 35:23	Bone Pin	1-P.29	—
Ish. 35:24	Cylinder Seal	1-R.29	OIP 72, pl. 86:904
Ish. 35:25	Cylinder Seal	Surface	OIP 72, p. 61
Ish. 35:26	Cylinder Seal	2-Q.29	OIP 72, pl. 86:906
Ish. 35:27	Cylinder Seal	Surface	OIP 72, pl. 89:956
Ish. 35:28	Duck Weight	Surface	44o
Ish. 35:29	Weight	6-Q.30	—
Ish. 35:30	Cylinder Seal	Street (P.33)	—
Ish. 35:31	Cylinder Seal	3-V.31	OIP 72, pl. 88:939
Ish. 35:32	Cylinder Seal	Surface	OIP 72, pl. 89:954
Ish. 35:33	Duck Weight	Street (P.32)	44g
Ish. 35:34	Cylinder Seal (inscribed)	2-T.30	OIP 72, p. 61
Ish. 35:35	Cylinder Seal	Dump	OIP 72, pl. 89:958
Ish. 35:36	Relief Fragment	2-V.30 (Top)	25 (OIP 60, fig. 75A)
Ish. 35:37	Weight(?)	2-V.30 (Top)	46a
Ish. 35:38	Cylinder Seal	Street (W of Kitûtum Temple)	—
Ish. 35:39	Cylinder Seal	Surface	OIP 72, pl. 89:955
Ish. 35:40	Plaque	Outside Gate to 1-Q.32	38c
Ish. 35:41	Duck Weight	Surface	44p
Ish. 35:42	Cylinder Seal	3-S.30	OIP 72, pl. 86:909
Ish. 35:43	Weight	3-V.30 (Top)	—
Ish. 35:44	Weight	3-V.30 (Top)	45e
Ish. 35:45	Weight	3-V.30 (Top)	—
Ish. 35:46	Weight	3-V.30 (Top)	—
Ish. 35:47	Weight	City Wall (Surface)	45b

Catalogue of Ishchali Object Register Numbers (*cont.*)

Ish. No.	Object	Locus	Plate/Figure
1935 EXCAVATIONS (*cont.*)			
Ish. 35:48	Statuette	2-S.29	40e, f (OIP 60, pl. 74A, B)
Ish. 35:49	Cylinder Seal	W 30 (Street NE corner, Shamash Temple)	—
Ish. 35:50	Cylinder Seal	Surface	OIP 72, pl. 89:951
Ish. 35:51	Bead	2-S.29	43c
Ish. 35:52	Cylinder Seal	2-V.32	OIP 72, pl. 89:944
Ish. 35:53	Cylinder Seal	Large Court (Kitîtum Temple)	OIP 72, pl. 87:927
Ish. 35:54	Bone Pin	City Wall	—
Ish. 35:55	Metal Pin	2-T.30	—
Ish. 35:56	Plaque	6-V.32	38d
Ish. 35:57	Shell Fragment	Well (Kitîtum Main Court)	—
Ish. 35:58	Duck Weight	14-V.32 (Top)	—
Ish. 35:59	Model Bed	16-V.32	—
Ish. 35:60	Metal Cup	3-V.32 (Top)	30i
Ish. 35:61	Metal Cup	3-V.32 (Top)	30h
Ish. 35:62	Plaque	10-V.32	34q
Ish. 35:63	Cylinder Seal	10-V.32 (Top)	—
Ish. 35:64	Duck Weight	16-V.32 (Top)	—
Ish. 35:65	Cylinder Seal	12-V.32 (Top)	OIP 72, pl. 89:949
Ish. 35:66	Plaque	City Wall (SE corner)	35i
Ish. 35:67	Cylinder Seal	W. 33 (Inside City Wall)	OIP 72, pl. 89:945
Ish. 35:68	Metal Cup	15-V.32	—
Ish. 35:69	Metal Bands	1-S.32 (Top)	30j
Ish. 35:70	Cylinder Seal	4-T.30	OIP 72, pl. 86:905
Ish. 35:71	Cylinder Seal	2-S.30	OIP 72, pl. 86:900
Ish. 35:72	Cylinder Seal	5-T.30	OIP 72, pl. 86:913
Ish. 35:73	Cylinder Seal	3-T.32	OIP 72, p. 60
Ish. 35:74	Cylinder Seal	1-U.30	OIP 72, pl. 87:920
Ish. 35:75	Plaque	2-V.31	33e
Ish. 35:76	Stone Bowl	5-T.30	—
Ish. 35:77	Seal Impression	4-V.31	OIP 72, pl. 88:942
Ish. 35:78	Cylinder Seal	9-R.29	OIP 72, p. 60
Ish. 35:79	Plaque	3-V.31	35a
Ish. 35:80	Macehead	4-V.30	41h
Ish. 35:81	Macehead	4-V.30	41g
Ish. 35:82	Macehead	4-V.30	41f
Ish. 35:83	Macehead	4-V.30	—
Ish. 35:84	Metal Lamp	4-V.30	30f, g
Ish. 35:85	Cylinder Seal	*Kîsu* (N of 7-S.29)	OIP 72, pl. 88:930
Ish. 35:86	Plaque	2-S.30	—
Ish. 35:87	Plaque	5-V.31	35e

Catalogue of Ishchali Object Register Numbers (*cont.*)

Ish. No.	Object	Locus	Plate/Figure
1935 EXCAVATIONS (*cont.*)			
Ish. 35:88	Figurine	Surface	36b
Ish. 35:89	Plaque	Dump	34p
Ish. 35:90	Plaque	Surface	38j
Ish. 35:91	Plaque	9-V.31 (Top)	34d
Ish. 35:92	Plaque	2-T.29	—
Ish. 35:93	Plaque	2-T.29	36g
Ish. 35:94	Cylinder Seal	Behind *Kîsu* (N of Kitîtum Temple)	OIP 72, pl. 88:934
Ish. 35:95	Cylinder Seal	2-W.30 (Top)	OIP 72, pl. 88:938
Ish. 35:96-203	(nos. not used)		
Ish. 35:204	Plaque	5-S.30 (Top)	37d
Ish. 35:205	Macehead	Surface	—
Ish. 35:206	Figurine	City Gate (Top)	34m
Ish. 35:207	Worked Stone	1-R.31 (Top)	41b
Ish. 35:208	Plaque	Dump	33i
Ish. 35:209	Mold	Surface	—
Ish. 35:210	Plaque	Surface	34e
Ish. 35:211	Plaque	Surface (NW corner of *Kîsu*)	35h
Ish. 35:212	Plaque	2-W.31 (Top)	34l
Ish. 35:213	Figurine	8-Q.30	36f
Ish. 35:214	Plaque	1-R.29	36e
Ish. 35:215	Plaque	1-R.29	35q
Ish. 35:216	Plaque	1-W.31 (Top)	34g
Ish. 35:217	Eye Fragment	3-S.30 (Top)	—
Ish. 35:218	Plaque	Dump	38i
Ish. 35:219	Plaque	2-T.29	38e
Ish. 35:220	Plaque	Dump	34i
Ish. 35:221	Plaque	1-T.31	36c
Ish. 35:222	Plaque	2-S.30	—
Ish. 35:223	Plaque	Surface	34j
1937 EXCAVATIONS			
Ish. 37:1	Cylinder Seal	Trench B(?)	39a
Ish. 37:2	Cylinder Seal	Trench B(?)	39b
Ish. 37:224	Beads	6-Q.30	43d
Ish. 37:225	Beads	6-Q.30	—

APPENDIX 2

CATALOGUE OF ISHCHALI 1934 REFERENCE NUMBERS

Ish. No.	Object	Locus	Plate/Figure
Ref. 34:1	Metal Lump	N side of survey mark	—
Ref. 34:2	Metal Lumps	NE-E side of survey mark	—
Ref. 34:3	Weight	Dig house excavation	—
Ref. 34:4	Weight	Survey mark hill	—
Ref. 34:5	Bead	Survey mark hill	—
Ref. 34:6	Bead	Survey mark hill	—
Ref. 34:7	Plaque (Bull)	Dig house excavation	—
Ref. 34:8	Model Boat	Dig house excavation	—
Ref. 34:9	Figurine	Dig house excavation	—
Ref. 34:10	Votive Adze	Dig house excavation	—
Ref. 34:11	Figurine	City Wall (Top)	—
Ref. 34:12	Clay Bottle	6-R.35 (Top)	—
Ref. 34:13	Metal Pin	3-R.34 (Top)	—
Ref. 34:14	(see app. 1, Ish. 34:115)	8-R.35 (Top)	38k
Ref. 34:15	Model Boat	2-Q.35 (Top)	—
Ref. 34:16	(see app. 1, Ish. 34:5)	1-S.36 (Top)	33j (OIC 20, fig. 69a)
Ref. 34:17	(see app. 1, Ish. 34:7)	1-R.33 (Top)	33k
Ref. 34:18	(see app. 1, Ish. 34:59)	1-S.36 (Top)	33q (OIC 20, fig. 69b)
Ref. 34:19	Silver Wire	2-R.34	—
Ref. 34:20	(see app. 1, Ish. 34:6)	1-R.33 (Top)	35c
Ref. 34:21	Cylinder Seal Fragment	Surface	—
Ref. 34:22	(see app. 1, Ish. 34:200)	7-R.35 (Top)	—
Ref. 34:23-32	(nos. not used)		
Ref. 34:33	Plaque	Surface	—
Ref. 34:34	Plaque	6-R.35 (Top)	—
Ref. 34:35	Figurine	Surface	—
Ref. 34:36	Plaque	8-R.34 (Top)	—
Ref. 34:37	Model Bed	Dump	—
Ref. 34:38	Spindle Whorl	9-R.34	—
Ref. 34:39	Model Chisel	Surface	—
Ref. 34:40	Plaque	Surface	—
Ref. 34:41	Plaque	9-R.33 (Top)	—
Ref. 34:42	Figurine (Male)	Surface	—
Ref. 34:43	Metal Nail Head	6-R.33 (Top)	—

117

Catalogue of Ishchali 1934 Reference Numbers (*cont.*)

Ish. No.	Object	Locus	Plate/Figure
Ref. 34:44	Figurine (Male)	Surface	—
Ref. 34:45	(see app. 1, Ish. 34:95)	Surface	33o
Ref. 34:46	(see app. 1, Ish. 34:94)	Surface	33a (OIC 20, fig. 69c)
Ref. 34:47	Plaque	Surface	—
Ref. 34:48	Plaque	1-S.36 (Top)	—
Ref. 34:49	(see app. 1, Ish. 34:93)	1-S.36 (Top)	36d
Ref. 34:50	Clay Stand	Surface	—
Ref. 34:51	Figurine (Animal)	4-R.29 (Top)	—
Ref. 34:52	Model Chariot	4-R.29 (Top)	—
Ref. 34:53	Plaque	Surface	—
Ref. 34:54	Figurine (Human)	Surface	—
Ref. 34:55	Model Boat	2-R.29 (Top)	—
Ref. 34:56	Figurine (Human)	Surface	—
Ref. 34:57	Figurine (Human Head)	1-S.36 (Top)	—
Ref. 34:58	Plaque	Temple dump	—
Ref. 34:59	Model Boat	2-R.29 (Top)	—
Ref. 34:60	(see app. 1, Ish. 34:203)	4-R.29 (Top)	30e
Ref. 34:61	Bronze Nails	2-R.29 (Top)	—
Ref. 34:62	Metal Pin	1-R.30 (Top)	—
Ref. 34:63	(see app. 1, Ish. 34:201)	4-Q.30 (Top)	41a
Ref. 34:64	(see app. 1, Ish. 34:202)	Temple dump	41c
Ref. 34:65	Model Bed	1-R.29 (Top)	—
Ref. 34:66	Plaque	Dump	—
Ref. 34:67	Plaque	Surface	—
Ref. 34:68	Plaque	3-Q.30 (Top)	—
Ref. 34:69	Shell	1-R.29 (Top)	—
Ref. 34:70	Shell Pendant(?)	5-Q.29 (Top)	—
Ref. 34:71	Metal Pin	1-R.29 (Top)	—
Ref. 34:72	(see app. 1, Ish. 34:60)	2-R.30 (Top)	38g
Ref. 34:73	Figurine (Animal)	4-R.29 (Top)	—
Ref. 34:74	Model Chariot	3-Q.29 (Top)	—
Ref. 34:75	Metal Nail	4-Q.29 (Top)	—
Ref. 34:76	Plaque	1-S.36 (Top)	—
Ref. 34:77	Metal Coil	2-R.30 (Top)	—
Ref. 34:78	Ostrich Egg Shell	4-Q.30 (Top)	—
Ref. 34:79	Alabaster Fragments	4-Q.30 (Top)	—
Ref. 34:80	Metal Plate(?)	4-Q.30 (Top)	—
Ref. 34:81	(see app. 1, Ish. 34:105)	Surface	33d (OIC 20, fig. 69f)
Ref. 34:82	Plaque	Surface	—
Ref. 34:83	Figurine (Human)	1-Q.29	—
Ref. 34:84	Plaque	Surface	—
Ref. 34:85	Figurine (Animal)	1-Q.29	—

Catalogue of Ishchali 1934 Reference Numbers (*cont.*)

Ish. No.	Object	Locus	Plate/Figure
Ref. 34:86	Model Chariot	Surface	—
Ref. 34:87	(see app. 1, Ish. 34:89)	1-R.32 (Top)	37b
Ref. 34:88	Metal Nail Heads	2-R.29	—
Ref. 34:89	Model Wheel	2-Q.29	—
Ref. 34:90	Cylinder Seal	6-Q.30	—
Ref. 34:91	Metal Knife Blade	6-Q.30	—
Ref. 34:92	Bead	2-Q.31 (Top)	—
Ref. 34:93	Metal Pincers	5-Q.30	—
Ref. 34:94	Metal Spike Head	5-Q.30	—
Ref. 34:95	Plaque	Temple dump	—
Ref. 34:96	Figurine (Human Female)	2-R.29	—
Ref. 34:97	Figurine (Human)	4-Q.30 (Top)	—
Ref. 34:98	Clay Vase	5-Q.30	—
Ref. 34:99	Clay Jar	Temple dump	—
Ref. 34:100	Cylinder Seal	4-Q.30 (Top)	—
Ref. 34:101	Weight	2-R.29	—
Ref. 34:102	Model Bed	2-R.29	—
Ref. 34:103	Cylinder Seals	1-P.30	—
Ref. 34:104	Metal Nail	2-Q.31	—
Ref. 34:105	Bead	5-Q.30	—
Ref. 34:106	Cylinder Seal	6-Q.30	—
Ref. 34:107	Ostrich Egg Shell	6-Q.30	—
Ref. 34:108	Cylinder Seal	6-Q.30	—
Ref. 34:109	Metal Pin	6-Q.30	—
Ref. 34:110	Metal Pin	6-Q.30	—
Ref. 34:111	(see app. 1, Ish. 34:58)	5-Q.30	38b
Ref. 34:112	(see app. 1, Ish. 34:57)	5-Q.30	38a (OIC 20, fig. 72d)
Ref. 34:113	Beads and Shells	1-P.30	—
Ref. 34:114	Ostrich Egg Shell	6-Q.30 (Robber dump)	—
Ref. 34:115	(see app. 1, Ish. 34:106)	2-R.29	35n (OIC 20, fig. 70d)
Ref. 34:116	Plaque	4-Q.30 (Top)	—
Ref. 34:117	Shells	4-Q.30 (Top)	—
Ref. 34:118	Cylinder Seal	4-Q.30 (Top)	—
Ref. 34:119	Shells	1-P.29 (Top)	—
Ref. 34:120	Bead(?)	1-P.29 (Surface)	—
Ref. 34:121	Figurine (Human Female)	Surface	—
Ref. 34:122	Figurine (Human Head)	2-Q.31 (Top)	—
Ref. 34:123	Plaque (Hunter)	3-P.30 (Top)	—
Ref. 34:124	Alabaster Inlay(?)	5-Q.30	—
Ref. 34:125	Loomweight(?)	2-Q.31	—
Ref. 34:126	Plaque	Temple dump	—
Ref. 34:127	Model Wheel	1-Q.29 (Top)	—

Catalogue of Ishchali 1934 Reference Numbers (*cont.*)

Ish. No.	Object	Locus	Plate/Figure
Ref. 34:128	(see app. 1, Ish. 34:108)	1-Q.29 (Top)	35o
Ref. 34:129	Figurine (Charioteer)	Surface	—
Ref. 34:130	Figurine (Human Head)	Temple dump	—
Ref. 34:131	Bone Pin	1-R.29	—
Ref. 34:132	Bone Pin	1-R.29	—
Ref. 34:133	Metal Nail	2-Q.31	—
Ref. 34:134	Figurine (Human Head)	1-R.30	—
Ref. 34:135	Model Chariot	1-R.30 (Top)	—
Ref. 34:136	Model Chariot	1-P.30	—
Ref. 34:137	Alabaster Bowl Fragment	2-P.30	—
Ref. 34:138	Alabaster Jar Stopper	6-Q.30	—
Ref. 34:139	Cylinder Seal	6-Q.30	—
Ref. 34:140	Clay Jar	3-P.31	—
Ref. 34:141	Figurine (Human Female?)	2-P.30	—
Ref. 34:142	Figurine (Human Female?)	3-P.31	—
Ref. 34:143	Figurine (Seated Human Female)	Temple dump	—
Ref. 34:144	Bead	6-Q.30	—
Ref. 34:145	Model Bed	1-Q.32 (Top)	—
Ref. 34:146	Plaque	City Wall	—
Ref. 34:147	Relief Fragment	Temple dump	—
Ref. 34:148	Plaque	Surface	—
Ref. 34:149	Metal Strips	2-S.30 (Top)	—
Ref. 34:150	(see app. 1, Ish. 34:101)	6-R.29 (Top)	33f
Ref. 34:151	Plaque	5-R.30 (Top)	—
Ref. 34:152	(see app. 1, Ish. 34:61)	Dump	36a (OIC 20, fig. 73a)
Ref. 34:153	Relief Fragment	Dump	—
Ref. 34:154	Shell Inlay	2-S.30 (Top)	—
Ref. 34:155	Figurine (Human Female)	1-P.33 (Top)	—
Ref. 34:156	Metal Ring	2-S.30 (Top)	—
Ref. 34:157	Bone Pin	6-R.29 (Top)	—
Ref. 34:158	Model Bed	6-R.30 (Top)	—
Ref. 34:159	Zoomorphic Pot	6-R.30 (Top)	—
Ref. 34:160	Ostrich Egg Shell	1-R.32 (Top of door socket)	—
Ref. 34:161	Beads	4-R.30	—
Ref. 34:162	Macehead	Temple dump	—
Ref. 34:163	Plaque	Surface	—
Ref. 34:164	Weight	Temple dump	—
Ref. 34:165	Clay Lamp	6-R.30 (Top)	—
Ref. 34:166	Plaque	2-P.30	—
Ref. 34:167	Plaque	Surface	—
Ref. 34:168	Plaque	Surface	—
Ref. 34:169	Plaque	2-P.32 (Top)	—

Catalogue of Ishchali 1934 Reference Numbers (*cont.*)

Ish. No.	Object	Locus	Plate/Figure
Ref. 34:170	Figurine (Animal)	2-P.32 (Top)	—
Ref. 34:171	Plaque	Surface	—
Ref. 34:172	(see app. 1, Ish. 35:204)	5-S.30 (Top)	37d
Ref. 34:173	(see app. 1, Ish. 34:107)	2-S.30 (Top)	35m
Ref. 34:174	Metal Strips	2-S.30 (Top)	—
Ref. 34:175	Plaque	3-P.32	—
Ref. 34:176	Plaque	1-S.29 (Top)	—
Ref. 34:177	(see app. 1, Ish. 34:98)	3-P.32	35d (OIC 20, fig. 72c)
Ref. 34:178	Plaque	Dump	—
Ref. 34:179	Plaque	Surface	—
Ref. 34:180	Figurine (Human)	3-P.32 (Top)	—
Ref. 34:181	(see app. 1, Ish. 34:97)	Dump	35d (OIC 20, fig. 72c)
Ref. 34:182	(see app. 1, Ish. 34:114)	3-S.30 (Top)	34o (OIC 20, fig. 70b)
Ref. 34:183	(see app. 1, Ish. 34:111)	Dump	35j (OIC 20, fig. 72b)
Ref. 34:184	Plaque	2-Q.31	—
Ref. 34:185	Stone Horn Fragment	3-S.30 (Top)	—
Ref. 34:186	Stone Horn Fragment	3-S.30 (Top)	—
Ref. 34:187	Metal Nails	3-S.30 (Top)	—
Ref. 34:188	Beads	2-R.32 (Top)	—
Ref. 34:189	Plaque	3-P.32 (Top)	—
Ref. 34:190	Model Bed	3-P.32 (Top)	—
Ref. 34:191	(see app. 1, Ish. 34:109)	2-T.29 (Top)	35p
Ref. 34:192	(see app. 1, Ish. 34:112)	Dump	34k (OIC 20, fig. 72a)
Ref. 34:193	(see app. 1, Ish. 34:91)	2-S.29 (Top)	34l
Ref. 34:194	Beads	3-R.32 (Top)	—
Ref. 34:195	Metal Nail	1-T.29 (Top)	—
Ref. 34:196	(see app. 1, Ish. 34:104)	3-S.30 (Top)	35g
Ref. 34:197	Figurine (Animal)	3-R.31 (Top)	—
Ref. 34:198	Figurine (Human Female)	Surface	—
Ref. 34:199	Plaque	Dump	—
Ref. 34:200	(see app. 1, Ish. 34:67)	2-U.30 (Top)	38h
Ref. 34:201	Model Boat	Dump	—
Ref. 34:202	Figurine (Human Male)	Dump	—
Ref. 34:203	Figurine (Human Female)	Dump	—
Ref. 34:204	Model Axe(?)	2-Q.31	—
Ref. 34:205	Figurine(?) Fragment	3-P.32 (Top)	—
Ref. 34:206	Figurine (Animal)	1-R.30	—
Ref. 34:207	Figurine (Human)	4-S.29 (Top)	—
Ref. 34:208	Metal Nails	1-R.31 (Top)	—
Ref. 34:209	Stone Cube	City Wall	—
Ref. 34:210	Stone Cube	City Wall	—
Ref. 34:211	Bone Pin	7-S.29 (Top)	—

Catalogue of Ishchali 1934 Reference Numbers (*cont.*)

Ish. No.	Object	Locus	Plate/Figure
Ref. 34:212	Bone Pin	7-S.29 (Top)	—
Ref. 34:213	Duck Weight	City Wall	—
Ref. 34:214	Bead	City Wall	—
Ref. 34:215	Figurine (Human Female)	Surface	—
Ref. 34:216	Figurine (Human Female)	Surface	—
Ref. 34:217	Plaque	Dump	—
Ref. 34:218	Figurine (Horse Head)	6-T.29 (Top)	—
Ref. 34:219	Plaque	Dump	—
Ref. 34:220	(see app. 1, Ish. 34:100)	5-T.29 (Top)	33g (OIC 20, fig. 70c)
Ref. 34:221	Model Bed	1-R.29 (Top)	—
Ref. 34:222	Plaque	[Keshem]	—
Ref. 34:223	(see app. 1, Ish. 34:99)	4-T.29 (Top)	33c (OIC 20, fig. 69e)
Ref. 34:224	Plaque	[Keshem]	—
Ref. 34:225	Plaque	City Wall	—
Ref. 34:226	Figurine Stand	City Wall	—
Ref. 34:227	Bone Pin	1-S.30	—
Ref. 34:228	Stone Relief	1-P.31 (Top)	—
Ref. 34:229	Stone Relief	1-P.31 (Top)	—
Ref. 34:230	Metal Earring	Dump	—
Ref. 34:231	Metal Earring	City Wall	—
Ref. 34:232	(see app. 1, Ish. 34:75)	Kitîtum Temple dump	OIP 72, pl. 88:937
Ref. 34:233	(see app. 1, Ish. 34:113)	2-P.31 (W wall)	33p
Ref. 34:234	(see app. 1, Ish. 34:102)	Surface	33b (OIC 20, fig. 69d)
Ref. 34:235	(see app. 1, Ish. 34:96)	2-T.31 (Top)	33h
Ref. 34:236	Plaque	Surface	—
Ref. 34:237	Figurine (Human Female)	6-T.29 (Top)	—
Ref. 34:238	Plaque Fragment	Dump	—
Ref. 34:239	Plaque Fragment	1-R.29	—
Ref. 34:240	(see app. 1, Ish. 34:116)	Surface	38f
Ref. 34:241	Plaque	2-R.32 (Top)	—
Ref. 34:242	Model Bed	Surface	—
Ref. 34:243	Plaque	3-P.32 (Top)	—
Ref. 34:244	Metal Spear(?) Blade	Large Court (Kitîtum)	—
Ref. 34:245	Stone Conglomerate	2-U.30 (Top)	—
Ref. 34:246	Clay Jar Stopper	2-T.31 (Top)	—
Ref. 34:247	Plaque	Dump	—
Ref. 34:248	Vase Sherd	Dump	—
Ref. 34:249	Model Bed	Surface	—
Ref. 34:250	Figurine (Bird Head)	6-R.30 (Top)	—
Ref. 34:251	Figurine (Human Male)	2-S.30 (Top)	—
Ref. 34:252	Figurine (Animal)	Kitîtum Court (Smaller?)	—
Ref. 34:253	Figurine (Animal)	Surface	—

Catalogue of Ishchali 1934 Reference Numbers (*cont.*)

Ish. No.	*Object*	*Locus*	*Plate/Figure*
Ref. 34:254	Plaque	Surface	—
Ref. 34:255	Plaque	Dump	—
Ref. 34:256	Alabaster Fragment	Kitîtum Court (Smaller?)	—
Ref. 34:257	Alabaster Vase Fragment	4-Q.30	—
Ref. 34:258	Plaque	Dump	—
Ref. 34:259	Metal Sickle Blade	1-Q.30 (Top)	—
Ref. 34:260	Figurine (Human Female)	Surface	—
Ref. 34:261	Bone Pin	City Gate (Top)	—
Ref. 34:262	(see app. 1, Ish. 34:92)	City Gate (Top)	33n (OIC 20, fig. 70a)
Ref. 34:263	Cylinder Seal	4-Q.30 (Top of wall)	—
Ref. 34:264	Cylinder Seal	4-Q.30 (Top of wall)	—
Ref. 34:265	Cylinder Seal	4-Q.30 (Top)	—
Ref. 34:266	Shells	1-Q.30 (Top)	—
Ref. 34:267	Zoomorphic Head Spout	2-Q.31	—
Ref. 34:268	Cylinder Seal	4-Q.30 (Libn bench)	—
Ref. 34:269	Figurine (Animal)	1-T.31 (Top)	—
Ref. 34:270	Plaque	Surface	—
Ref. 34:271	Plaque	Temple dump	—
Ref. 34:272	Plaque	Dump	—
Ref. 34:273	Bead	5-P.30 (Top)	—
Ref. 34:274	Plaque	4-V.30 (Top)	—
Ref. 34:275	Bead	1-R.31	—
Ref. 34:276	Metal Nails	3-R.31	—
Ref. 34:277	Figurine Fragment	3-R.31	35d (OIC 20, fig. 72c)
Ref. 34:278	Seal Impression	Dump	—
Ref. 34:279	Plaque	Surface	—
Ref. 34:280	Figurine (Human Female)	Dump	—
Ref. 34:281	Plaque	Surface	—
Ref. 34:282	Figurine (Human Head)	Surface	—
Ref. 34:283	Figurine Fragment	Surface	—
Ref. 34:284	Bone Disc	Dump	—
Ref. 34:285	Alabaster Sphere	Dump	—
Ref. 34:286	Plaque	5-P.30	—
Ref. 34:287	Cylinder Seal	4-Q.30	—
Ref. 34:288	Figurine (Animal)	2-T.31 (Top)	—
Ref. 34:289	Zoomorphic Spout	Dump	—
Ref. 34:290	Figurine (Horse? Head)	Surface	—
Ref. 34:291	Plaque	Dump	—
Ref. 34:292	Alabaster Fragment (=316)	6-R.30	—
Ref. 34:293	Metal Nail	2-P.30	—
Ref. 34:294	(see app. 1, Ish. 34:88)	Dump	37c
Ref. 34:295	Model Wheel	3-P.32 (Top)	—

Catalogue of Ishchali 1934 Reference Numbers (*cont.*)

Ish. No.	Object	Locus	Plate/Figure
Ref. 34:296	Bone Pin	2-R.32 (Top)	—
Ref. 34:297	Model Chariot	3-P.32 (Top)	—
Ref. 34:298	Plaque	Surface	—
Ref. 34:299	Bone (Stag's Horn)	1-P.30	—
Ref. 34:300	Bone (Stag's Horn)	6-Q.30	—
Ref. 34:301	Knuckle Bones	6-Q.30 (Robber dump)	—
Ref. 34:302	Model Chariot	City Gate	—
Ref. 34:303	(see app. 1, Ish. 34:103 and 110)	City Gate (Top)	34c (OIC 20, fig. 71)
Ref. 34:304	Model Wheel	6-R.30 (Top)	—
Ref. 34:305	Rattle (Ram-Shaped)	Surface	—
Ref. 34:306	Shell Cap	City Gate	—
Ref. 34:307	Model Chariot	Dump	—
Ref. 34:308	Figurine Fragment	2-R.31	—
Ref. 34:309	Plaque	Surface	—
Ref. 34:310	Model Boat	Surface	—
Ref. 34:311	Plaque	Surface	—
Ref. 34:312	Figurine Fragment	City Gate	—
Ref. 34:313	(see app. 1, Ish. 35:5)	1-R.32 (Top of wall)	OIP 72, pl. 87:926
Ref. 34:314	Bone Pin	City Gate (Top)	—
Ref. 34:315	Bone Pin	City Gate (Top)	—
Ref. 34:316	Alabaster Fragment (=292)	2-T.30 (Top)	—
Ref. 34:317	Figurine (Human Female)	Dump	—
Ref. 34:318	Model Boat	Surface	—
Ref. 34:319	Figurine (Hollow, Human)	Dump	—
Ref. 34:320	Plaque	Surface	—
Ref. 34:321	Plaque	Surface	—
Ref. 34:322	Plaque	Surface	—
Ref. 34:323	Figurine (Animal)	2-P.30	—
Ref. 34:324	Plaque	Surface	—
Ref. 34:325	Bone Pin	City Gate (Outside)	—
Ref. 34:326	Bone Tool	1-V.32 (Top)	—
Ref. 34:327	Figurine (Horse and Rider)	Surface	—
Ref. 34:328	Plaque	2-P.29	—
Ref. 34:329	Bead	4-Q.30 (E bench)	—
Ref. 34:330	Plaque	Dump	—
Ref. 34:331	Shell Beads and Rings	4-Q.30 (E bench)	—
Ref. 34:332	Plaque (Head)	Dump	—
Ref. 34:333	(see app. 1, Ish. 35:205)	Surface	—
Ref. 34:334	Plaque	Surface	—
Ref. 34:335	Agate Lump	—	—
Ref. 34:336	Plaque (Head)	Surface	—
Ref. 34:337	Alabaster Vase	—	—

Catalogue of Ishchali 1934 Reference Numbers (*cont.*)

Ish. No.	Object	Locus	Plate/Figure
Ref. 34:338	Alabaster Vase Fragment	—	—
Ref. 34:339	Plaque (Head)	Surface	—
Ref. 34:340	Model Bed	Surface	—
Ref. 34:341	Stone Relief	4-R.30	—
Ref. 34:342	Plaque	Dump	—
Ref. 34:343	Figurine (Human)	Dump	—
Ref. 34:344	Plaque	Surface	—
Ref. 34:345	Model Bed	Surface	—
Ref. 34:346	Plaque	1-P.30	—
Ref. 34:347	Plaque	Street (Kitîtum Temple)	—
Ref. 34:348	Plaque (Rider Type)	Dump	—
Ref. 34:349	Figurine (Human)	Dump	—
Ref. 34:350	Figurine (Human)	Street (P.32)	—
Ref. 34:351	Plaque	3-T.32	—
Ref. 34:352	Figurine (Human)	5-Q.30	—
Ref. 34:353	Metal Fragment	1-T.31 (W pivotstone box)	—
Ref. 34:354a	Bead	6-Q.30	—
Ref. 34:354b	Plaque	Dump	—
Ref. 34:355	Stone Disc with Inlay	Dump	—
Ref. 34:356	Model Chariot	3-Q.33 (Top)	—
Ref. 34:357	Bead	Street (S of 1-S.32)	—
Ref. 34:358	Bone Pin Fragments	City Gate (Top)	—
Ref. 34:359	Bone Pin Fragments	City Gate (Top)	—
Ref. 34:360	Rubbing Stone(?)	Surface	—
Ref. 34:361	Plaque	Room opposite Kitîtum Gate	—
Ref. 34:362	Figurine (Human Female)	Dump	—
Ref. 34:363	Figurine (Animal)	2-P.31	—
Ref. 34:364	Figurine (Human)	Kitîtum Court (Smaller?)	—
Ref. 34:365	Plaque	Surface	—
Ref. 34:366	Figurine (Male Head)	4-P.30	—
Ref. 34:367	Plaque	Surface	—
Ref. 34:368	Plaque	City Gate	—
Ref. 34:369	(see app. 1, Ish. 35:206)	City Gate (Top)	34m
Ref. 34:370	(no. not used)		
Ref. 34:371	(see app. 1, Ish. 35:6)	Street (Outside 1-T.31)	—
Ref. 34:372	Weight	4-T.29 (E door)	—
Ref. 34:373	(see app. 1, Ish. 35:207)	1-R.31 (Top)	41b
Ref. 34:374	Plaque	Dump	—
Ref. 34:375	Figurine (Animal?)	2-P.31	—
Ref. 34:376	Stone Cup	[Abu Obeid]	—
Ref. 34:377	Plaque	Surface	—
Ref. 34:378	(see app. 1, Ish. 35:208)	Dump	33i

Catalogue of Ishchali 1934 Reference Numbers (*cont.*)

Ish. No.	*Object*	*Locus*	*Plate/Figure*
Ref. 34:379	(see app. 1, Ish. 35:209)	Surface	—
Ref. 34:380	(see app. 1, Ish. 35:210)	Surface	34e
Ref. 34:381	(see app. 1, Ish. 35:7)	Dump	44c
Ref. 34:382	(see app. 1, Ish. 35:211)	Surface (NE corner of *Kîsu*)	35h

APPENDIX 3

CATALOGUE OF ISHCHALI 1935 REFERENCE NUMBERS

Ish. No.	Object	Locus	Plate
Ref. 35:1	Figurine (Human with Tambourine?)	Surface	—
Ref. 35:2	(see app. 1, 35:88)	Surface	36b
Ref. 35:3	Figurine (Human Male)	1-Q.29 (Niche)	—
Ref. 35:4	Model Bed	Surface	—
Ref. 35:5	Figurine (Animal)	1-Q.29	—
Ref. 35:6	Marble Head (Female)	[Abu Hamam]	—
Ref. 35:7	Plaque	1-R.29	—
Ref. 35:8	Bone Needle	1-R.29	—
Ref. 35:9	Plaque	Surface	—
Ref. 35:10	(see app. 1, 35:212)	2-W.31 (Top)	34l
Ref. 35:11	Model Boat	2-W.31 (Top)	—
Ref. 35:12	Plaque	[Abu Trachia]	—
Ref. 35:13	Clay Implement	6-Q.30	—
Ref. 35:14	(see app. 1, 35:213)	8-Q.30	36f
Ref. 35:15	(see app. 1, 35:214)	1-R.29	36e
Ref. 35:16	Plaque	Surface	—
Ref. 35:17	Metal Pin	2-Q.29	—
Ref. 35:18	(see app. 1, 35:215)	1-R.29	35q
Ref. 35:19	(see app. 1, 35:216)	1-W.31 (Top)	34g
Ref. 35:20	Clay Rattle Fragment	1-R.29	—
Ref. 35:21	Clay Vessel	1-R.29	—
Ref. 35:22	Plaque	Dump	—
Ref. 35:23	Figurine (Human)	1-R.29	—
Ref. 35:24	Clay Object(?)	2-V.31 (Top)	—
Ref. 35:25	Figurine (Human)	1-R.29	—
Ref. 35:26	Clay Jar	1-R.29	—
Ref. 35:27	Plaque	2-Q.29	—
Ref. 35:28	Weight	Surface	—
Ref. 35:29	Pendant	Dump	—
Ref. 35:30	Plaque	City Gate	—
Ref. 35:31	Figurine (Human)	1-R.29	—
Ref. 35:32	(see app. 1, 35:86)	2-S.30	—
Ref. 35:33	Bone Pin	1-R.29	—
Ref. 35:34	Bone Pin	1-R.29	—

Catalogue of Ishchali 1935 Reference Numbers (*cont.*)

Ish. No.	Object	Locus	Plate
Ref. 35:35	Plaque	6-Q.30	—
Ref. 35:36	Model Chariot	6-R.30	—
Ref. 35:37	Plaque	6-R.30	—
Ref. 35:38	(see app. 1, 35:87)	5.V.31	35e
Ref. 35:39	(see app. 1, 35:217)	3-S.30 (Top)	—
Ref. 35:40	Figurine (Animal)	1-R.29	—
Ref. 35:41	Figurine (Human)	6-R.30	—
Ref. 35:42	Bone Pin	6-Q.30	—
Ref. 35:43	Model Chariot	6-S.29	—
Ref. 35:44	Plaque	Surface	—
Ref. 35:45	Plaque	5-R.30	—
Ref. 35:46	Metal Pin	6-V.31 (Top)	—
Ref. 35:47	Bead	Kitîtum Small Temple	—
Ref. 35:48	Figurine (Animal)	Surface	—
Ref. 35:49	Model Boat	6-T.29 (Outside)	—
Ref. 35:50	Figurine (Human)	6-T.29 (Outside)	—
Ref. 35:51	Model Bed	Street (Kitîtum SW corner)	—
Ref. 35:52	Figurine (Male?)	Dump	—
Ref. 35:53	(see app. 1, 35:218)	Dump	38i
Ref. 35:54	Model Bed	6-T.29 (Outside)	—
Ref. 35:55	Figurine (Male)	6-V.31 (Top)	—
Ref. 35:56	Plaque	Street (Kitîtum SW corner)	—
Ref. 35:57	Plaque	6-T.29 (Outside)	—
Ref. 35:58	Figurine (Human)	Street (V.31)	—
Ref. 35:59	Plaque	Street (V.31)	—
Ref. 35:60	Metal Nail	3-V.30 (Top)	—
Ref. 35:61	Votive Model Leg	3-V.30 (Top)	—
Ref. 35:62	Clay Object(?)	Street (SW Kitîtum)	—
Ref. 35:63	Plaque	2-S.29	—
Ref. 35:64	Plaque	1-S.30 (Outside)	—
Ref. 35:65	Figurine (Human)	6-Q.30 (Floor below Kitîtum)	—
Ref. 35:66	Figurine (Human)	Street (Outside 6-T.29)	—
Ref. 35:67	Plaque	7-V.31 (Top)	—
Ref. 35:68	Metal Pin	Street (Outside 7-T.29)	—
Ref. 35:69	Metal Nail	2-S.29	—
Ref. 35:70	Metal Nail	3-V.30 (Top)	—
Ref. 35:71	Metal Pin	3-V.30 (Top)	—
Ref. 35:72	Metal Object(?)	2-S.29	—
Ref. 35:73	Bead	2-S.29	—
Ref. 35:74	Plaque	3-S.30	—
Ref. 35:75	Figurine (Human Head)	Surface	—
Ref. 35:76	Plaque	Surface	—
Ref. 35:77	Bone Pin	2-S.29	—

Catalogue of Ishchali 1935 Reference Numbers (*cont.*)

Ish. No.	Object	Locus	Plate
Ref. 35:78	Model Axe	City Wall	—
Ref. 35:79	Plaque	Dump	—
Ref. 35:80	Plaque	Street (NW corner of Kitîtum)	—
Ref. 35:81	Figurine (Human Head)	Street (NW corner of Kitîtum)	—
Ref. 35:82	Figurine (Human Head)	Street (NE corner of Kitîtum)	—
Ref. 35:83	Pot Sherd	6-Q.30	—
Ref. 35:84	Marble Vessel Fragment	3-S.30	—
Ref. 35:85	Plaque	3-S.30	—
Ref. 35:86	Metal Ring	2-S.30	—
Ref. 35:87	Bone Object(?)	2-S.30	—
Ref. 35:88	Bead	2-T.29	—
Ref. 35:89	Bead	3-S.30	—
Ref. 35:90	Bead	6-Q.30	—
Ref. 35:91	Metal Fragment	Street (S.32)	—
Ref. 35:92	Bead	3-S.30	—
Ref. 35:93	Bead	Kitîtum Court	—
Ref. 35:94	(see app. 1, 35:89)	Dump	34p
Ref. 35:95	Clay Rattle	Dump (Shamash Temple)	—
Ref. 35:96	Figurine (Human)	9-V.31 (Top)	—
Ref. 35:97	Figurine (Human Female)	5-V.30 (Top)	—
Ref. 35:98	Plaque (Human Female)	Surface	—
Ref. 35:99	Figurine (Human Female)	South end of Tell	—
Ref. 35:100	Clay Rattle	Street (E of Shamash Temple)	—
Ref. 35:101	Bone Ring	9-V.31 (Top)	—
Ref. 35:102	Figurine (Human)	Street (N of 7-S.29)	—
Ref. 35:103	Metal Tool	5-V.30	—
Ref. 35:104	(see app. 1, 35:91)	9-V.31 (Top)	34d
Ref. 35:105	Metal Ring	Street (City Gate)	—
Ref. 35:106	Plaque	Street (City Gate)	—
Ref. 35:107	Plaque	Surface	—
Ref. 35:108	Figurine (Human)	City Wall (SW end)	—
Ref. 35:109	Figurine (Human Female)	Kitîtum Court	—
Ref. 35:110	Plaque	2-V.31 (Top)	—
Ref. 35:111	(see app. 1, 35:219)	2-T.29	38e
Ref. 35:112	Plaque	5-V.30 (Top)	—
Ref. 35:113	(see app. 1, 35:92)	2-T.29	—
Ref. 35:114	Metal Ring	5-V.32 (Top)	—
Ref. 35:115	(see app. 1, 35:220)	Dump	34i
Ref. 35:116	Plaque	4-V.32 (Top)	—
Ref. 35:117	Plaque	2-V.32	—
Ref. 35:118	Plaque	4-V.32	—
Ref. 35:119	Plaque	5-V.32 (Top)	—
Ref. 35:120	Metal Ring	5-V.32 (Top)	—

Catalogue of Ishchali 1935 Reference Numbers (*cont.*)

Ish. No.	Object	Locus	Plate
Ref. 35:121	Metal Tweezers	6-V.32 (Top)	—
Ref. 35:122	Clay Rattle	4-V.32 (Top)	—
Ref. 35:123	Figurine(?)	2-T.29	—
Ref. 35:124	Metal Lump	2-T.29	—
Ref. 35:125	Plaque	7-V.32	—
Ref. 35:126	Plaque Fragment	Kitîtum Court	—
Ref. 35:127	Metal Bundle	Kitîtum Court	—
Ref. 35:128	Figurine (Human)	3-V.30	—
Ref. 35:129	Clay Saucer Fragment	1-R.29	—
Ref. 35:130	Plaque	City Wall	—
Ref. 35:131	Plaque	Well (Kitîtum Court)	—
Ref. 35:132	(see app. 1, 35:221)	1-T.31	36c
Ref. 35:133	(joins Ref. 35:131)	Kitîtum Court	—
Ref. 35:134	Plaque	5-R.29	—
Ref. 35:135	Metal Bowl	15-V.32 (Top)	—
Ref. 35:136	Model Boat	1-R.29	—
Ref. 35:137	Plaque	1-R.29	—
Ref. 35:138	Figurine (Animal)	Building north of Shamash Temple	—
Ref. 35:139	Plaque	3-R.32	—
Ref. 35:140	Plaque	2-R.29	—
Ref. 35:141	Plaque(?) Fragment	2-T.29	—
Ref. 35:142	Plaque (Head)	2-T.30	—
Ref. 35:143	Weight (Square)	South Kitîtum Wall (Outside)	—
Ref. 35:144	Plaque	1-T.32 (E of)	—
Ref. 35:145	Plaque	2-V.29 (Top)	—
Ref. 35:146	Figurine (Seated)	4-S.29	—
Ref. 35:147	Figurine (Human Head)	1-T.32	—
Ref. 35:148	Plaque	Dump	—
Ref. 35:149	Plaque (Head)	2-S.30	—
Ref. 35:150	Model Chariot	2-S.30	—
Ref. 35:151	Metal Arrowhead	2-V.29	—
Ref. 35:152	Bone Pin	3-V.31	—
Ref. 35:153	Figurine (Horseman)	2-S.30	—
Ref. 35:154	Plaque	2-S.30	—
Ref. 35:155	(see app. 1, 35:222)	2-S.30	—
Ref. 35:156	Bead	2-T.32	—
Ref. 35:157	Plaque	Dump	—
Ref. 35:158	Clay Bowl Fragment	2-R.30	—
Ref. 35:159	Bone Needle	2-R.30	—
Ref. 35:160	Plaque	2-V.31 (Top)	—
Ref. 35:161	Figurine (Human Head)	3-V.31 (Top)	—
Ref. 35:162	Plaque Fragment	Kitîtum (Central Court)	—
Ref. 35:163	Plaque Fragment	Surface	—

Catalogue of Ishchali 1935 Reference Numbers (*cont.*)

Ish. No.	Object	Locus	Plate
Ref. 35:164	Plaque Fragment	1-S.29	—
Ref. 35:165	Clay Lamp	2-R.30	—
Ref. 35:166	Figurine (Human Female)	7-S.29	—
Ref. 35:167	Figurine (Animal)	2-V.31	—
Ref. 35:168	(see app. 1, 35:90)	Surface	38j
Ref. 35:169	Figurine (Human Head)	4-R.32	—
Ref. 35:170	Figurine (Human Female)	*Kîsu* (Opposite 3-Q.29)	—
Ref. 35:171	(see app. 1, 35:93)	2-T.29	36g
Ref. 35:172	Plaque	Surface	—
Ref. 35:173	Model Bed	4-V.31	—
Ref. 35:174	Plaque Fragment	Shamash Temple (Top)	—
Ref. 35:175	Spindle Whorl	5-V.31	—
Ref. 35:176	(see app. 1, 35:223)	Surface	34j
Ref. 35:177	Plaque	Ziqqurat	—

APPENDIX 4

CATALOGUE OF ISHCHALI OBJECTS BY PERIOD*

Plate	Object	Ish. / Ref. No.	Locus	Material	Remarks	Museum

KITÎTUM PERIOD I-A

Plate	Object	Ish. / Ref. No.	Locus	Material	Remarks	Museum
34b	Plaque	Ish. 34:40	2-R.29	terracotta	god fragment	OI: A16972
—	Plaque	Ish. 35:92	2-T.29	terracotta	god fragment	Baghdad
36g	Plaque	Ish. 35:93	2-T.29	terracotta	fragment	Baghdad
—	Figurine(?)	Ref. 35:123	2-T.29	terracotta	animal fragment	—
—	Metal	Ref. 35:124	2-T.29	bronze/ copper	lump fragment	—
—	Bowl	Ish. 35:76	5-T.30	stone	—	Baghdad

KITÎTUM PERIOD I-B

Plate	Object	Ish. / Ref. No.	Locus	Material	Remarks	Museum
36f	Figurine	Ish. 35:213	8-Q.30	terracotta	male fragment	Baghdad
36e	Plaque	Ish. 35:214	1-R.29	terracotta	female fragment	OI: A21201
35q	Plaque	Ish. 35:215	1-R.29	terracotta	fragment	Baghdad
—	Cylinder Seal	Ish. 35:78	9-R.29	terracotta	see OIP 72, p. 60	OI: A17675
43c	Bead	Ish. 35:51	2-S.29	gold	discoid-shaped	OI: A17669
—	Cylinder Seal	Ish. 35:71	2-S.30	hematite	—	OI: A17673
35f	Plaque	Ish. 35:86	2-S.30	terracotta	lion and man fragment	Baghdad
34f	Plaque	Ish. 35:222	2-S.30	terracotta	female fragment	OI: A21205
—	Figurine	Ref. 35:153	2-S.30	terracotta	horseman	—

KITÎTUM PERIOD I-II

Plate	Object	Ish. / Ref. No.	Locus	Material	Remarks	Museum
—	Pin	Ish. 35:23	1-P.29	bone	12 × 0.90 cm	—
—	Plaque	Ref. 34:346	1-P.30	terracotta	fragment	—
—	Figurine	Ref. 34:366	4-P.30	terracotta	male head	—
—	Cylinder Seal	Ish. 34:68	1-P.31	stone	—	Baghdad

* Two object registers were kept, one for objects to be divided with Baghdad, and one for duplicates and fragments that seemed too trivial to divide. They were turned over to Baghdad without division. This latter register was designated as "Reference Collection." "Ish." refers to objects recorded in the large Object Registers in the 1934 and 1935 seasons. "Ref." refers to objects only recorded in the smaller Reference Collection Register for the same seasons.

Catalogue of Ishchali Objects by Period (*cont.*)

Plate	Object	Ish. / Ref. No.	Locus	Material	Remarks	Museum

KITÎTUM PERIOD I-II (*cont.*)

Plate	Object	Ish. / Ref. No.	Locus	Material	Remarks	Museum
—	Figurine	Ref. 35:3	1-Q.29	terracotta	male fragment (in niche)	—
—	Figurine	Ref. 35:5	1-Q.29	terracotta	animal fragment	—
—	Pin	Ref. 35:17	2-Q.29	bronze/copper	—	—
—	Bowl	Ish. 34:30	4-Q.30	marble	carved and inlaid fragments, 5.60 × 10.10 cm, thickness of wall 0.80 cm	—
42e	Stamp Seal	Ish. 34:133	4-Q.30	limestone	—	Baghdad
42d	Stamp Seal	Ish. 34:134	4-Q.30	limestone	—	OI: A17007
42g	Stamp Seal	Ish. 34:136	4-Q.30	crystal	—	Baghdad
42b	Stamp Seal	Ish. 34:137	4-Q.30	stone	—	OI: A17008
42f	Stamp Seal	Ish. 34:135	6-Q.30	marble	—	Baghdad
—	Jar Stopper	Ref. 34:138	6-Q.30	alabaster	—	—
—	Cylinder Seal	Ref. 34:139	6-Q.30	(?)	worn	—
—	Bead	Ref. 34:354a	6-Q.30	faience	globular-shaped	—
—	Clay Implement	Ref. 35:13	6-Q.30	clay	—	—
—	Plaque	Ref. 35:35	6-Q.30	terracotta	female fragment	—
—	Pin	Ref. 35:42	6-Q.30	bone	—	—
—	Jar Sherd	Ref. 35:83	6-Q.30	terracotta	painted birds(?)	—
—	Bead	Ref. 35:90	6-Q.30	stone	ovoid-shaped	—
—	Cylinder Seal	Ish. 35:24	1-R.29	terracotta	—	—
—	Rattle	Ref. 35:20	1-R.29	terracotta	fragment	—
—	Vessel	Ref. 35:21	1-R.29	terracotta	—	—
—	Figurine	Ref. 35:23	1-R.29	terracotta	male fragment	—
—	Figurine	Ref. 35:25	1-R.29	terracotta	male fragment	—
—	Jar	Ref. 35:26	1-R.29	terracotta	—	—
—	Figurine	Ref. 35:31	1-R.29	terracotta	female fragment	—
—	Pin	Ref. 35:33	1-R.29	bone	—	—
—	Pin	Ref. 35:34	1-R.29	bone	—	—
—	Figurine	Ref. 35:40	1-R.29	terracotta	animal fragment	—
—	Plaque	Ref. 35:140	2-R.29	terracotta	fragment	—
—	Plaque	Ref. 35:134	5-R.29	terracotta	fragment	—
—	Bowl	Ref. 35:158	2-R.30	terracotta	incised fragment	—
—	Needle	Ref. 35:159	2-R.30	bone	—	—
—	Lamp	Ref. 35:165	2-R.30	terracotta	—	—
—	Plaque	Ref. 35:45	5-R.30	terracotta	god fragment	—
—	Model Chariot	Ref. 35:36	6-R.30	terracotta	fragment	—
—	Plaque	Ref. 35:37	6-R.30	terracotta	female fragment	—
—	Figurine	Ref. 35:41	6-R.30	terracotta	female with child, fragment	—
37b	Model Bed	Ish. 34:89	1-R.32	terracotta	with female figure, fragment	Baghdad

Catalogue of Ishchali Objects by Period (*cont.*)

Plate	Object	Ish. / Ref. No.	Locus	Material	Remarks	Museum

KITÎTUM PERIOD I-II (*cont.*)

Plate	Object	Ish. / Ref. No.	Locus	Material	Remarks	Museum
—	Plaque	Ref. 35:164	1-S.29	terracotta	female fragment	—
—	Figurine	Ref. 35:146	4-S.29	terracotta	female seated fragment	—
—	Model Chariot	Ref. 35:43	6-S.29	terracotta	fragment	—
—	Figurine	Ref. 35:166	7-S.29	terracotta	female fragment	—
—	Plaque	Ref. 35:64	1-S.30 (outside)	terracotta	male fragment	—
—	Weight	Ref. 34:372	4-T.29	hematite	date-shaped (from east door)	—
—	Plaque	Ref. 35:142	2-T.30	terracotta	god fragment	—

KITÎTUM PERIOD II-A

Plate	Object	Ish. / Ref. No.	Locus	Material	Remarks	Museum
40e, f	Statuette	Ish. 35:48	2-S.29	alabaster	seated monkey	Baghdad
—	Pin	Ref. 35:77	2-S.29	bone	—	—
—	Cylinder Seal	Ish. 34:129	3-T.30	hematite	—	—
—	Cylinder Seal	Ish. 35:70	4-T.30	stone	—	—
36c	Plaque	Ish. 35:221	1-T.31	terracotta	male fragment	OI: A21204

KITÎTUM PERIOD II-B

Plate	Object	Ish. / Ref. No.	Locus	Material	Remarks	Museum
—	Shells	Ref. 34:119	1-P.29	shell	—	—
—	Cylinder Seal	Ish. 35:26	2-Q.29	stone	—	OI: A17659
—	Plaque	Ref. 35:27	2-Q.29	terracotta	musician fragment	—
35l	Plaque	Ish. 35:8	1-R.29	terracotta	man on bovine	Baghdad
—	Plaque	Ref. 35:7	1-R.29	terracotta	female fragment	—
—	Needle	Ref. 35:8	1-R.29	bone	—	—
—	Model Boat	Ref. 35:136	1-R.29	terracotta	fragment	—
—	Plaque	Ref. 35:137	1-R.29	terracotta	fragment	—
—	Plaque	Ref. 35:63	2-S.29	terracotta	lion fragment	—
—	Nail	Ref. 35:69	2-S.29	bronze/copper	—	—
—	Metal Object	Ref. 35:72	2-S.29	bronze/copper	—	—
—	Bead	Ref. 35:73	2-S.29	(?)	cylinder	—
38e	Plaque	Ish. 35:219	2-T.29	terracotta	bull-man fragment	OI: A21202
—	Bead	Ref. 35:88	2-T.29	shell	rectangular	—
—	Metal Fragments	Ref. 34:353	1-T.31	bronze/copper	in west pivotstone box	—
—	Cylinder Seal	Ish. 35:73	3-T.32	shell	—	—

Catalogue of Ishchali Objects by Period (*cont.*)

Plate	Object	Ish. / Ref. No.	Locus	Material	Remarks	Museum

KITÎTUM PERIOD III

Plate	Object	Ish. / Ref. No.	Locus	Material	Remarks	Museum
—	Cylinder Seal	Ish. 34:69	5-Q.30	stone	east pivotstone box	Baghdad
—	Bead	Ish. 34:70	5-Q.30	shell	date-shaped (east pivotstone box)	—
—	Beads	Ish. 34:71	5-Q.30	stone+ bronze/ copper	17 carnelian + 3 stone + bronze/copper clasp(?) (from east pivotstone box)	—
—	Cylinder Seal	Ish. 34:72	5-Q.30	crystal	fragment (from east pivotstone box)	—
42c	Stamp Seal	Ish. 34:73	5-Q.30	stone	beside east pivotstone box	OI: A16982
35n	Plaque	Ish. 34:106	2-R.29	terracotta	human fragment	—
—	Nail Heads	Ref. 34:88	2-R.29	bronze/ copper	2 exx.	—
—	Figurine	Ref. 34:96	2-R.29	terracotta	female fragment	—
—	Weight	Ref. 34:101	2-R.29	stone	date-shaped	—
—	Model Bed	Ref. 34:102	2-R.29	terracotta	fragment	—
39c	Relief	Ish. 34:79	2-R.30	terracotta	painted musician fragment	Baghdad
34a	Plaque	Ish. 34:124	5-R.30	terracotta	god fragment	Baghdad
—	Cylinder Seal	Ish. 34:127	5-R.30	stone	—	Baghdad
40a-c	Statuette Head	Ish. 34:139	2-R.31	granite	painted	OI: A17009
—	Figurine	Ref. 34:308	2-R.31	terracotta	male(?) fragment	—
—	Figurine	Ref. 35:169	4-R.32	terracotta	male head	—
—	Cylinder Seal	Ish. 35:42	3-S.30	stone	—	OI: A17666
—	Vessel	Ref. 35:84	3-S.30	marble	fragment	—
—	Plaque	Ref. 35:85	3-S.30	terracotta	human fragment	—
—	Bead	Ref. 35:89	3-S.30	stone	ovoid-shaped	—
—	Bead	Ref. 35:92	3-S.30	(?)	bugle-shaped	—
—	Pin	Ish. 35:55	2-T.30	lead(?)	6.40 x 0.40 cm	Baghdad
—	Cylinder Seal	Ish. 35:72	5-T.30	lapis lazuli	—	Baghdad
—	Plaque	Ref. 34:351	3-T.32	terracotta	god fragment (top of west pivotstone box)	—

KITÎTUM PERIOD III-IV

Plate	Object	Ish. / Ref. No.	Locus	Material	Remarks	Museum
—	Cylinder Seal	Ish. 34:34	1-P.29	shell	—	OI: A16970
—	Cylinder Seal	Ish. 34:35	1-P.29	shell	see OIP 72, p. 60	—
—	Cylinder Seal	Ish. 34:36	1-P.29	shell	—	OI: A16971
—	Plaque	Ref. 34:328	2-P.29	terracotta	female fragment	—
—	Cylinder Seal	Ish. 34:53	1-P.30	shell	—	—
—	Cylinder Seal	Ish. 34:54	1-P.30	shell	—	—
—	Bead	Ish. 34:131	1-P.30	stone	conical spacer	OI: A17006
—	Bead	Ish. 34:132	1-P.30	stone	conical spacer fragment	Baghdad
—	Cylinder Seals	Ref. 34:103	1-P.30	shell	2 exx. (unfinished)	—

Catalogue of Ishchali Objects by Period (*cont.*)

Plate	Object	Ish. / Ref. No.	Locus	Material	Remarks	Museum

KITÎTUM PERIOD III-IV (*cont.*)

Plate	Object	Ish. / Ref. No.	Locus	Material	Remarks	Museum
—	Beads + Shells	Ref. 34:113	1-P.30	(?) + shell	—	—
—	Model Chariot	Ref. 34:136	1-P.30	terracotta	—	—
—	Stag horn	Ref. 34:299	1-P.30	bone	—	—
30a, b	Lamp	Ish. 34:51	2-P.30	bronze/copper	animal-shaped	Baghdad
30c, d	Lamp	Ish. 34:52	2-P.30	bronze/copper	animal-shaped head fragment	OI: A16977
—	Bowl	Ref. 34:137	2-P.30	alabaster	fragment	—
—	Plaque	Ref. 34:166	2-P.30	terracotta	fragment	—
—	Nail	Ref. 34:293	2-P.30	bronze/copper	—	—
—	Figurine	Ref. 34:323	2-P.30	terracotta	animal (gazelle) head	—
—	Bead	Ref. 34:273	5-P.30	agate	ovoid-shaped	—
33m	Plaque	Ref. 34:286	5-P.30	terracotta	male fragment	—
—	Cylinder Seal	Ish. 34:128	1-P.31	limestone	—	OI: A17003
—	Relief	Ref. 34:228	1-P.31	stone	fragment	—
—	Relief	Ref. 34:229	1-P.31	stone	fragment	—
—	Jar	Ref. 34:140	3-P.31	terracotta	bag-shaped body, cylindrical neck	—
—	Plaque	Ref. 34:169	2-P.32	terracotta	lion fragment	—
—	Figurine	Ref. 34:170	2-P.32	terracotta	animal fragment	—
—	Figurine	Ref. 34:83	1-Q.29	terracotta	male fragment	—
—	Figurine	Ref. 34:85	1-Q.29	terracotta	bird fragment	—
—	Model Wheel	Ref. 34:89	2-Q.29	terracotta	—	—
—	Model Chariot	Ref. 34:74	3-Q.29	terracotta	fragment	—
—	Pendant(?)	Ref. 34:70	5-Q.29	shell	pierced	—
—	Sickle Blade	Ref. 34:259	1-Q.30	bronze/copper	—	—
—	Cylinder Seal	Ref. 34:265	1-Q.30	terracotta	—	—
—	Plaque	Ref. 34:68	3-Q.30	terracotta	fragment	—
—	Ostrich Egg	Ish. 34:31	4-Q.30	shell	fragments	—
40g, h	Bowl	Ish. 34:32	4-Q.30	alabaster	base	OI: A21190
43b	Beads	Ish. 34:33	4-Q.30	agate, crystal carnelian, shell	43 exx.	OI: A16969
—	Cylinder Seal	Ish. 34:37	4-Q.30	shell	—	—
—	Cylinder Seal	Ish. 34:38	4-Q.30	shell	—	—
—	Cylinder Seal	Ish. 34:39	4-Q.30	shell	—	Baghdad
—	Cylinder Seal	Ish. 34:48	4-Q.30	shell	—	Baghdad
—	Cylinder Seal	Ish. 34:49	4-Q.30	limestone	—	Baghdad
—	Cylinder Seal	Ish. 34:50	4-Q.30	shell	see OIP 72, p. 61	OI: A16976

Catalogue of Ishchali Objects by Period (*cont.*)

Plate	Object	Ish. / Ref. No.	Locus	Material	Remarks	Museum

KITÎTUM PERIOD III–IV (*cont.*)

Plate	Object	Ish. / Ref. No.	Locus	Material	Remarks	Museum
—	Cylinder Seal	Ish. 34:86	4-Q.30	shell	—	Baghdad
—	Cylinder Seal	Ish. 34:87	4-Q.30	stone	—	OI: A16986
31, 32	Bowl	Ish. 34:117	4-Q.30	stone	fragment with carved mouflon, 13 × 19.20 cm	Baghdad
41e	Amulet	Ish. 34:130	4-Q.30	limestone	pig-shaped	OI: A17005
—	Ostrich Egg	Ref. 34:78	4-Q.30	shell	fragments	—
—	Unidentified	Ref. 34:79	4-Q.30	alabaster	2 fragments	—
—	Plate(?)	Ref. 34:80	4-Q.30	bronze/copper	fragments	—
—	Figurine	Ref. 34:97	4-Q.30	terracotta	female fragment	—
—	Cylinder Seal	Ref. 34:100	4-Q.30	(?)	worn	—
—	Plaque	Ref. 34:116	4-Q.30	terracotta	fragment	—
—	Shells	Ref. 34:117	4-Q.30	shell	—	—
—	Cylinder Seal	Ref. 34:118	4-Q.30	(?)	worn	—
—	Cylinder Seal	Ref. 34:263	4-Q.30	stone	from top of wall	—
—	Cylinder Seal	Ref. 34:264	4-Q.30	stone	from top of wall	—
—	Shells	Ref. 34:266	4-Q.30	shell	two pierced	—
—	Cylinder Seal	Ref. 34:268	4-Q.30	stone	from libn bench	—
—	Cylinder Seal	Ref. 34:287	4-Q.30	shell	—	—
—	Bead	Ref. 34:329	4-Q.30	stone	fragment (east bench)	—
—	Beads + Rings	Ref. 34:331	4-Q.30	shell	east bench	—
35b	Plaque	Ish. 34:41	5-Q.30	terracotta	2 male figures	Baghdad
—	Cylinder Seals	Ish. 34:46	5-Q.30	stone	—	OI: A16975
—	Cylinder Seal	Ish. 34:47	5-Q.30	stone	unfinished (see OIP 72, p. 61)	—
—	Macehead	Ish. 34:55	5-Q.30	marble	—	Baghdad
42a	Stamp Seal	Ish. 34:56	5-Q.30	stone	—	Baghdad
38a	Plaque	Ish. 34:57	5-Q.30	terracotta	lion fragments top of W pivotstone box	OI: A16978
38b	Plaque	Ish. 34:58	5-Q.30	terracotta	lion fragments top of W pivotstone box	Baghdad
—	Pincers	Ref. 34:93	5-Q.30	bronze/copper	—	—
—	Spike Head	Ref. 34:94	5-Q.30	bronze/copper	—	—
—	Vase	Ref. 34:98	5-Q.30	terracotta	—	—
—	Bead	Ref. 34:105	5-Q.30	carnelian	barrel-shaped	—
—	Inlay(?)	Ref. 34:124	5-Q.30	alabaster	fragment	—
—	Figurine	Ref. 34:352	5-Q.30	terracotta	female fragment	—
44a	Amulet (Weight?)	Ish. 34:42	6-Q.30	carnelian	lion-shaped (1,496 gm)	OI: A16974

Catalogue of Ishchali Objects by Period (*cont.*)

Plate	Object	Ish. / Ref. No.	Locus	Material	Remarks	Museum

KITÎTUM PERIOD III-IV (*cont.*)

Plate	Object	Ish. / Ref. No.	Locus	Material	Remarks	Museum
44b	Amulet (Weight?)	Ish. 34:43	6-Q.30	carnelian	lion-shaped (1,362 gm)	Baghdad
—	Cylinder Seal	Ish. 34:45	6-Q.30	amethyst	—	Baghdad
46d	Ring + Fragments	Ish. 35:21	6-Q.30	shell	—	—
—	Cylinder Seal	Ref. 34:90	6-Q.30	shell	—	—
—	Knife Blade	Ref. 34:91	6-Q.30	bronze/copper	—	—
—	Cylinder Seal	Ref. 34:106	6-Q.30	shell	—	—
—	Ostrich Egg	Ref. 34:107	6-Q.30	shell	fragments	—
—	Cylinder Seal	Ref. 34:108	6-Q.30	shell	—	—
—	Disc	Ref. 34:109	6-Q.30	bronze/copper	nail head(?)	—
—	Pin	Ref. 34:110	6-Q.30	bronze/copper	—	—
—	Bead	Ref. 34:144	6-Q.30	faience	rectangular-shaped	—
—	Bead	Ref. 34:92	2-Q.31	white stone	—	—
—	Nail	Ref. 34:104	2-Q.31	bronze/copper	—	—
—	Figurine	Ref. 34:122	2-Q.31	terracotta	male head	—
—	Loomweight(?)	Ref. 34:125	2-Q.31	stone	—	—
—	Nail	Ref. 34:133	2-Q.31	bronze/copper	—	—
—	Model Bed	Ref. 34:145	1-Q.32	terracotta	fragment	—
—	Model Bed	Ref. 34:65	1-R.29	terracotta	fragment	—
—	Shell	Ref. 34:69	1-R.29	shell	pierced	—
—	Pin	Ref. 34:71	1-R.29	bronze/copper	—	—
—	Pin	Ref. 34:131	1-R.29	bone	—	—
—	Pin	Ref. 34:132	1-R.29	bone	—	—
—	Model Bed	Ref. 34:221	1-R.29	terracotta	fragment	—
—	Plaque	Ref. 34:239	1-R.29	terracotta	fragment	—
—	Model Boat	Ref. 34:55	2-R.29	terracotta	fragment	—
—	Model Boat	Ref. 34:59	2-R.29	terracotta	fragment	—
—	Nail Heads	Ref. 34:61	2-R.29	bronze/copper	3 exx.	—
—	Pin	Ref. 34:212	7-S.29	bone	—	—
—	Pin	Ref. 34:62	1-R.30	bronze/copper	—	—
—	Figurine	Ref. 34:134	1-R.30	terracotta	human head	—
—	Model Chariot	Ref. 34:135	1-R.30	terracotta	—	—
—	Figurine	Ref. 34:206	1-R.30	terracotta	animal fragment	—
—	Beads	Ref. 34:161	4-R.30	green stone	—	—

Catalogue of Ishchali Objects by Period (*cont.*)

Plate	Object	Ish. / Ref. No.	Locus	Material	Remarks	Museum

KITÎTUM PERIOD III-IV (*cont.*)

Plate	Object	Ish. / Ref. No.	Locus	Material	Remarks	Museum
—	Plaque	Ref. 34:151	5-R.30	terracotta	female fragment	—
—	Model Bed	Ref. 34:158	6-R.30	terracotta	with female figure	—
—	Zoomorphic Pot	Ref. 34:159	6-R.30	terracotta	lion-shaped	—
—	Lamp	Ref. 34:165	6-R.30	terracotta	—	—
—	Figurine	Ref. 34:250	6-R.30	terracotta	bird head	—
—	Model Wheel	Ref. 34:304	6-R.30	terracotta	—	—
—	Nails	Ref. 34:208	1-R.31	bronze/ copper	in door to court	—
—	Figurine	Ref. 34:197	3-R.31	terracotta	animal fragment	—
—	Ostrich Egg	Ref. 34:160	1-R.32	shell	fragments (top of door socket)	—
—	Plaque	Ref. 34:176	1-S.29	terracotta	female fragment	—
—	Pin	Ref. 34:211	7-S.29	bone	—	—
—	Ring	Ref. 35:86	2-S.30	bronze/ copper	open at ends	—
—	Ring	Ref. 35:86	2-S.30	bronze/ copper	open at ends	—
—	(?)	Ref. 35:87	2-S.30	bone	piece	—
—	Plaque	Ref. 35:74	3-S.30	terracotta	fragment	—
—	Nail	Ref. 34:195	1-T.29	bronze/ copper	broken	—
—	Figurine	Ref. 34:218	6-T.29	terracotta	animal (horse?) fragment	—
—	Figurine	Ref. 34:237	6-T.29	terracotta	goddess fragment	—
—	Figurine	Ref. 34:269	1-T.31	terracotta	animal fragment	—

KITÎTUM PERIOD IV

Plate	Object	Ish. / Ref. No.	Locus	Material	Remarks	Museum
—	Cylinder Seal	Ish. 34:121	1-P.30	hematite	—	Baghdad
35o	Plaque	Ish. 34:108	1-Q.29	terracotta	—	—
—	Model Wheel	Ref. 34:127	1-Q.29	terracotta	—	—
—	Cylinder Seal	Ish. 34:26	2-Q.30	—	—	—
41a	Plaque	Ish. 34:201	4-Q.30	stone	relief fragment	OI: A21193
30e	Arrowhead	Ish. 34:203	4-R.29	copper	3.90×1.40 cm	OI: A21195
—	Cylinder Seal	Ish. 34:64	5-R.29	hematite	—	Baghdad
33f	Plaque	Ish. 34:101	6-R.29	terracotta	god fragment	Baghdad
—	Pin	Ref. 34:157	6-R.29	bone	—	—
—	Bulla	Ish. 34:65	7-R.29	unbaked clay	4 seal impressions	—
—	Pendant	Ish. 34:66	7-R.29	stone	axe-shaped	Baghdad
—	Jar Lid	Ish. 34:28	2-R.30	alabaster	fragment	—
44d	Weight	Ish. 34:29	2-R.30	carnelian	duck-shaped (519 gm)	Baghdad

Catalogue of Ishchali Objects by Period (*cont.*)

Plate	Object	Ish. / Ref. No.	Locus	Material	Remarks	Museum

KITÎTUM PERIOD IV (*cont.*)

Plate	Object	Ish. / Ref. No.	Locus	Material	Remarks	Museum
38g	Plaque	Ish. 34:60	2-R.30	terracotta	animal-shaped	OI: A16980
—	Wire Coil	Ref. 34:77	2-R.30	metal	—	—
41b	Plaque	Ish. 35:207	1-R.31	stone	relief fragment	Baghdad
—	Cylinder Seal	Ish. 34:82	4-R.32	stone	—	OI: A16984
34l	Plaque	Ish. 34:91	2-S.29	terracotta	goddess fragment	OI: A16989
—	Cylinder Seal	Ish. 34:74	4-S.29	stone	—	Baghdad
—	Figurine	Ref. 34:207	4-S.29	terracotta	human fragment	—
44m	Weight	Ish. 34:62	2-S.30	carnelian	duck-shaped (4,375 gm)	OI: A16981
—	Weights	Ish. 34:63	2-S.30	hematite	10 exx.	Baghdad
35m	Plaque	Ish. 34:107	2-S.30	terracotta	rider fragment (joins Ish. 34:90)	OI: A16995
—	Metal Strips	Ref. 34:149	2-S.30	copper	—	—
—	Inlay	Ref. 34:154	2-S.30	shell	petal-shaped	—
—	Ring	Ref. 34:156	2-S.30	bronze/copper	open at ends	—
—	Metal Strips	Ref. 34:174	2-S.30	bronze/copper	—	—
—	Figurine	Ref. 34:251	2-S.30	terracotta	male fragment	—
35g	Plaque	Ish. 34:104	3-S.30	terracotta	musician fragment	OI: A16994
34o	Plaque	Ish. 34:114	3-S.30	terracotta	god fragment	Baghdad
—	Eye	Ish. 34:217	3-S.30	stone	with shell inlay (3.50 × 5.40 cm)	Baghdad
—	Horn	Ref. 34:185	3-S.30	stone	fragment	—
—	Horn	Ref. 34:186	3-S.30	stone	fragment	—
—	Nails	Ref. 34:187	3-S.30	bronze/copper	—	—
37d	Model Bed	Ish. 35:204	5-S.30	terracotta	fragment	OI: A21196
30j	Metal Bands	Ish. 35:69	1-S.32	copper	lump with cloth impressions	—
35p	Plaque	Ish. 34:109	2-T.29	terracotta	fragment	OI: A16996
33c	Plaque	Ish. 34:99	4-T.29	terracotta	god fragment (joins Ish. 34:94, 102, 105)	Baghdad
33g	Plaque	Ish. 34:100	5-T.29	terracotta	male fragment	OI: A16992
—	Bead	Ish. 34:78	1-T.30	gold	ball-shaped (1 × 0.7 cm)	Baghdad
—	Pendant	Ish. 34:77	2-T.30	stone	jar-shaped	OI: A16983
—	Cylinder Seal	Ish. 35:34	2-T.30	crystal	fragment (see OIP 72, p. 61)	—
—	(?)	Ref. 34:316	2-T.30	alabaster	fragment (= Ref. 34:292 from 6-R.30, period undetermined)	—
33h	Plaque	Ish. 34:96	2-T.31	terracotta	god fragment	OI: A16991
—	Jar Stopper	Ref. 34:246	2-T.31	terracotta	—	—
—	Figurine	Ref. 34:288	2-T.31	terracotta	animal fragment, hollow	—
41d	Figurine	Ish. 34:80	3-T.32	stone	female(?)	Baghdad

Catalogue of Ishchali Objects by Period (*cont.*)

Plate	Object	Ish. / Ref. No.	Locus	Material	Remarks	Museum

KITÎTUM PERIOD IV (*cont.*)

Plate	Object	Ish. / Ref. No.	Locus	Material	Remarks	Museum
—	Cylinder Seal	Ish. 35:74	1-U.30	hematite	—	OI: A 17674
38h	Plaque	Ish. 34:67	2-U.30	terracotta	dog design	Baghdad
—	(?)	Ref. 34:245	2-U.30	conglom(?)	—	—

KITÎTUM (PERIOD UNDETERMINED)

Plate	Object	Ish. / Ref. No.	Locus	Material	Remarks	Museum
—	Figurine	Ref. 34:141	2-P.30	terracotta	female(?) figurine	—
—	Figurine	Ref. 34:363	2-P.31	terracotta	animal	—
—	Figurine	Ref. 34:375	2-P.31	terracotta	animal fragment (below floor II)	—
—	Figurine	Ref. 34:142	3-P.31	terracotta	female fragment	—
40d	Bowl	Ish. 34:44	4-Q.30	alabaster	fragment	OI: A21191
—	Vase	Ref. 34:257	4-Q.30	alabaster	fragment	—
43d	Beads	Ish. 37:224	6-Q.30	agate, granite, limestone	—	OI: A21206
—	Beads	Ish. 37:225	6-Q.30	agate, carnelian	—	Baghdad
—	Ostrich Egg	Ref. 34:114	6-Q.30	shell	fragments (robber dump)	—
—	Stag Horn	Ref. 34:300	6-Q.30	bone	fragments	—
—	Bones	Ref. 34:301	6-Q.30	bone	knuckle (robber dump)	—
—	Figurine	Ref. 35:65	6-Q.30	terracotta	fragment (floor below Kitîtum Temple)	—
—	Plaque	Ref. 34:184	2-Q.31	terracotta	fragment (floor II)	—
—	Model Axe(?)	Ref. 34:204	2-Q.31	terracotta	fragment (floor II)	—
—	Zoomorphic Spout	Ref. 34:267	2-Q.31	terracotta	lion's head (floor II)	—
—	Saucer	Ref. 35:129	1-R.29	pottery	fragment	—
—	Relief	Ref. 34:341	4-R.30	stone	fragment	—
—	(?)	Ref. 34:292	6-R.30	alabaster	fragment (joins Ref. 34:316, period IV)	—
—	Bead	Ref. 34:275	1-R.31	(?)	cylinder-shaped	—
—	Nails	Ref. 34:276	3-R.31	bronze/ copper	—	—
—	Figurine	Ref. 34:277	3-R.31	terracotta	fragment	—
—	Pin	Ref. 34:227	1-S.30	bone	fragment	—
—	Plaque	Ref. 35:149	2-S.30	terracotta	god fragment	—
—	Model Chariot	Ref. 35:150	2-S.30	terracotta	fragment	—
—	Plaque(?)	Ref. 35:141	2-T.29	terracotta	fragment	—
—	Shell	Ish. 35:57	2-T.30	shell	fragments (from well)	—
35k	Plaque	Ish. 34:85	3-T.31	terracotta	animal rider (from robber dump)	Baghdad
—	Figurine	Ref. 35:147	1-T.32	terracotta	male fragment	—

Catalogue of Ishchali Objects by Period (*cont.*)

Plate	Object	Ish. / Ref. No.	Material	Remarks	Museum

KITÎTUM COMPLEX (PERIOD UNDETERMINED)

Plate	Object	Ish. / Ref. No.	Material	Remarks	Museum
	From 1-P.30 and 4- and 5-Q.30				
43a	Beads	Ish. 34:138	carnelian, shell, stone	43 exx.	Baghdad
	Small temple on north side (2-S.29?)				
—	Bead	Ref. 35:47	stone	transparent cylinder	—
	Large court of Kitîtum Temple				
—	Cylinder Seal	Ish. 35:53	stone	—	Baghdad
	Large court 15 m west of 1-T.31				
—	Spear(?) Blade	Ref. 34:244	bronze/copper	with tang	—
	Large court at well				
—	Plaque	Ref. 35:131	terracotta	fragment (man + tree)	—
	Central court (larger)				
—	Plaque	Ref. 35:162	terracotta	male fragment	—
	Middle of Kitîtum court (smaller?)				
—	Figurine	Ref. 34:252	terracotta	animal fragment	—
	Middle of Kitîtum court (smaller?)				
—	Unidentified	Ref. 34:256	alabaster	fragment	—
	Kitîtum court SE corner (smaller?)				
—	Figurine	Ref. 34:364	terracotta	male with animal	—
	Court of Kitîtum complex(?)				
—	Figurine	Ref. 35:109	terracotta	female fragment	—
	Kitîtum complex court(?)				
—	Wire Bundle	Ref. 35:127	bronze/copper	—	—
	Court(?)				
—	Bead	Ref. 35:93	—	cube-shaped	—
	Court center(?)				
—	Plaque	Ref. 35:126	terracotta	fragment	—

Catalogue of Ishchali Objects by Period (*cont.*)

Plate	Object	Ish. / Ref. No.	Material	Remarks	Museum

KITÎTUM COMPLEX (PERIOD UNDETERMINED) (*cont.*)

Inside kisû *north of 7-S.29*

	Cylinder Seal	Ish. 35:85	black stone	—	—

Inside kisû *north of 3-Q.29*

	Figurine	Ref. 35:170	terracotta	female fragment	—

Behind kisû *north of complex*

	Cylinder Seal	Ish. 35:94	black stone	—	OI: A17681

East of 1-T.32

	Plaque	Ref. 35:144	terracotta	fragment	—

Plate	Object	Ish. / Ref. No.	Locus	Material	Remarks	Museum

KITÎTUM TEMPLE AREA (TOP LAYER)

Plate	Object	Ish. / Ref. No.	Locus	Material	Remarks	Museum
—	Bead(?)	Ref. 34:120	1-P.29	stone	square-shaped	—
—	Cylinder Seal	Ish. 34:120	north of 2-P.29	hematite	—	Baghdad
—	Plaque	Ref. 34:123	3-P.30	terracotta	hunter fragment	—
33p	Plaque	Ish. 34:113	outside 2-P.31	terracotta	fragment	OI: A16998
35d	Plaque	Ish. 34:97	3-P.32	terracotta	god fragment (joins Ish. 34:98, 50 cm below surface)	Baghdad
35d	Plaque	Ish. 34:98	3-P.32	terracotta	god fragment (joins Ish. 34:97, 50 cm below surface)	Baghdad
—	Plaque	Ref. 34:175	3-P.32	terracotta	female fragment (60 cm below surface)	—
—	Figurine	Ref. 34:180	3-P.32	terracotta	fragment	—
—	Plaque	Ref. 34:189	3-P.32	terracotta	female fragment	—
—	Model Bed	Ref. 34:190	3-P.32	terracotta	fragment	—
—	Figurine	Ref. 34:205	3-P.32	terracotta	female fragment	—
—	Plaque	Ref. 34:243	3-P.32	terracotta	female fragment	—
—	Model Wheel	Ref. 34:295	3-P.32	terracotta	—	—
—	Model Chariot	Ref. 34:297	3-P.32	terracotta	fragment	—
—	Cylinder Seal	Ish. 34:24	north of 2-Q.29	black stone	—	OI: A16968

Catalogue of Ishchali Objects by Period (*cont.*)

Plate	Object	Ish. / Ref. No.	Locus	Material	Remarks	Museum

KITÎTUM TEMPLE AREA (TOP LAYER) (*cont.*)

Plate	Object	Ish. / Ref. No.	Locus	Material	Remarks	Museum
—	Weight	Ish. 35:29	6-Q.30	hematite	date-shaped	Baghdad
38c	Plaque	Ish. 35:40	1-Q.32	terracotta	painted lion fragment	Baghdad
—	Weight	Ish. 35:19	1-R.29	hematite	ovoid	Baghdad
—	Figurine	Ref. 34:51	4-R.29	terracotta	animal fragment	—
—	Model Chariot	Ref. 34:52	4-R.29	terracotta	fragment	—
—	Figurine	Ref. 34:73	4-R.29	terracotta	animal fragment	—
—	Cylinder Seal	Ish. 35:5	1-R.32	stone	—	—
—	Beads	Ref. 34:188	2-R.32	(?)	3 exx.	—
—	Plaque	Ref. 34:241	2-R.32	terracotta	female fragment	—
—	Pin	Ref. 34:296	2-R.32	bone	fragment	—
—	Beads	Ref. 34:194	3-R.32	(?)	various	—
—	Plaque	Ref. 35:139	3-R.32	terracotta	fragment	—
—	Model Boat	Ref. 35:49	north of 6-T.29	terracotta	fragment	—
—	Figurine	Ref. 35:50	north of 6-T.29	terracotta	male fragment	—
—	Model Bed	Ref. 35:54	north of 6-T.29	terracotta	—	—
—	Figurine	Ref. 35:57	north of 6-T.29	terracotta	male fragment	—
—	Bead	Ref. 35:156	2-T.32	stone	ovoid oblong-shaped	—
35h	Plaque	Ish. 35:211	NW corner of *kisû*	terracotta	female fragment (seated)	Baghdad
—	Cylinder Seal	Ish. 34:119	N of temple	stone	—	OI: A17000
—	Weight	Ref. 35:143	S wall of temple (outside)	stone	rectangular-shaped	—

KITÎTUM STREETS

Northeast corner of Kitîtum Temple

Plate	Object	Ish. / Ref. No.	Locus	Material	Remarks	Museum
—	Cylinder Seal	Ish. 34:123	T.28	stone	—	Baghdad
—	Figurine	Ref. 35:66	T.28	terracotta	male fragment	—
—	Figurine	Ish. 35:82	(?)	terracotta	fragment	—

East of Kitîtum Temple

Plate	Object	Ish. / Ref. No.	Locus	Material	Remarks	Museum
—	Cylinder Seal	Ish. 35:6	U.31	stone	—	Baghdad
—	Figurine	Ref. 35:58	U.31	terracotta	male fragment	—
—	Plaque	Ref. 35:59	U.31	terracotta	female fragment	—

Catalogue of Ishchali Objects by Period (*cont.*)

Plate	Object	Ish. / Ref. No.	Locus	Material	Remarks	Museum

KITÎTUM STREETS (*cont.*)

Southeast corner of Kitîtum Temple

Plate	Object	Ish. / Ref. No.	Locus	Material	Remarks	Museum
44f	Weight	Ish. 34:122	U.32	hematite	duck-shaped (1,709 gm)	OI: A17001

South of Kitîtum Temple

	Cylinder Seal	Ish. 34:76	2-R.32	stone	—	—
—	Bead	Ref. 34:357	S.32	stone	—	—
	Unidentified	Ref. 35:91	S.32	bronze/copper	fragment	—

Southwest corner of Kitîtum Temple

—	Cylinder Seal	Ish. 35:30	P.32(?)	stone	—	—
44g	Weight	Ish. 35:33	P.32	hematite	duck-shaped	OI: A17664

Street in front of door to Kitîtum Temple

—	Plaque	Ref. 34:347	P.32	terracotta	female fragment	—
—	Figurine	Ref. 34:350	P.32	terracotta	fragment	—
—	Model Bed	Ref. 35:51	P.32	terracotta	with female figure	—
—	Figurine	Ref. 35:56	P.32	terracotta	female fragment	—
—	(?)	Ref. 35:62	P.32	terracotta	—	—

West of Kitîtum Temple

—	Cylinder Seal	Ish. 35:38	(?)	terracotta	—	—

Northwest corner of Kitîtum Temple

—	Plaque	Ref. 35:80	0.29	terracotta	female fragment	—
—	Figurine	Ref. 35:81	0.29	terracotta	male fragment	—

North of Kitîtum Temple

—	Pin	Ref. 35:68	T.28	bronze/copper	—	—
—	Figurine	Ref. 35:102	S.29	terracotta	male fragment	—

Northeast corner of Shamash Temple

—	Cylinder Seal	Ish. 35:49	W.30	terracotta	—	Baghdad

East of Shamash Temple

—	Rattle	Ref. 35:100	U.31	terracotta	—	—

South end of Tell

—	Figurine	Ref. 35:99	(?)	terracotta	female fragment	—

Catalogue of Ishchali Objects by Period (*cont.*)

Plate	Object	Ish. / Ref. No.	Locus	Material	Remarks	Museum

KITÎTUM STREETS (*cont.*)

Street at City Gate

—	Ring	Ref. 35:105	X.33	bronze/ copper	enclosed circle	—
—	Plaque	Ref. 35:106	X.33	terracotta	with two figures	—

CITY WALL (TOP)

45b	Weight	Ish. 35:47	(?)	hematite	date-shaped	OI: A17668
35i	Plaque	Ish. 35:66	SE corner	terracotta	musician fragment	Baghdad
—	Cylinder Seal	Ish. 35:67	W.33	terracotta	—	Baghdad

CITY WALL (PERIOD UNDETERMINED)

—	Pin	Ish. 35:54	(?)	bone	—	—
—	Plaque	Ref. 34:146	(?)	terracotta	female fragment	—
—	Model Axe	Ref. 35:78	(?)	terracotta	—	—
—	Figurine	Ref. 35:108	SW end	terracotta	fragment	—
—	Plaque	Ref. 35:130	(?)	terracotta	god fragment	—
—	Cube	Ref. 34:209	3-W.29	stone	—	—
—	Cube	Ref. 34:210	(?)	stone	—	—
—	Weight	Ref. 34:213	(?)	stone	duck-shaped	—
—	Bead	Ref. 34:214	(?)	stone	spacer type (short cylinder)	—
—	Plaque	Ref. 34:225	(?)	terracotta	female fragment	—
—	Earring	Ref. 34:231	(?)	copper	—	—

CITY GATE (TOP)

33n	Plaque	Ish. 34:92	(?)	terracotta	god fragment	OI: A16990
34c	Plaque	Ish. 34:103	(?)	terracotta	male fragment (joins Ish. 34:110)	Baghdad
34c	Plaque	Ish. 34:110	(?)	terracotta	male fragment (joins Ish. 34:103)	—
—	Pin	Ref. 34:261	(?)	bone	—	—
—	Pin	Ref. 34:314	(?)	bone	—	—
—	Pin	Ref. 34:315	(?)	bone	—	—
—	Pin	Ref. 34:358	(?)	bone	fragments (3 exx.)	—
—	Pin	Ref. 34:359	(?)	bone	fragments	—

Catalogue of Ishchali Objects by Period (*cont.*)

Plate	Object	Ish. / Ref. No.	Locus	Material	Remarks	Museum

CITY GATE (TOP) (*cont.*)

Plate	Object	Ish. / Ref. No.	Locus	Material	Remarks	Museum
	Period II					
—	Metal	Ish. 34:118	(?)	bronze	oblong-shaped, 2.10 × 2.30 cm	—
	Period Undetermined					
34m	Plaque	Ish. 34:206	(?)	terracotta	female fragment	OI: A21197
—	Model Chariot	Ref. 34:302	(?)	terracotta	fragment	—
—	Cap	Ref. 34:306	(?)	shell	—	—
—	Figurine	Ref. 34:312	(?)	terracotta	fragment	—
—	Plaque	Ref. 34:368	(?)	terracotta	fragment	—
—	Plaque	Ref. 35:30	(?)	terracotta	female fragment	—
	Outside City Gate					
—	Pin	Ref. 34:325	(?)	bone	fragment	—

SHAMASH GATE TEMPLE (TOP LEVEL)

Plate	Object	Ish. / Ref. No.	Locus	Material	Remarks	Museum
—	Plaque	Ref. 35:145	2-V.29	terracotta	female fragment	—
—	Arrowhead	Ref. 35:151	2-V.29	bronze/ copper	triangle-shaped with short tang	—
25	Relief	Ish. 35:36	2-V.30	limestone	fragment	Baghdad
46a	Animal Head (Weight?)	Ish. 35:37	2-V.30	hematite	lion-shaped	OI: A17665
—	Weight	Ish. 35:43	3-V.30	hematite	date-shaped (1,362 gm)	Baghdad
45e	Weight	Ish. 35:44	3-V.30	hematite	date-shaped	OI: A17667
—	Weight	Ish. 35:45	3-V.30	hematite	date-shaped	Baghdad
—	Weight	Ish. 35:46	3-V.30	hematite	date-shaped	Baghdad
—	Nail	Ref. 35:60	3-V.30	bronze/ copper	—	—
—	Model Leg	Ref. 35:61	3-V.30	terracotta	—	—
—	Nail	Ref. 35:70	3-V.30	bronze/ copper	—	—
—	Pin	Ref. 35:71	3-V.30	bronze/ copper	—	—
41h	Macehead	Ish. 35:80	4-V.30	marble	—	Baghdad
41g	Macehead	Ish. 35:81	4-V.30	marble	—	OI: A21199
41f	Macehead	Ish. 35:82	4-V.30	black stone	—	OI: A21200
—	Macehead	Ish. 35:83	4-V.30	marble	fragment	—
30f, g	Lamp	Ish. 35:84	4-V.30	bronze	height 2.20, length 10, width 5.60 cm	OI: A17677
—	Plaque	Ref. 34:274	4-V.30	terracotta	male fragment	—

Catalogue of Ishchali Objects by Period (*cont.*)

Plate	Object	Ish. / Ref. No.	Locus	Material	Remarks	Museum

SHAMASH GATE TEMPLE (TOP LEVEL) (*cont.*)

Plate	Object	Ish. / Ref. No.	Locus	Material	Remarks	Museum
—	Figurine	Ref. 35:97	5-V.30	terracotta	female fragment	—
—	Plaque	Ref. 35:112	5-V.30	terracotta	bull-man fragment	—
—	Figurine	Ref. 34:226	8-V.30	terracotta	fragment	—
—	Unidentified	Ref. 35:24	2-V.31	terracotta	—	—
—	Plaque	Ref. 35:110	2-V.31	terracotta	male fragment	—
—	Plaque	Ref. 35:160	2-V.31	terracotta	lion fragment	—
—	Figurine	Ref. 35:167	2-V.31	terracotta	ram's head	Baghdad
33e	Plaque	Ish. 35:75	2-V.31	terracotta	god fragment	—
—	Cylinder Seal	Ish. 35:31	3-V.31	stone	—	OI: A17662
—	Pin	Ref. 35:152	3-V.31	bone	—	—
—	Figurine	Ref. 35:161	3-V.31	terracotta	male head	—
—	Seal Impression	Ish. 35:77	4-V.31	unbaked clay	—	—
—	Model Bed	Ref. 35:173	4-V.31	terracotta	fragment	—
35e	Plaque	Ish. 35:87	5-V.31	terracotta	man carrying gazelle	OI: A17678
—	Spindle Whorl	Ref. 35:175	5-V.31	terracotta	—	—
—	Pin	Ref. 35:46	6-V.31	terracotta	—	—
—	Figurine	Ref. 35:55	6-V.31	terracotta	male fragment	—
—	Plaque	Ref. 35:67	7-V.31	terracotta	god fragment	—
34d	Plaque	Ish. 35:91	9-V.31	terracotta	god fragment	Baghdad
—	Figurine	Ref. 35:96	9-V.31	terracotta	male fragment	—
—	Ring	Ref. 35:101	9-V.31	bone	—	—
—	Tool	Ref. 34:326	1-V.32	bone	point fragment	—
—	Cylinder Seal	Ish. 35:52	2-V.32	marble	fragment	Baghdad
30i	Cup	Ish. 35:60	3-V.32	bronze	with handle and pedestal base	Baghdad
30h	Cup	Ish. 35:61	3-V.32	bronze	fragment	Baghdad (IM. 27735)
—	Plaque	Ref. 35:116	4-V.32	terracotta	male fragment	—
—	Rattle	Ref. 35:122	4-V.32	terracotta	—	—
—	Ring	Ref. 35:114	5-V.32	bronze	—	—
—	Plaque	Ref. 34:41	9-R.33	terracotta	female fragment	—
—	Ring	Ref. 35:120	5-V.32	bronze/copper	open at ends	—
—	Tweezers	Ref. 35:121	6-V.32	bronze/copper	—	—
34q	Plaque	Ish. 35:62	10-V.32	terracotta	female	OI: A17672
—	Cylinder Seal	Ish. 35:63	10-V.32	terracotta	—	—
—	Cylinder Seal	Ish. 35:65	12-V.32	terracotta	—	—
—	Weight	Ish. 35:58	14-V.32	stone	duck-shaped fragment	—
—	Bowl	Ref. 35:135	15-V.32	bronze	flat base, shallow circle	—

Catalogue of Ishchali Objects by Period (*cont.*)

Plate	Object	Ish. / Ref. No.	Locus	Material	Remarks	Museum

SHAMASH GATE TEMPLE (TOP LEVEL) (*cont.*)

Plate	Object	Ish. / Ref. No.	Locus	Material	Remarks	Museum
—	Weight	Ish. 35:64	16-V.32	hematite	duck-shaped	Baghdad
—	Cylinder Seal	Ish. 35:95	2-W.30	stone	—	—
34g	Plaque	Ish. 35:216	1-W.31	terracotta	god fragment	Baghdad
34l	Plaque	Ish. 35:212	2-W.31	terracotta	god fragment	Baghdad
—	Model Boat	Ref. 35:11	2-W.31	terracotta	fragment	—
—	Cylinder Seal	Ish. 34:83	1-W.32	stone	—	OI: A16985
—	Cylinder Seal	Ish. 34:84	1-W.32	hematite	—	Baghdad
	Plaque	Ref. 35:174	(?)	terracotta	fragment	—

SHAMASH GATE TEMPLE (PERIOD UNDETERMINED)

Plate	Object	Ish. / Ref. No.	Locus	Material	Remarks	Museum
—	Figurine	Ref. 35:128	3-V.30	terracotta	female fragment	—
—	Tool	Ref. 35:103	5-V.30	bronze	perforated circles on both ends of bar	—
35a	Plaque	Ish. 35:79	3-V.31	terracotta	fragment with god in chariot	OI: A17676
—	Plaque	Ref. 35:117	2-V.32	terracotta	female fragment	—
—	Plaque	Ref. 35:118	4-V.32	terracotta	female fragment	—
38d	Plaque	Ish. 35:56	6-V.32	terracotta	lion design	OI: A17670
—	Plaque	Ref. 35:125	7-V.32	terracotta	god fragment	—
—	Cup	Ish. 35:68	15-V.32	copper	carinated just above disc base	—
—	Model Bed	Ish. 35:59	16-V.32	terracotta	—	OI: A17671

BUILDING NORTH OF THE SHAMASH GATE TEMPLE (PERIOD UNDETERMINED)

Plate	Object	Ish. / Ref. No.	Locus	Material	Remarks	Museum
—	Figurine	Ref. 35:138	(?)	terracotta	animal fragment	—

THE "SERAI" (TOP LEVEL)

Plate	Object	Ish. / Ref. No.	Locus	Material	Remarks	Museum
34h	Mold	Ish. 34:125	3-Q.33	terracotta	for god plaque	OI: A17002
—	Model Chariot	Ref. 34:356	3-Q.33	terracotta	fragment	—
—	Model Boat	Ref. 34:15	2-Q.35	terracotta	fragment	—
35c	Plaque	Ish. 34:6	1-R.33	terracotta	male fragment	—
33k	Plaque	Ish. 34:7	1-R.33	terracotta	male fragment	Baghdad
44h	Weight	Ish. 34:23	6-R.33	agate	duck-shaped (2,859 gm)	OI: A16967
—	Nail Head	Ref. 34:43	6-R.33	bronze/ copper	—	—
—	Jar	Ish. 34:27	7-R.33	terracotta	painted	—
—	Plaque	Ref. 34:41	9-R.33	terracotta	female fragment	—

Catalogue of Ishchali Objects by Period (*cont.*)

Plate	Object	Ish. / Ref. No.	Locus	Material	Remarks	Museum

THE "SERAI" (TOP LEVEL) (*cont.*)

Plate	Object	Ish. / Ref. No.	Locus	Material	Remarks	Museum
—	Pin	Ref. 34:13	3-R.34	bronze/copper	—	—
—	Cylinder Seal	Ish. 34:16	8-R.34	steatite	—	—
—	Cylinder Seal	Ish. 34:20	8-R.34	steatite	—	—
44i	Weight	Ish. 34:21	8-R.34	hematite	duck-shaped (1,544 gm)	Baghdad
—	Weights	Ish. 34:22	8-R.34	hematite	12 exx.	—
—	Plaque	Ref. 34:36	8-R.34	terracotta	female	—
—	Model Wheel	Ref. 34:38	9-R.34	terracotta	—	—
46b	Weight	Ish. 34:17	1-R.35	stone	conical-shaped	OI: A21189
—	Bottle	Ref. 34:12	6-R.35	terracotta	—	—
—	Plaque	Ref. 34:34	6-R.35	terracotta	goddess fragment	—
—	Arrowhead	Ish. 34:200	7-R.35	copper	2.60 × 9.20 cm	Baghdad
38k	Figurine	Ish. 34:115	8-R.35	terracotta	lion fragment	Baghdad
33j	Plaque	Ish. 34:5	1-S.36	terracotta	male fragment	OI: A16965
33q	Figurine	Ish. 34:59	1-S.36	terracotta	human fragment	OI: A16979
36d	Plaque	Ish. 34:93	1-S.36	terracotta	female fragment	Baghdad
—	Plaque	Ref. 34:48	1-S.36	terracotta	bull-man fragment	—
—	Figurine	Ref. 34:57	1-S.36	terracotta	male fragment	—
—	Plaque	Ref. 34:76	1-S.36	terracotta	female fragment	—

THE "SERAI" (PERIOD UNDETERMINED)

Plate	Object	Ish. / Ref. No.	Locus	Material	Remarks	Museum
—	Figurine	Ref. 34:155	1-P.33	terracotta	female fragment	—
—	Wire	Ref. 34:19	2-R.34	silver	—	—
—	Spindle Whorl	Ref. 34:38	9-R.34	terracotta	—	—
—	Cylinder Seal	Ish. 34:15	7-R.35	bone	—	—
26, 27	Statuette	—	7-R.35	bronze	four-faced god, 17.30 cm high	OI: A7119
28, 29	Statuette	—	7-R.35	bronze	four-faced goddess, 16.20 cm high	OI: A7120

Objects from Grave, Group I

Plate	Object	Ish. / Ref. No.	Locus	Material	Remarks	Museum
44q	Weight	Ish. 34:8	10-R.35	faience	duck-shaped	—
—	Weight	Ish. 34:9	10-R.35	hematite	duck-shaped	OI: A21188
—	Weights	Ish. 34:10	10-R.35	hematite	5 exx.	—
—	Metal Pieces	Ish. 34:11	10-R.35	bronze/copper	4 exx.	—
—	Stones	Ish. 34:12	10-R.35	stone	17 exx.	—
—	Shell pieces	Ish. 34:13	10-R.35	shell	3 exx.	—
—	Weight	Ish. 34:14	10-R.35	obsidian	triangle-shaped	Baghdad

Catalogue of Ishchali Objects by Period (*cont.*)

Plate	Object	Ish. / Ref. No.	Locus	Material	Remarks	Museum

MISCELLANEOUS AREAS (PERIOD UNDETERMINED)

Hill with Survey Mark (S.36)

Plate	Object	Ish. / Ref. No.	Locus	Material	Remarks	Museum
—	Metal	Ref. 34:1	N side	bronze/ copper plus wood	charred lump	—
—	Nails + Bands	Ref. 34:2	NE side	bronze/ copper	lumps	—
45a	Weight	Ish. 34:4	W side	stone	ovoid-shaped	OI: A21187
—	Weight	Ish. 34:2	NW side	stone	duck-shaped	—
—	Weight	Ref. 34:4	(?)	hematite	globular-shaped	—
—	Bead	Ref. 34:5	(?)	stone	oval-shaped	—
—	Bead	Ref. 34:6	(?)	stone	cylinder-shaped	—

West side of Mound

44k	Weight	Ish. 35:9	Surface	hematite	duck-shaped	Baghdad
44l	Weight	Ish. 35:10	Surface	hematite	duck-shaped	OI: A17651
46c	Bead	Ish. 35:11	Surface	brown stone	transparent	OI: A17652
44j	Weight	Ish. 35:12	Surface	hematite	duck-shaped	Baghdad

West side of Mound (cont.)

—	Weight	Ish. 35:13	Surface	hematite	oblong-shaped	Baghdad
—	Weight	Ish. 35:14	Surface	hematite	date-shaped	—
45d	Weight	Ish. 35:15	Surface	hematite	date-shaped	OI: A17653
45c	Weight	Ish. 35:16	Surface	hematite	date-shaped	OI: A17654
—	Cylinder Seal	Ish. 35:17	Surface	hematite	—	OI: A17655

City Wall

| — | Figurine | Ref. 34:11 | Surface | terracotta | male head | — |

"Room Opposite Kititum Gate"

| — | Plaque | Ref. 34:361 | (?) | terracotta | rider type | — |

"Trench B" (Not identified on final plans)

| 39a | Cylinder Seal | Ish. 37:1 | — | stone | — | Baghdad |
| 39b | Cylinder Seal | Ish. 37:2 | — | stone | — | P* |

* University Museum, Pennsylvania

Catalogue of Ishchali Objects by Period (*cont.*)

Plate	Object	Ish. / Ref. No.	Material	Remarks	Museum

UNKNOWN SURFACE AREAS (PERIOD UNDETERMINED)

Plate	Object	Ish. / Ref. No.	Material	Remarks	Museum
—	Cylinder Seal	Ish. 34:1	stone	—	Baghdad
—	Weight	Ish. 34:18	stone	oblong-shaped (16,077 gm)	Baghdad
—	Weight	Ish. 34:19	hematite	conical-shaped	Baghdad
—	Cylinder Seal	Ish. 34:25	stone	—	Baghdad
44e	Weight	Ish. 34:81	hematite	duck-shaped (5,933 gm)	Baghdad
33a	Plaque	Ish. 34:94	terracotta	god fragment (joins Ish. 34:99, 102, 105)	Baghdad
33o	Plaque	Ish. 34:95	terracotta	male fragment	Baghdad
33b	Plaque	Ish. 34:102	terracotta	god fragment (joins Ish. 34:94, 99, 105)	OI: A16993
33d	Plaque	Ish. 34:105	terracotta	god fragment (joins Ish. 34:94, 99, 102)	Baghdad
38f	Plaque	Ish. 34:116	terracotta	bull-man fragment	OI: A16999
—	Stamp Seal	Ish. 35:2	carnelian	—	—
37a	Model Bed	Ish. 35:3	terracotta	fragment with female figure	Baghdad
—	Cylinder Seal	Ish. 35:4	stone	—	Baghdad
44n	Weight	Ish. 35:22	hematite	duck-shaped	OI: A17657
—	Cylinder Seal	Ish. 35:25	stone	see OIP 72, p. 61	OI: A17658
—	Cylinder Seal	Ish. 35:27	hematite	fragment	OI: A17660
44o	Weight	Ish. 35:28	stone	duck-shaped	OI: A17661
—	Cylinder Seal	Ish. 35:32	hematite	—	OI: A17663
—	Cylinder Seal	Ish. 35:39	stone	—	Baghdad
44p	Weight	Ish. 35:41	agate	duck-shaped	Baghdad
—	Cylinder Seal	Ish. 35:50	lapis lazuli	—	Baghdad
36b	Figurine	Ish. 35:88	terracotta	male fragment	OI: A17679
38j	Plaque	Ish. 35:90	terracotta	fragment with winged lion and man	OI: A17680
—	Macehead	Ish. 35:205	black stone	—	Baghdad
—	Mold	Ish. 35:209	terracotta	figurine fragment	Baghdad
34e	Plaque	Ish. 35:210	terracotta	fragment	Baghdad
34j	Plaque	Ish. 35:223	terracotta	god fragment	Baghdad
—	Cylinder Seal	Ref. 34:21	(?)	fragment	—
—	Plaque	Ref. 34:33	terracotta	bird fragment	—
—	Figurine	Ref. 34:35	terracotta	fragment	—
—	Chisel	Ref. 34:39	bronze	—	—
—	Plaque	Ref. 34:40	terracotta	god type	—
—	Figurine	Ref. 34:42	terracotta	male fragment	—
—	Figurine	Ref. 34:44	terracotta	male fragment	—
—	Plaque	Ref. 34:47	terracotta	female type	—
—	Pot Stand	Ref. 34:50	terracotta	triangle-shaped	—

Catalogue of Ishchali Objects by Period (*cont.*)

Plate	Object	Ish. / Ref. No.	Material	Remarks	Museum

UNKNOWN SURFACE AREAS (PERIOD UNDETERMINED) (*cont.*)

Plate	Object	Ish. / Ref. No.	Material	Remarks	Museum
—	Plaque	Ref. 34:53	terracotta	female fragment	—
—	Figurine	Ref. 34:54	terracotta	male fragment	—
—	Figurine	Ref. 34:56	terracotta	male fragment	—
—	Plaque	Ref. 34:67	terracotta	fragment	—
—	Plaque	Ref. 34:82	terracotta	female fragment	—
—	Plaque	Ref. 34:84	terracotta	fragment	—
—	Model Chariot	Ref. 34:86	terracotta	fragment	—
—	Figurine	Ref. 34:121	terracotta	female fragment	—
—	Figurine	Ref. 34:129	terracotta	charioteer	—
—	Plaque	Ref. 34:148	terracotta	female fragment	—
—	Plaque	Ref. 34:163	terracotta	bull-man fragment	—
—	Plaque	Ref. 34:167	terracotta	lion fragment	—
—	Plaque	Ref. 34:168	terracotta	female fragment	—
—	Plaque	Ref. 34:171	terracotta	fragment	—
—	Plaque	Ref. 34:179	terracotta	female fragment	—
—	Figurine	Ref. 34:198	terracotta	female fragment	—
—	Figurine	Ref. 34:215	terracotta	female fragment	—
—	Figurine	Ref. 34:216	terracotta	female fragment	—
—	Plaque	Ref. 34:236	terracotta	animal fragment	—
—	Model Bed	Ref. 34:242	terracotta	fragment	—
—	Model Bed	Ref. 34:249	terracotta	fragment	—
—	Figurine	Ref. 34:253	terracotta	animal	—
—	Plaque	Ref. 34:254	terracotta	fragment	—
—	Figurine	Ref. 34:260	terracotta	female fragment	—
—	Plaque	Ref. 34:270	terracotta	lion fragment	—
—	Plaque	Ref. 34:279	terracotta	female fragment	—
—	Plaque	Ref. 34:281	terracotta	fragment	—
—	Figurine	Ref. 34:282	terracotta	human head fragment	—
—	Figurine	Ref. 34:283	terracotta	fragment	—
—	Figurine	Ref. 34:290	terracotta	animal (horse? head)	—
—	Plaque	Ref. 34:298	terracotta	god fragment	—
—	Rattle	Ref. 34:305	terracotta	ram-shaped	—
—	Plaque	Ref. 34:309	terracotta	female fragment	—
—	Model Boat	Ref. 34:310	terracotta	fragment	—
—	Plaque	Ref. 34:311	terracotta	lion fragment	—
—	Model Boat	Ref. 34:318	terracotta	fragment	—
—	Plaque	Ref. 34:320	terracotta	male fragment	—
—	Plaque	Ref. 34:321	terracotta	female fragment	—
—	Plaque	Ref. 34:322	terracotta	female fragment	—
—	Plaque	Ref. 34:324	terracotta	fragment	—

Catalogue of Ishchali Objects by Period (*cont.*)

Plate	Object	Ish. / Ref. No.	Material	Remarks	Museum

UNKNOWN SURFACE AREAS (PERIOD UNDETERMINED) (*cont.*)

Plate	Object	Ish. / Ref. No.	Material	Remarks	Museum
—	Figurine	Ref. 34:327	terracotta	horse and rider fragment	—
—	Plaque	Ref. 34:334	terracotta	male fragment	—
—	Plaque	Ref. 34:336	terracotta	god fragment	—
—	Plaque	Ref. 34:339	terracotta	male fragment	—
—	Model Bed	Ref. 34:340	terracotta	fragment	—
—	Model Bed	Ref. 34:344	terracotta	fragment with female figure	—
—	Model Bed	Ref. 34:345	terracotta	fragment	—
—	Cube	Ref. 34:360	stone	rubbing stone(?)	—
—	Plaque	Ref. 34:365	terracotta	male fragment	—
—	Plaque	Ref. 34:367	terracotta	female fragment	—
—	Plaque	Ref. 34:377	terracotta	dog design	—
—	Figurine	Ref. 35:1	terracotta	human with tambourine(?)	—
—	Model Bed	Ref. 35:4	terracotta	fragment with two human figures	—
—	Plaque	Ref. 35:9	terracotta	male fragment	—
—	Plaque	Ref. 35:16	terracotta	fragment	—
—	Weight	Ref. 35:28	stone(?)	oblong-shaped	—
—	Figurine	Ref. 35:44	terracotta	female fragment	—
—	Figurine	Ref. 35:48	terracotta	ram head fragment	—
—	Figurine	Ref. 35:75	terracotta	human head fragment	—
—	Plaque	Ref. 35:76	terracotta	musician fragment	—
—	Plaque	Ref. 35:98	terracotta	female fragment	—

DUMP (PERIOD UNDETERMINED)

Plate	Object	Ish. / Ref. No.	Material	Remarks	Museum
—	Plaque	Ref. 35:107	terracotta	male fragment	—
—	Plaque	Ref. 35:163	terracotta	female fragment	—
—	Plaque	Ref. 35:172	terracotta	fragment	—
36a	Plaque	Ish. 34:61	terracotta	male fragment	Baghdad
—	Cylinder Seal	Ish. 34:75	lapis lazuli	fragment	—
37c	Model Bed	Ish. 34:88	terracotta	fragment with female figure	OI: A16987
35m	Plaque	Ish. 34:90	terracotta	rider fragment (joins Ish. 34:107)	OI: A16988
35j	Plaque	Ish. 34:111	terracotta	seated figure fragment	Baghdad
34k	Plaque	Ish. 34:112	terracotta	god fragment	OI: A16997
34n	Mold	Ish. 34:126	terracotta	figurine fragment	Baghdad
41c	Inlay	Ish. 34:202	stone	fragment	OI: A21194
33i	Plaque	Ish. 35:208	terracotta	god fragment	OI: A21198
—	Amulet	Ish. 35:1	agate	frog-shaped	Baghdad
44c	Amulet (Weight?)	Ish. 35:7	carnelian	lion-shaped	Baghdad

Catalogue of Ishchali Objects by Period (*cont.*)

Plate	Object	Ish. / Ref. No.	Material	Remarks	Museum

DUMP (PERIOD UNDETERMINED) (*cont.*)

Plate	Object	Ish. / Ref. No.	Material	Remarks	Museum
45f	Weight	Ish. 35:18	stone	date-shaped	OI: A17656
—	Cylinder Seal	Ish. 35:35	hematite	—	Baghdad
34p	Plaque	Ish. 35:89	terracotta	god fragment	Baghdad
38i	Plaque	Ish. 35:218	terracotta	bird fragment	Baghdad
34i	Plaque	Ish. 35:220	terracotta	god fragment	OI: A21203
—	Model Bed	Ref. 34:37	terracotta	—	—
—	Plaque	Ref. 34:58	terracotta	fragment	—
—	Plaque	Ref. 34:66	terracotta	fragment	—
—	Plaque	Ref. 34:95	terracotta	female fragment	—
—	Jar	Ref. 34:99	terracotta	—	—
—	Plaque	Ref. 34:126	terracotta	fragment	—
—	Figurine	Ref. 34:130	terracotta	male fragment	—
—	Figurine	Ref. 34:143	terracotta	female fragment, seated	—
—	Relief	Ref. 34:147	stone	fragment	—
—	Relief	Ref. 34:153	stone	fragment	—
—	Macehead	Ref. 34:162	stone	fragment	—
—	Weight	Ref. 34:164	stone	date-shaped	—
—	Plaque	Ref. 34:178	terracotta	female fragment	—
—	Plaque	Ref. 34:199	terracotta	fragment	—
—	Model Boat	Ref. 34:201	terracotta	fragment	—
—	Figurine	Ref. 34:202	terracotta	male head	—
—	Figurine	Ref. 34:203	terracotta	female fragment	—
—	Plaque	Ref. 34:217	terracotta	male fragment	—
—	Plaque	Ref. 34:219	terracotta	dog fragment	—
—	Earring	Ref. 34:230	copper(?)	—	—
—	Plaque	Ref. 34:238	terracotta	fragment	—
—	Plaque	Ref. 34:247	terracotta	female fragment	—
—	Vase Sherd	Ref. 34:248	terracotta	—	—
—	Plaque	Ref. 34:255	terracotta	female fragment	—
—	Plaque	Ref. 34:258	terracotta	fragment	—
—	Plaque	Ref. 34:271	terracotta	fragment	—
—	Plaque	Ref. 34:272	terracotta	male fragment	—
—	Seal Impression	Ref. 34:278	unbaked clay	—	—
—	Figurine	Ref. 34:280	terracotta	female fragment	—
—	Disc	Ref. 34:284	bone	pierced	—
—	Sphere	Ref. 34:285	alabaster	fragment	—
—	Zoomorphic Vessel	Ref. 34:289	terracotta	ram's head spout	—
—	Plaque	Ref. 34:291	terracotta	god fragment	—
—	Model Chariot	Ref. 34:307	terracotta	fragment	—

Catalogue of Ishchali Objects by Period (*cont.*)

Plate	Object	Ish. / Ref. No.	Material	Remarks	Museum

DUMP (PERIOD UNDETERMINED) (*cont.*)

Plate	Object	Ish. / Ref. No.	Material	Remarks	Museum
—	Figurine	Ref. 34:317	terracotta	female fragment	—
—	Figurine	Ref. 34:319	terracotta	hollow fragment	—
—	Plaque	Ref. 34:330	terracotta	fragment	—
—	Plaque	Ref. 34:332	terracotta	head fragment	—
—	Plaque	Ref. 34:342	terracotta	fragment	—
—	Figurine	Ref. 34:343	terracotta	fragment	—
—	Plaque	Ref. 34:348	terracotta	rider type	—
—	Figurine	Ref. 34:349	terracotta	female fragment	—
—	Plaque	Ref. 34:354b	terracotta	male fragment	—
—	Disc	Ref. 34:355	stone	fragment with inlaid rosette	—
—	Figurine	Ref. 34:362	terracotta	female fragment	—
—	Plaque	Ref. 34:374	terracotta	male fragment	—
—	Figurine	Ref. 35:22	terracotta	female fragment	—
—	Pendant	Ref. 35:29	stone	rectangular-shaped	—
—	Figurine	Ref. 35:52	terracotta	male fragment	—
—	Plaque	Ref. 35:79	terracotta	fragment	—
—	Rattle	Ref. 35:95	terracotta	—	—
—	Plaque	Ref. 35:148	terracotta	male fragment	—
—	Plaque	Ref. 35:157	terracotta	male fragment	—

OTHER PROVENIENCES

Plate	Object	Ish. / Ref. No.	Material	Remarks	Museum
	Keshem (surface)				
—	Plaque	Ref. 34:222	terracotta	fragment (cf. pl. 62e)	—
—	Plaque	Ref. 34:224	terracotta	female fragment	—
	Abu Obeid (surface)				
—	Cup	Ref. 34:376	stone	—	—
	Abu Hamam (surface)				
—	Statuette Head	Ref. 35:6	marble	female	—
	Abu Trachia (surface)				
—	Plaque	Ref. 35:12	terracotta	male fragment	—
	Ziqqurat				
—	Plaque	Ref. 35:177	terracotta	female fragment	—
	Unknown				
—	Stone Lump	Ref. 34:335	agate	—	—
—	Vase	Ref. 34:337	alabaster	fragments	—
—	Vase	Ref. 34:338	alabaster	fragments	—

PLATE 1

(*a*) Ishchali—View of Antecella (5-Q.30) and Cella (6-Q.30) of Periods I-II

(*b*) Ishchali—Cult Niche and Two Mudbrick Pillars of Periods I-II in 6-Q.30, the Cella of the Upper Temple

PLATE 2

(*a*) Ishchali—Period I-A Staircase at 2-R.31 Leading Up to the Upper Temple,
Seen from the Main Court Looking West

(*b*) Ishchali—Detail of the Extension of the Main Court Terrace Face to the North Wall of the Court (4-R.30)
Showing Vertical Slot Decoration from the Southeast

PLATE 3

Ishchali—Part of the Brick Terrace of 4-R.30, Seen from the Northeast

PLATE 4

(*a*) Ishchali—Small Quadratic Niche in the North Wall of 1-S.30

(*b*) Ishchali—Court of the West Unit (North Wing, 1-R.29) of Period I-A, Viewed from the East

PLATE 5

(b) Ishchali—Room 1-Q.29 in Period I-A, Seen from the East

(a) Ishchali—Open Drain in 7-S.29, Seen from the Northeast

PLATE 6

(*a*) Ishchali—General View of the Eastern Unit of the North Wing,
Seen from the East with Court 2-T.29 in the Foreground

(*b*) Ishchali—Detail of the Recessed Wall Decoration ("Slotted Simulated Towers") in Court 2-T.29 of Period I-A,
Seen from the East

PLATE 7

(*a*) Ishchali—The "Seat" in the Niche of Room 2-S.29, Period I-B, Seen from the Northeast

(*b*) Ishchali—Cella of the Ninshubura Temple (2-S.29), Seen from the Court (2-T.29) During Period I-B

PLATE 8

(b) Ishchali—Detail of Room 3-T.30 (Northwest Corner)
Showing Relationship of Periods II-B, III, and IV

(a) Ishchali—Court 1-R.29 from the East Court of the West Unit of the North Wing
Showing the Tilt in the Pavement Caused by the Wall Settling

PLATE 9

(b) Ishchali—Detail of Room 3-T.31 Looking West Showing
Drain of Period II-B and a Pavement and Sill of Period III

(a) Ishchali—Detail of the Drain in the Eastern End of the Main
Court (T.30-31) During Period II-B, Seen from the Southeast

PLATE 10

(a) Ishchali—View of the Western Court in the North Wing (1-R.29)
Showing Secondary Shacks Built During Periods III and IV

(b) Ishchali—Oval Kitchen Stove in Room 1-Q.29 During Period III

PLATE 11

(a) Ishchali—Detail of the Northern Wall of Room 2-P.30 Showing Foundation Trench
for the Period III Wall with Lowest Courses of the Period IV Wall on Top

(b) Ishchali—View of the Period IV Cella (2-S.29) Looking East
Showing Paved Doorway with Steps into the Room

PLATE 12

(b) Ishchali—Remnants of a Charred Wooden Beam in Front of the Niche
in the Cella (2-S.29), Viewed from the South

(a) Ishchali—Cult Niche and Floor of the Cella (2-S.29)
of the Ninshubura Temple of Period IV

PLATE 13

(b) Ishchali—Detail in Southwest Court (1-P.31) Showing Vertical T-Shaped
Grooves on the Western Gate Tower at the Entrance to the Antecella (5-Q.30)
of Periods I-II, Seen from the South

(a) Ishchali—The Well in the Main Court (2-T.30) Looking North Showing
Upper and Lower Brickwork of Periods IV and II-B Down

PLATE 14

Ishchali—The Retaining Wall (*Kisû*) at the Northwest Corner of the Complex (3-P.29), Looking East

PLATE 15

(b) Ishchali—Detail Showing the Batter of the High *Kisû* (3-Q.29),
Looking West

(a) Ishchali—View of the First Buttress of the *Kisû* (3-Q.29) of Period I-A,
Seen from the East

PLATE 16

(b) Ishchali—North Side of the *Kisû* Outside of Room 7-S.29
Showing Outlets of Drains of Periods I-A and II-A

(a) Ishchali—Detail Showing Mode of Construction Inside the Battered
Top Portion of the *Kisû* (3-Q.29), Looking East

PLATE 17

(*a*) Ishchali—View of the Third Buttress of the *Kisû* from the Southwest Corner
Showing Row of Five Square Holes

(*b*) Ishchali—General View of the Antecella (5-Q.30) and Cella (6-Q.30) of Periods I-II
of the Upper Kitîtum Temple

PLATE 18

(b) Ishchali—View of Room 1-Q.29 with Kitchen Ranges of Period II-B, Seen from the West

(a) Ishchali—Detail of Westernmost Pivotstone Box in the Antecella (5-Q.30), Seen from the South

PLATE 19

(*a*) Ishchali—View of the Period II-B Northern Wing West Court (1-R.29)
Showing Multiple Fireplaces, Seen from the Northeast

(*b*) Ishchali—Brick Stairs Leading to the Upper Level of Room 8-Q.30,
Seen from the Southeast

PLATE 20

(b) Ishchali—Detail of the Corbeled Arch in Room 2-R.29 that Supported the Upper Part of the Stairway, Looking East

(a) Ishchali—Mudbrick Staircase in Room 2-R.29, Viewed from the South

PLATE 21

(*a*) Ishchali—Detail of the Period II-A Mudbrick Foundation for the Stairway in Room 2-R.29
Showing Bricks Placed on Edge, Seen from the Northeast

(*b*) Ishchali—General View of the Period IV Ninshubura Temple (2-T.29), Seen from the East,
with Portions of the Pivotstone Boxes in 4-T.29 in the Foreground

PLATE 22

Ishchali—Detail of the Northwest Corner of the Main Court (4-R.30), Seen from the South, Showing the Period I-A Pavement
and the Stairs of Periods II-A and III

PLATE 23

Ishchali—Detail of the Northeast Corner of the Main Court (2-T.30), Seen from the South, Showing Period II-B Baked Bricks with the Stamp of Ipiq-Adad II in Foreground, and Pivotstone Box of Room 4-T.30, Period IV, in Upper Background

PLATE 24

(a) Ishchali—General View of the Period IV Well in the Northeast Part of the Main Court (2-T.30),
Viewed from the West

(b) Ishchali—General View of the Shamash "Gate" (Sîn) Temple, Seen from the North

a

b

(*a*) Ishchali—Fragment of an Alabaster Carved Cylindrical Cup or Vase from Kitûtum Room 4-Q.30 and (*b*) Fragment of a Limestone Stela from the Antecella 2-V.30 in the Shamash "Gate" (Sîn) Temple. Scales (*a*) 1:1 and (*b*) 1:4

PLATE 25

PLATE 26

Ishchali—Bronze Statue of a Four-Faced God from the "Serai," Top of Room 7-R.35

PLATE 27

Ishchali—Side and Back Views of the Bronze Statue of a Four-Faced God from the "Serai," Top of Room 7-R.35

PLATE 28

Ishchali—Bronze Statue of a Four-Faced Goddess from the "Serai," Top of Room 7-R.35

PLATE 29

Ishchali—Side and Back Views of the Bronze Statue of a Four-Faced Goddess from the "Serai," Top of Room 7-R.35

PLATE 30

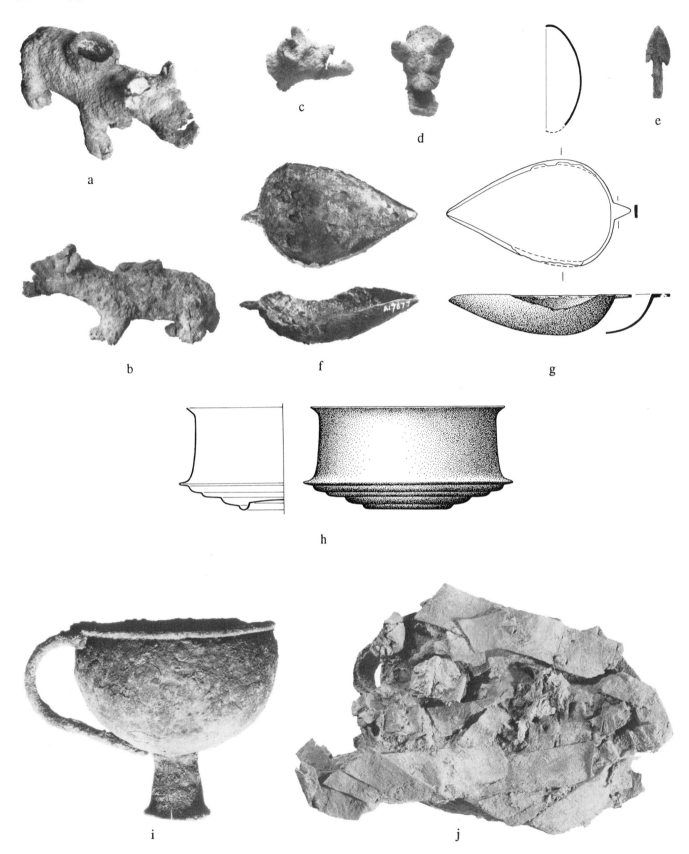

Ishchali—Metal Objects: (*a, b*) Lion-Shaped Lamp, Ish. 34:51 (Top and Side Views), (*c, d*) Lion-Shaped Lamp Fragment, Ish. 34:52 (Side and Front View of Head), (*e*) Arrowhead, Ish. 34:203, (*f, g*) Leaf-Shaped Lamp, Ish. 35:84 (Photographs and Drawings, Side and Top Views), (*h*) Cup, Ish. 35:61 (Reconstruction), (*i*) Cup, Ish. 35:60, and (*j*) Bundle of Metal Bands Wrapped in Cloth, Ish. 35:69. Scale 1:2

PLATE 31

Ishchali—Two Views of Mouflon Bowl Fragment (Ish. 34:117) of Bituminous Stone from 4-Q.30, Floor of Periods III-IV

PLATE 32

Ishchali—Reconstruction of Mouflon Bowl Fragment (Ish. 34:117). (From water-color paintings by G. Rachel Levy)

PLATE 33

Ishchali—Clay Plaques with God-Like Images: (*a-d*) Plaque in Four Pieces, Ish. 34:94, 102, 99, and 105, (*e*) Ish. 35:75, (*f*) Ish. 34:101, (*g*) Ish. 34:100, (*h*) Ish. 34:96, (*i*) Ish. 34:208, (*j*) Ish. 34:5, (*k*) Ish. 34:7, (*l*) Ish. 35:212, (*m*) Ish. 34:286, (*n*) Ish. 34:92, (*o*) Ish. 34:95, (*p*) Ish. 34:113, and (*q*) Ish. 34:59. Scale 1:2

PLATE 34

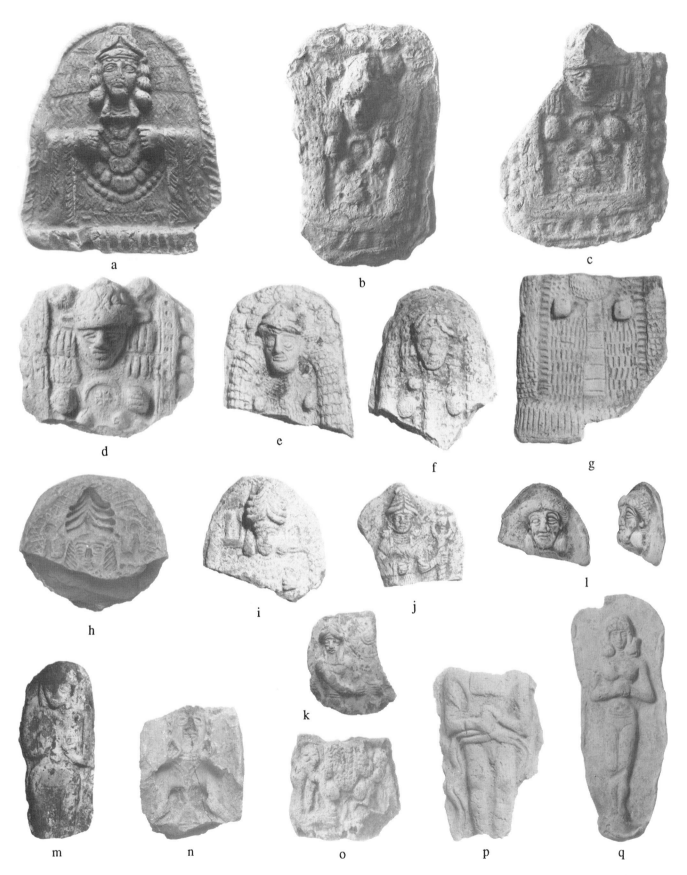

Ishchali—Clay Plaques with God-Like Images: (*a*) Ish. 34:124, (*b*) Ish. 34:40, (*c*) Ish. 34:103 + 110, (*d*) Ish. 35:91, (*e*) Ish. 34:210, (*f*) Ish. 35:222, (*g*) Ish. 35:216, (*h*) Ish. 34:125, (*i*) Ish. 35:220, (*j*) Ish. 35:223, (*k*) Ish. 34:112, (*l*) Ish. 34:91, (*m*) Ish. 35:206, (*n*) Ish. 34:126, (*o*) Ish. 34:114, (*p*) Ish. 35:89, and (*q*) Ish. 35:62. Scale 1:2

PLATE 35

Ishchali—Miscellaneous Clay Plaques: (*a*) Ish. 35:79, (*b*) Ish. 34:41, (*c*) Ish. 34:6, (*d*) Ish. 34:97-98, (*e*) Ish. 35:87, (*f*) Ish. 35:86, (*g*) Ish. 34:104, (*h*) Ish. 35:211, (*i*) Ish. 35:66, (*j*) Ish. 34:111, (*k*) Ish. 34:85, (*l*) Ish. 35:8, (*m*) Ish. 34:90 + 107, (*n*) Ish. 34:106, (*o*) Ish. 34:108, (*p*) Ish. 34:109, and (*q*) Ish. 35:215. Scale 1:2

PLATE 36

Ishchali—Miscellaneous Clay Plaques and Figurines: (*a*) Ish. 34:61, (*b*) Ish. 35:88, (*c*) Ish. 35:221, (*d*) Ish. 34:93, (*e*) Ish. 35:214, (*f*) Ish. 35:213, and (*g*) Ish. 35:93. Scale 1:1

PLATE 37

a

b

c

d

Ishchali—Clay Model Bed Plaques with Goddess Images: (*a*) Ish. 35:3, (*b*) Ish. 34:89, (*c*) Ish. 34:88, and (*d*) Ish. 35:204.
Scale 1:1

PLATE 38

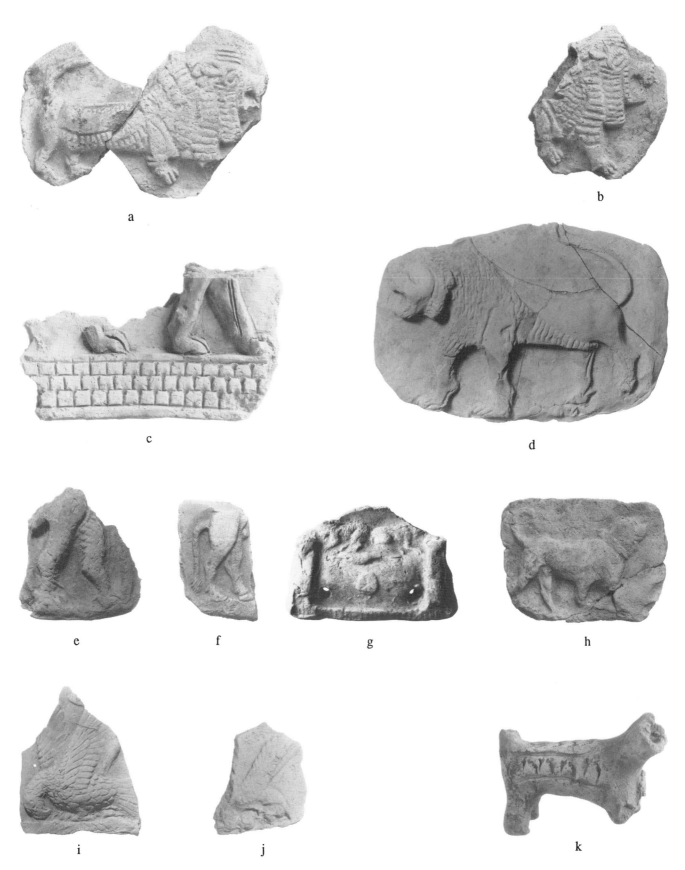

Ishchali—Miscellaneous Clay Plaques and Figurines Depicting Animals and Birds: (*a*) Ish. 34:57, (*b*) Ish. 34:58, (*c*) Ish. 35:40, (*d*) Ish. 35:56, (*e*) Ish. 35:219, (*f*) Ish. 34:116, (*g*) Ish. 34:60, (*h*) Ish. 34:67, (*i*) Ish. 35:218, (*j*) Ish. 35:90, and (*k*) Ish. 35:115. Scale 1:2

PLATE 39

a

b

c

Ishchali—(*a, b*) Cylinder Seal Impressions, Ish. 37:1, 2, and (*c*) Fragment of Terracotta Relief
Depicting a Musician, Ish. 34:79. Scale 1:1

PLATE 40

a

b

c

d

g

e

f

h

Ishchali—Stone Objects: (*a-c*) Human Statuette Fragment, Ish. 34:139 (Right Side, Front, and Left Side Views of Head);
(*d*) Bowl Rim Fragment, Ish. 34:44, (*e, f*) Seated Alabaster Monkey Statuette, Ish. 35:48 (Front and Left Side Views),
and (*g, h*) Alabaster Vessel(?) Fragment, Ish. 34:32 (Top and Side Views). Scale 1:2

PLATE 41

a

b

c

d

e

f

g

h

Ishchali—Stone Objects: (*a-c*) Relief Fragments, Ish. 34:201, 35:207, and 34:202, (*d*) Female(?) Figurine, Ish. 34:80, (*e*) Pig-Shaped Amulet, Ish. 34:130, and (*f-h*) Maceheads, Ish. 35:82, 81, and 80. Scale 1:1

PLATE 42

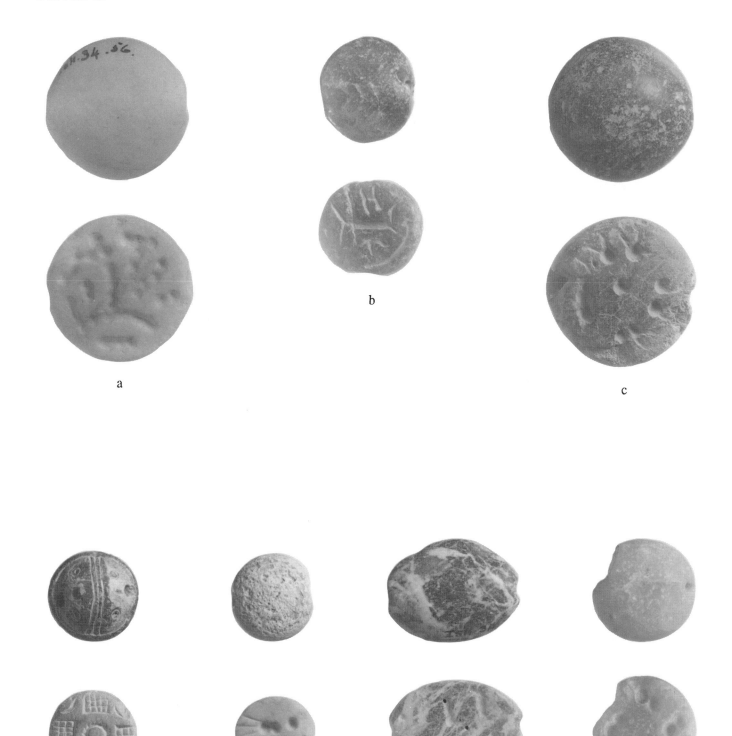

a

b

c

d

e

f

g

Ishchali—Stone Stamp Seals: (*a*) Ish. 34:56, (*b*) Ish. 34:137, (*c*) Ish. 34:73, (*d*) Ish. 34:134, (*e*) Ish. 34:133, (*f*) Ish. 34:135, and (*g*) Ish. 34:136. Scale 1:1

PLATE 43

Ishchali—Stone Beads: (*a*) Ish. 34:138, (*b*) Ish. 34:33, (*c*) Ish. 35:51, and (*d*) Ish. 37:224.
Scales (*a, b*) 1:2, (*c*) 2:1, and (*d*) 1:1

PLATE 44

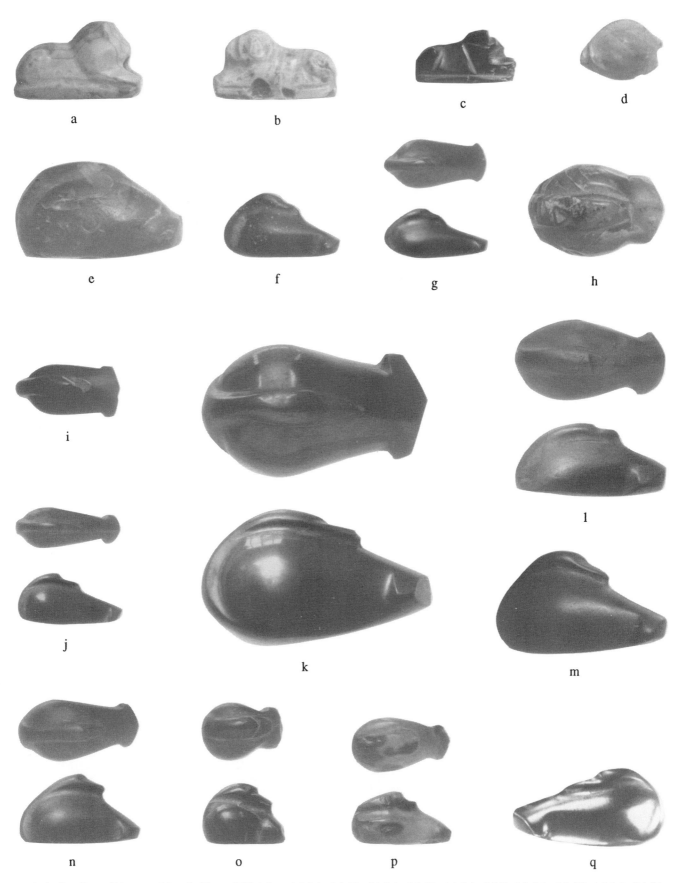

Ishchali—Stone Lion- and Duck-Shaped Weights: (*a*) Ish. 34:42, (*b*) Ish. 34:43, (*c*) Ish. 35:7, (*d*) Ish. 34:29, (*e*) Ish. 34:81, (*f*) Ish. 34:122, (*g*) Ish. 35:33, (*h*) Ish. 34:23, (*i*) Ish. 34:21, (*j*) Ish. 35:12, (*k*) Ish. 35:9, (*l*) Ish. 35:10, (*m*) Ish. 34:62, (*n*) Ish. 35:22, (*o*) Ish. 35:28, (*p*) Ish. 35:41, and (*q*) Ish. 34:8. Scale 2:1

PLATE 45

Ishchali—Stone Date-Shaped Weights: (*a*) Ish. 34:4, (*b*) Ish. 35:47, (*c*) Ish. 35:16, (*d*) Ish. 35:15, (*e*) Ish. 35:44, and (*f*) Ish. 35:18. Scale 2:1

PLATE 46

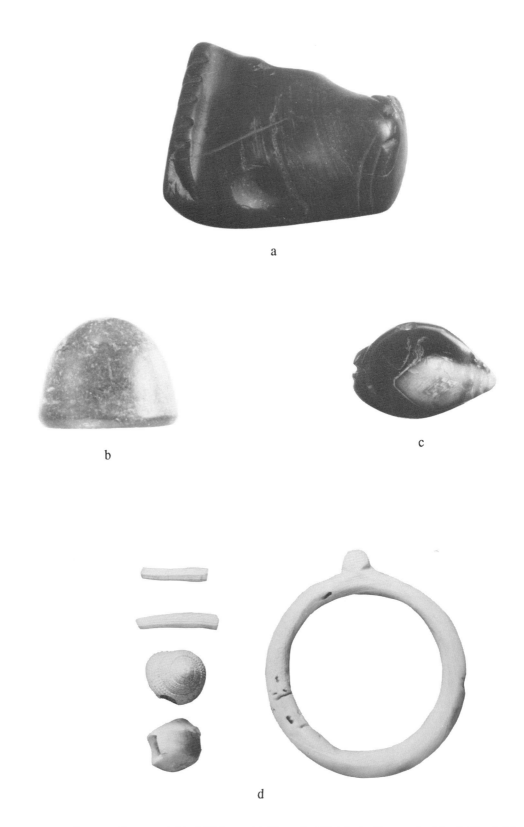

a

b

c

d

Ishchali—Miscellaneous Stone and Shell Objects: (*a*) Hematite Weight in Shape of a Lion's Head, Ish. 35:37, (*b*) Conical-Shaped Weight, Ish. 34:17, (*c*) Transparent Stone Bead, Ish. 35:11, and (*d*) Shell Beads and Ring, Ish. 35:21. Scales (*a-c*) 2:1 and (*d*) 1:1

PART TWO:

EXCAVATIONS AT KHAFĀJAH
MOUNDS B, C, AND D

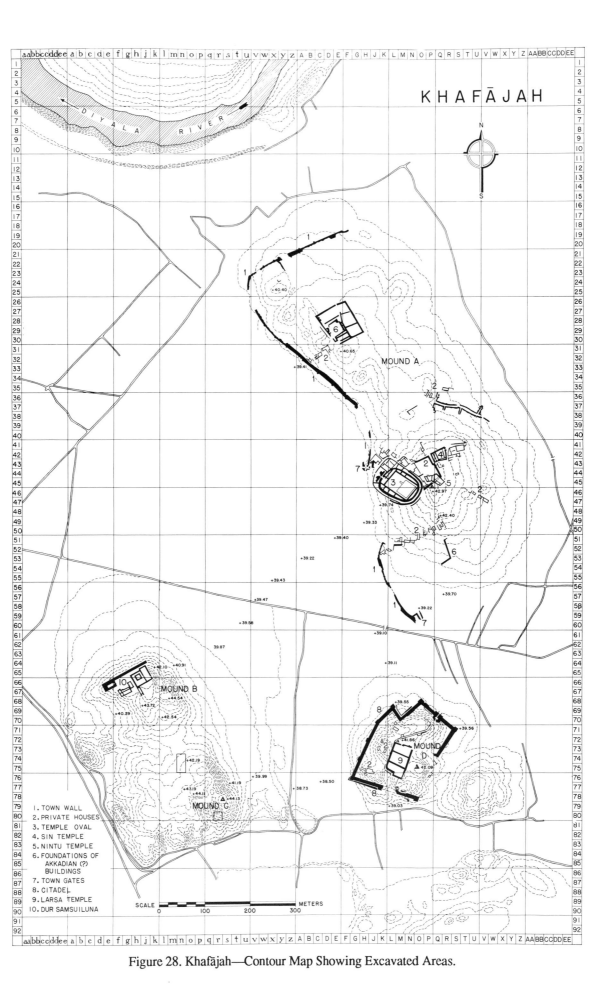

KHAFĀJAH

MOUND A

MOUND B

MOUND C

MOUND D

DIYALA RIVER

1. TOWN WALL
2. PRIVATE HOUSES
3. TEMPLE OVAL
4. SIN TEMPLE
5. NINTU TEMPLE
6. FOUNDATIONS OF
   AKKADIAN (?)
   BUILDINGS
7. TOWN GATES
8. CITADEL
9. LARSA TEMPLE
10. DUR SAMSUILUNA

SCALE   0   100   200   300   METERS

Figure 28. Khafājah—Contour Map Showing Excavated Areas.

CHAPTER 8

KHAFĀJAH MOUND B

by Pinhas Delougaz[†]

DUR SAMSUILUNA

Mound B, located at the southwest end of Khafājah Mound A (fig. 28), could be dated by surface finds to a period later than Mounds C and D. Since two other sites in the Diyala region concession, Tell Asmar and Ishchali, contained extensive ruins of similarly dated periods, no excavations on this mound and Mounds C and D were undertaken during the seven seasons of The Oriental Institute's Iraq expedition in the field except for a few soundings at the highest parts of the mounds after heavy rains when other work was impossible. The first regular excavations on Mound B were undertaken only in the spring of 1937 under the auspices of The University Museum, The University of Pennsylvania and the American School of Oriental Research in Baghdad.

A closer examination of the surface of Mound B near its summit revealed, even before excavations began, the presence of comparatively thick walls which could be discerned by a slight difference in color between the surface above them and the surface above the interior of the rooms (pl. 47). Upon excavation these walls proved to be built of large flat rectangular or square unbaked bricks in contrast to the plano-convex bricks of which the ruins of Mound A consisted. The masonry was fairly good although the bonding was not always regular. The tracing of these ruins was a comparatively easy task for our workmen who were trained for several seasons in the tracing of irregular masonry of the pre-Sargonid remains on Mound A. We had by the end of the season a fairly complete plan of a large building covering an area of over 1,000 square meters in squares g, h, and j, 64-67.

In the second season under the new auspices (1937-38) the excavations on Mound B were continued with a small group of men. This resulted in the discovery of part of a thick fortification wall (pl. 48a) to the northwest of the large building and remains of a second, apparently isolated, building within the same enclosure (fig. 28). However, the most important find on this mound was the discovery in situ (1-e.66) of a complete historical inscription on a baked clay cylinder (pl. 48b) that identified the ruins as those of Dur Samsuiluna (see pls. 49 and 50 for detailed views of the cylinder and impressions of the inscription). The existence of this fortress was previously known from other inscriptions, one of which is practically a duplicate of an inscription found by us (35-T.86). It is now in

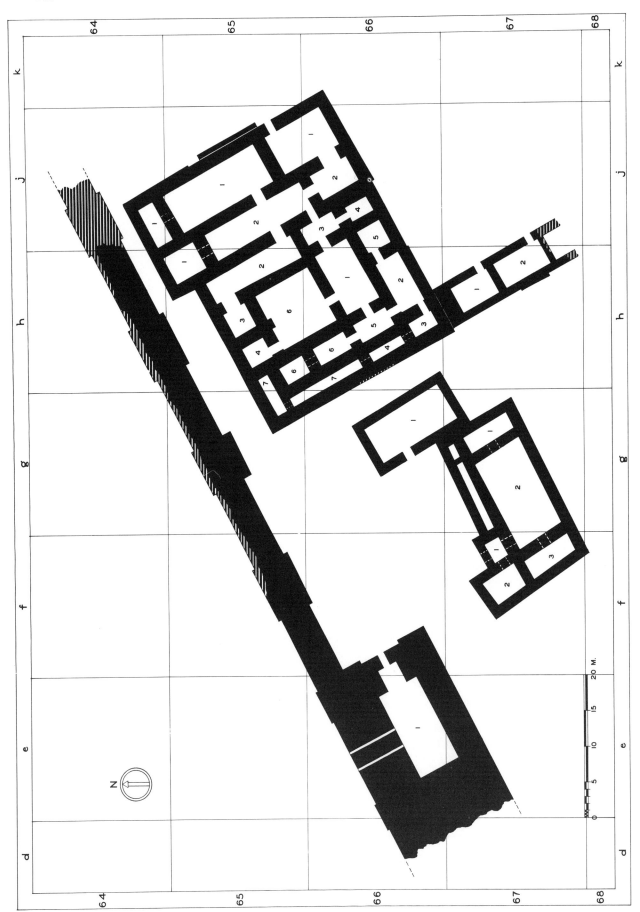

Figure 29. Khafājah Mound B—Plan of the Fortification Wall and Buildings of Dur Samsuiluna.

Berlin and was published by Dr. Poebel (1933/34), but its precise findspot is a matter of speculation. It is most probable that the previously published inscription came from the same location as did the one we found even though it was supposedly found at Babylon.

Though the outline of the buildings on this mound is fairly clear it should be noted that in most cases only the walls were traced in each of the rooms while the rooms themselves were not completely cleared. The slope of the ground toward the northwest accounts for the building remains at the southeastern part being much better preserved than those on the other side; in fact, only the foundations of the northwestern side of the larger buildings were found while the retaining wall was denuded below foundations and we were able to restore the main length of its northwestern side only by continuation of the line of the partly preserved brickwork in square f.65 and by considering the course of the inner face of the same wall. The shape of the mound is a result of the position of these ruins. The contour map (see fig. 28) shows that in k.63 the mound forms approximately a right angle, its side facing the northeast. Just before this point in j.64 the brickwork of the enclosure wall completely disappears. The shape of the mound, however, suggests that at a point not far from this, this wall probably turned a right angle and ran parallel to the northeastern side of the large building.

The plan of the building (see fig. 29) is fairly regular and presented several interesting points. Only one entrance existed into the hall. This was from the northeastern side through 1-j.66. It was in no way emphasized architecturally. From this room a rather wide doorway led into a smaller room 2-j.66 and from the latter a doorway of normal width led in its turn into a large and low room, 2-j.65. A doorway from this large room in its southwestern wall led into a suite of two rooms, 2- and 3-h.65. Another doorway in its northeastern wall opened into a large and regular room (1-j.65) approximately 6 × 14.50 meters which was undoubtedly the main room of this part of the building. A smaller chamber 1-j.64 was situated to the north of room 1-j.65 in the northern corner of the building. Northwest of 2-j.65 was one more room 1-j.65 which is the last room in this unit. No doorway into this was found but apparently it was connected with 2-j.65 through a doorway in the latter northwestern wall. It is interesting to note that six of the rooms mentioned above were situated in a double row in a rectangle of approximately 15 × 32 meters which projected northwest approximately 3.50 meters from the rest of the building to the southwest. The second unit of the building was also roughly rectangular and measured approximately 24 × 29 meters. Apart from the two rooms 2- and 3-h.65 which were obviously connected with the unit, the main part of which was in the northeast side of the building, this area contained a well-planned group of rooms which were undoubtedly living quarters. Only one entrance led into this second unit from j.65 through a small antechamber 3-j.66 and thence to a large room 1-h.66. This, in its turn, communicated with a roughly square space approximately 8 × 9 meters which seems to have been a court open to the sky, 6-j.65. It is interesting, however, that unlike similar courts in other ancient buildings, which usually were surrounded by a series of rooms around them, this court had only one more door leading to a rather small and apparently unimportant room 4-h.65. A third doorway in the southwestern wall of 1-h.66 led into a small room, 5-h.66, which was one of three intercommunicating rooms, 6-h.66 and 6-h.65, parallel to the southwestern side of the building. A doorway through the southeastern wall of 5-h.66

connected the latter with a suite of rooms alongside the southeastern side of the building of which the larger 2-h.66 was the central room and had two smaller rooms, 3-h.66 and 5-j.66, on both its sides. Finally, a series of three narrow and oblong spaces, two alongside the southwestern wall of the building, 4-h.66 and 7-h.66, and one oblong space along side its northwestern wall, 7-h.65, conclude the series of these rooms.

The few objects recovered from this building gave no clue as to its use. However, the plan can be interpreted as that of a secular building rather than that of a temple. That this was not one of the regular private houses of the city is indicated by its size and the exceptionally thick walls and perhaps, also, by its position at the highest part of the mound and presumably in a corner formed by the fortification wall. We are led to assume, therefore, that this might have been the palace or the residence of the governor of the city or of the fort. This assumption is supported to some extent by the plan of the building itself which, as we have seen, consists of two distinct units. Undoubtedly the six rooms at the northeastern end of the building together with the two rooms, 2- and 3-h.65, were the formal part of the building. The largest room in the whole building, 1-j.65, could have been the audience chamber with a small room for private use behind it (1-j.64). The other rooms of this unit might have served for officials and perhaps archives. The entrance into the second unit is so planned that it can be reached from the outside through the two rooms 1-and 2-j.66, which probably served only as guard rooms. On the other hand, the first formal unit of the building could be reached without one having to be outside the building. The isolated room, 4-j.66, near the antechamber, could have been a guard's room where a guard on duty could watch and control the approach to the rest of this building. The actual living quarters were probably confined to the three rooms alongside the southeastern wall and the row of three rooms parallel to the southwestern side of the building. The largest room in this second unit, 1-h.66, was probably also for more formal use as indicated by its size and proximity to the entrance. Area 6-h.65 was obviously an open court which was probably reserved for domestic use for which room 4-h.65 to the northwest of it might also have been reserved. The latter might have been a store room while the court perhaps served for preparing food. The function of the three narrow rooms is not clear. Such narrow rooms often occur in public buildings of similar or even earlier date. In most cases they are taken to be no more than spaces between two series of walls built probably more for strategical than for practical purposes. Perhaps one of them could have served as a base for a stairway to the roof of the building. The narrowness of these rooms certainly made roof construction comparatively easy and inexpensive. It is possible to assume, therefore, that in some cases such rooms were built not for their own use but for the additional solid surface of roof which they provided which could have been used as a terrace while the roofs over the larger rooms were perhaps not solid enough for such use.

At the outside, this building does not seem to have been ornamented. The monotony of its straight walls was, however, relieved by the projection of one part of the building at its northeastern corner. Also there was a shallow recess in the brickwork on its southeastern side and possibly a similar recess on the southwestern side. At the northeastern side there was originally also a very shallow recess in the brickwork. It seems, however, that the later part of the brickwork here was thickened forming a shallow buttress to the right of the main entrance. Against the southern corner of the building a few rooms were added at some later time but obviously while the main building was still in use. These rooms, of which two were cleared (1- and 2-h.65), were fairly large and regular but their walls were somewhat thinner than the walls of the main building. These rooms were not intercommunicating and the position of the doorways near their southeastern corners indicate, perhaps, that they were isolated rooms or storerooms. Their southwest walls were aligned with that of the main building and possibly faced a street or an open space in the town.

A group of rooms southwest of the main building was separated from it by a passage or street approximately 3.50 meters wide. Apparently this group of rooms consisted of two separate units one of which was a large single room, 1-g.66; the thickness of the brickwork between it and the second group of rooms to the southwest suggests that this room was added against the northeastern corner of the other group. It was also somewhat higher and the traces of a doorway into it were found; of the second group only the foundations were found and the arrangement of doorways must be purely conjectural. The largest room in the second unit was 2-g.67. It was flanked on both sides by smaller rooms, 1-g.67 and 3-f.67. At the northwestern side of this room was a long narrow corridor divided by a thin partition wall and two more rooms 1- and 2-f.67 at the western end. If the entrance was through 1-f.67, then 2-f.67 could have served as a guard room while the long passage might have contained a stairway to the roof. The arrangement of rooms and the size of 2-g.67 suggest that this unit had some official use rather than its serving as a dwelling house.

The fortification wall was found only to the northwest of this group of buildings at a point where both the inner and outer faces were still preserved; we could ascertain that the thickness of this wall was 4.70 meters. At intervals varying from 10 to 12 meters the walls were thickened by buttresses on both sides to a thickness of 6 to 6.50 meters. In square e.66 the brickwork was thickened to approximately 7 meters and against the inner face of the wall there was a large oblong room, 1-e.66, surrounded by thick brickwork. In the northeastern side of this room a rabbeted gateway led from it into the open space within the fortified enclosure. In the foundations, a similar gateway 3 meters wide was found in the brickwork of the outer wall to the northwest of this room. However, above the foundations this passage was completely blocked by solid brickwork. It is possible that this passage in the brickwork was left for carrying the building material while the fort was being built and that it was blocked up and built over when the building neared completion. However, the two symmetrically spaced shallow buttresses on both sides of the doorway, the exceptional thickness of the brickwork, and the presence of 1-e.66 suggest that a gateway existed here when the building was actually in use. It is possible, however, that the actual gateway contained a flight of stairs or a ramp which was higher than the lowest courses of the brickwork which were preserved. To the southwest of this gateway the brickwork had completely disappeared. However, traces of it still remained as a slight difference in color between the soil into which it had disintegrated and the debris inside the fortified area. One can distinguish this light difference and the roughly straight line between the differently colored earths. However, this difference is apparent only from a certain height and when the surface of the mound is in process of drying after a rain, it disappears completely most of the time and the only indication it provides is that the fortification wall originally ran for a certain length beyond the gateway in approximately a straight line. The point at which this wall turned could not be ascertained but if the contour of the mound can at all serve as an indication as to the original extension of the building on it, we might expect such a turn approximately in square b.68.

The inscribed cylinder which provided the evidence for the identification of this building was found in the northeast corner of the gate room, 1-e.66, at the level below the actual floor. Plate 48a is a general outside view of this room seen from the northeast. On plate 48b the workman is shown squatting on the floor which is only a few centimeters below the surface of the mound and which completely disappears at the other end (southwestern) of the room. It is seen also that the foundations were excavated below this floor. A closer observation will show that the surface of the wall at this point is damaged. The cylinder was found against the brickwork of the foundations. The northern doorjamb is shown to the right of the skeleton's feet. It is to be seen that the brickwork between the cylinder and the northern doorjamb was partly cut away by the hole dug for a grave. The feet and part of the legs of the skeleton still lay in this hole dug in the brickwork. The state of preservation and the position of the skeleton clearly indicate that this is not an ancient burial and it seems most likely that the cylinder now in Berlin was found while this burial was being dug. The placing of more than one such inscribed report at the foundations of a building is not uncommon. Plate 47a and b are general views of the palace seen from the northwest. In the foreground of both views is the shallow brickwork left of the foundations of the enclosure wall. The two workmen are standing behind the inner face of the same wall and in front of the northwestern wall of the palace. The central court, 6-h.65, is shown in the background to the left of the workman on plate 47b. In the distance shown on plate 47a and b, the dumps of Mound D can be distinguished.

CHAPTER 9

KHAFĀJAH MOUND C
by T. A. Holland

INTRODUCTION

Mound C, situated to the southeast of Mound B, is in close proximity to Mound B and is roughly similar to that mound in both height at its summit and in its overall dimensions. Although no major excavations were undertaken on the site, two large area soundings were made in grid squares n.74–75 and r.80 as well as a few unidentified soundings elsewhere on the mound. Surface and unstratified material also was included in the register of finds for seasons V, VI, and VIII (see app. 5, pp. 225–29).

With regard to any architectural details encountered in the soundings, it would appear, after a careful search of both The Oriental Institute and The University Museum of Pennsylvania archives, that plans and sections either were never made or were lost during the interval between the conclusion of excavations some fifty years ago and today. The register of finds certainly indicates that at least one house was found in square r.80, which was considered important as it contained one Old Babylonian cylinder seal,[1] and four pottery vessels which have been published,[2] as well as an unpublished bronze sickle (Reg. VI:88) ascribed to the period of Hammurabi.

THE FINDS

The pottery vessels[3] already published from sounding n.74–75, attributed to the Old Babylonian period, would now appear to date rather to the early Kassite period based upon more recent pottery evidence from sites such as Nippur.[4] Again, the one published

---

1. Seal no. 426, see Frankfort 1955, pl. 40:426. Note that this seal has been incorrectly attributed to Mound B.

2. See numbers VIII: 216, 217, 218, and 232 in appendix 5.

3. See Delougaz 1952, pls. 132a–c, 161, and 185.

4. Cf. Gibson et al. 1978, pp. 80ff., pls. 69 and 70:1–2, 8–10. But since the latest Old Babylonian pottery is still only slightly attested, this dating may not hold. Evidence from Tell ed-Dēr may allow the Khafājah types to date to the end of the Old Babylonian period (pers. comm. McG. Gibson).

cylinder seal from n.74–75 is attributed to the Old Babylonian period.[5] References to other already published finds from Mound C are listed in appendices 5 and 6. Previously unpublished finds from Mound C are presented in this volume on pls. 61–68.

5. Seal no. 427, see Frankfort 1955, pl. 40:427. Note that this seal also has been incorrectly attributed to Mound B.

CHAPTER 10

KHAFĀJAH MOUND D
by Pinhas Delougaz[†]

THE CITADEL

Since our main interest in the excavations at Khafājah lay in the elucidation of certain problems concerned with the pre-Sargonid period, excavations on Mound D (see fig. 28), which could be identified by surface finds as containing ruins of the Larsa period, were never regularly conducted for any considerable length of time. All the information which we possess from this mound and the plans of its ruins were obtained in sporadic operations lasting only a few days at a time after a spell of rain when excavations of the lower and less well-built ruins on Mound A were impossible.

Nearly all of the surface of Mound D was included within a thick enclosure wall which could be traced along the northeastern, northwestern, southwestern, and partly southeastern sides. The area thus fortified was undoubtedly a citadel of considerable importance. It was in the shape of an irregular polygon over 200 meters long and over 150 meters wide. Of the thick enclosure wall, which varied in thickness from 7 to nearly 12 meters (see fig. 30), only the foundations remained in most parts. However, the foundations apparently had features of all the details of the denuded wall, thus enabling us to gain a fairly clear idea about its appearance.

Only one entrance into the citadel was found and this was in its northeastern side in square Q.69 (pls. 51b and 52a, b). This main gateway was situated in the middle of thickened brickwork of the wall which had a projecting tower. The surface of this tower was decorated with small double recessed niches (see fig. 30 and pl. 52a and b). The two long screen walls flanking the entrance, 1- and 3-Q.69 might have originally served as a parapet for a stairway or a ramp of which, however, no traces were found. The actual face of the entrance through the wall was destroyed by water running off from the higher part of the mound and is shown restored on the plan by broken lines. A pottery drain ran through this gateway (pl. 51b) and though now exposed and partly destroyed it was obviously at a certain depth below the surface at the time the gateway was used. A large room, 1-Q.70, formed a gate chamber which opened in its turn into what also seems to have been a room, 2-Q.70. Both are surrounded by thick brickwork and were obviously parts of the fortified gate. The area marked 1 in square P.70 (fig. 30) seems to have been a small open

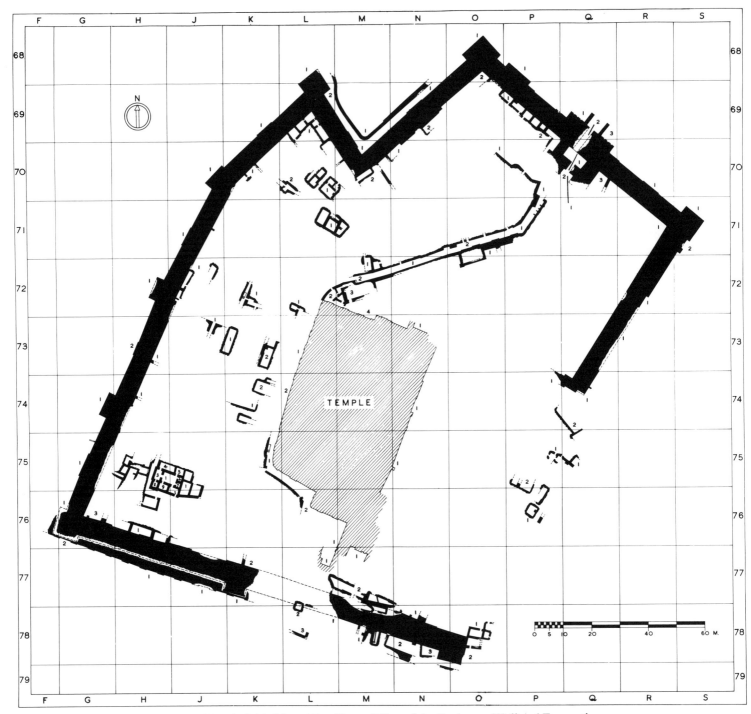

Figure 30. Khafājah Mound D—General Plan of the Enclosure Wall and Excavations.

space in the town from which at least two streets branched off. One was situated parallel to the northeastern wall as far as square O.70 but was not completely traced. The other was a long street straight in its main line and extending through squares P.71, O.71, N.72, and M.72 toward a large building in the center of the citadel which was identified from inscriptions on a group of tablets found in it as a temple of Sîn. The general outline of this building is shown on figure 30 as a hatched area but is reproduced on a larger scale on figure 31 and is discussed below. As mentioned above, the entire area within the citadel could not be excavated.

The numerous isolated soundings in which we tried to excavate whole rooms or groups of rooms and to ascertain the thickness of their walls seem to indicate that at least the area north and west of the Sîn temple and the street was occupied by private houses, the Sîn temple being most likely the largest and most important public building within the citadel. Several doorways opening off of the northern side of the long street leading from the gateway to the temple are of a size that indicate the buildings into which they led were also private houses and, therefore, the area beyond this street was not further investigated. No such doorways were found on the south side of the street, but a portion of a comparatively thick wall located in squares O-P.71 with three shallow buttresses and a large room adjoining it may indicate that here were the remains of a second though possibly smaller public building. However, due to the slope of the mound only the lowest courses of brickwork were found here and it is doubtful whether the rest of the building can be traced much further south. The area north of the temple was somewhat higher and the walls of the groups of rooms around 1-L.71 were found standing to a height between 0.80 to 1 meter and in some cases doorways were easily traced. However, even on this higher part of the mound the remaining brickwork was only that of foundations in which no doorways existed and the actual walls were completely destroyed. In all these soundings it was apparent that earlier building remains are to be found below those which are now exposed on the surface and that this part of the site must have been occupied for a considerable length of time. No deep soundings were undertaken here and we did not know whether this mound was occupied simultaneously with Mound A in pre-Sargonid times and what is the earliest date of its occupation. Most of the soundings in the area west of the temple were carried on only long enough to ascertain the character of the buildings in its vicinity and represent, therefore, isolated rooms, parts of rooms, or single walls.

Only near the southwestern corner of the citadel in H.75 and J.75 did we excavate a complete house (see fig. 30). This is bordered by a narrow street on its western side and possibly a second one on its southern side. The only entrance into this house is from the southern side through a single vestibule room, 1-J.76, into a central court, 1-H.75, which in its turn communicates with a suite of three rooms (2 to 4-H.75) to the west and north and four smaller single rooms (5 to 7-J.75 and 9-H.75) grouped on other sides apart from the vestibule. This house, though of modest size and obviously of no special importance, is well planned within an approximately square area of 10 × 10 meters and is typical of the better planned houses of the Larsa period.

The street leading from the gateway to the temple was apparently the main street within the citadel. A passage of similar width perhaps ran along the western side of the Sîn temple and parts of it were found at 1-K.75 and 2-L.75. Possibly narrower alleys and passage ways existed between the houses or groups of houses and of these the narrow passage around the house described above in squares H-J.75-76 is perhaps typical. No passage ways seem to have existed along the inner faces of the thick fortification walls for in all places where we investigated, for instance, in P.69 near the gateway, in L.69, one corner of the citadel, and in J.72 and H.76, we found groups of rooms abutting directly on the wall, which in all cases mentioned above actually served as a wall of each room. The implication of this is that all these rooms were built while the citadel already existed contrary to other instances where thick fortification walls were built to surround and protect an already existing group of buildings. The irregularity of the citadel, especially at its northern end, might therefore have been caused by some consideration other than the area of buildings which it had to enclose. A fairly thick and well-built wall in squares M.69 and N.69, running parallel to the outer face of the citadel wall at this corner, had no doorways in it and seemed to have no cross walls which would indicate the presence of rooms. Apparently it is a part of the fortification scheme, but we can offer no satisfactory explanation as to its probable use.

The northeastern wall in which the gateway is situated is perfectly straight and measures exactly 100 meters from the end of one corner tower to the other. The thickness of the wall itself is approximately 6.80 meters and the towers project between 2 to 2.80 meters from its main brickwork. The towers are not quite symmetrical; the one at the eastern corner (1-S.71, pl. 36a) is approximately 8 × 8 meters while that situated on the northern corner (1-O.68) is somewhat larger. The gateway was built exactly in the middle of this wall. The total length of the projecting brickwork or decorated towers in which the gateway is situated is nearly 20 meters. Two more shallow buttresses approximately 4 meters long are situated on each side of these towers; their brickwork projects only about 40 centimeters from the brickwork of the main wall. Two similarly shallow buttresses were symmetrically spaced between these secondary buttresses and the corner towers, one in 1-R.70 and the second in 1-P.68. The latter, however, had been covered partly by a more pronounced buttress approximately 10 meters long and projecting 1.60 meters from the surface of the wall, thus disturbing, to some extent, the symmetrical appearance of the front wall. In both corners, in squares O.68 and S.71, the walls turned toward the southwest. In both, the walls form an obtuse angle with the front wall; the northwestern more noticeably so than the southeastern one. The southeastern wall could be traced to a length of over 17 meters only. Parts of its inner and outer face have disappeared and are shown restored with a dotted line on the plan (see fig. 30). In Q.74 the brickwork of this wall completely disappeared and further soundings along the line which it should have taken if it were to meet the remaining wall discovered in O.78 produced only remains of thin walls, apparently of private houses. During the time at our disposal we were unable to investigate this area more thoroughly and it is, therefore, impossible to know whether at this point the wall was ruined or whether it turned at right angles to the northwest or southeast. The latter seems more likely since such a turn would have been in keeping with a symmetrical arrangement of the citadel, for a similar turn was observed on the other side in square M.70 where the northwestern wall, built in a straight line for approximately 60 meters from the northern corner, was constructed toward the northwest at not quite a right angle at M.70 (pl. 53a). This section of the wall, approximately 33 meters long, ended in a square tower 8 × 8 meters (1-L.68, pl. 53b). At this point the wall was angled again to the southwest and was built in a straight line for approximately 56 meters before ending in the brickwork of a projecting tower 1-J.70 (pl. 54a). Halfway between these two towers was a shallow buttress, 1-K.69, approximately 7 meters wide and projecting approximately 0.50 meters from the surface of the wall. A similar buttress also occurred halfway between the tower 1-O.68 and the corner 1-M.70. Another buttress northwest of corner 1-M.70 was not situated centrally between the corner and the tower 1-L.68.

From 1-J.70 the wall made again a slight deviation from the direction towards the south and continued approximately in a straight line for a distance of about 130 meters into square F.76 (pl. 54b). This space was relieved by two towers 1-H.72 and 1-G.74 and apparently also by a corner tower 1-G.76. The spaces between these towers were relieved by shallow buttresses 1-J.71, 2-H.73, and 1-G.75. A pottery drain was laid through the wall in square J.75. At the southern end of the citadel the wall attained a thickness of 11 meters. However, its outer surface was found to have been decorated at intervals of about 4 meters only by small buttresses approximately 2.50 meters wide and projecting only about 40 centimeters from the face of the wall. There were some indications that the wall face thus decorated did not belong to the same period as the main length of the citadel wall but probably was a later addition built against the earlier wall. This view is supported by some brickwork found at the back of one of such buttresses at 1-K.77, which we suggest may have been the face of one of the projecting towers of the original wall on this side. Accordingly, the face of the wall is restored with a dotted line on the plan which connects the fragment of brickwork in square K.77 with the restored corner tower 1-G.76 to the west and the remaining brickwork of the wall as found in squares M.78 and N.78. In squares L.77 and partly K.77, where there was a depression in the present surface of the mound through which the rain water ran into the fields, the brickwork of the enclosure wall seems to have been completely destroyed. Fragmentary brickwork found here (2- and 3-L.78) apparently belongs to some earlier occupation. In square N.78 the brickwork of the enclosure wall was partly destroyed by some later buildings, the plan of which is not clear. It seems, however, that at this point houses existed outside the citadel, perhaps when the latter stood in ruins. Rooms 2- and 3-N.78 and a group of rooms, 1- and 2-O.78, apparently belonged to such intrusive houses. If this view is correct it may also indicate that the building remains in squares P.75 and P.76 are of the same nature and were built after the wall at this point had been ruined.

The building as a whole can be dated to the Larsa period by the types of pottery vessels found in the various soundings. However, a more precise dating connecting this citadel with certain building strata at Tell Asmar and Ishchali was provided by a hoard of 112 tablets found in the upper strata of the Sîn temple, room 2-N.74[1] and which are discussed by R. Harris (1954).[2] The military character of the whole building is demonstrated vividly, apart from its general plan, by a great number of roughly made pottery maceheads found in front and in the vicinity of the gate (pls. 52 and 57b). The high proportion of broken specimens of this crude, but nevertheless efficient, weapon gives witness to a fierce battle in front of the gateway, perhaps the last before this stronghold was captured and finally destroyed.

---

1. [Note that the findspot for the tablets given by Harris, rooms 3- and 4-L.75, is not in accord with the locus 2-N.74 as given here and in the general discussion of the room presented on pp. 221f. by Delougaz. As the tablets are described below as coming from the "later building period" and on the evidence of the photographic record (pl. 58a), it would appear that the findspot should be room 2-N.74.—Gen. Ed.].

2. See also Harris 1955, pp. 31-88, 91-105, and Jacobsen in Harris 1955, pp. 70-81 and 106-20.

Figure 31. Khafājah Mound D—Plan of the Larsa Sîn Temple.

LARSA SÎN TEMPLE

The principal building in the citadel, as stated above, occupied a central position within it and covered an area approximately 45 × 75 meters. The plan of this building is given on figure 31 and a photographic view is shown on plate 55 and in closer detail on plates 56 and 57a. Two building periods of this large edifice could be distinguished. The later building period, which is represented by foundations only, is shown in solid black while the building remains of the earlier building is shown with horizontal hatching.

The Later Building Period

Apparently the later rebuilding was limited to an area of approximately 28 × 45 meters in the middle of the larger area, for no traces of similar foundations were found on either side of it. It is indeed possible that part of the building at the northwestern side was used simultaneously with the new rebuilding and that the foundations as found represent only the remains of a part of the building whose floors were artificially raised above the rest of the building as observed in the Kitîtum temple of approximately the same date at Ishchali (see chap. 1, fig. 2). The general plan of these foundations is quite regular and comparatively simple though it must be said that since the stumps of walls of the earlier building period were preserved to the same height as the foundations and were of exactly the same width and height of similar types of sun-dried bricks it was not always easy to distinguish between the remains of the two periods during the progress of excavation. Though we did not attempt to reconstruct the doorways between the different rooms it is not difficult to imagine how the rooms were grouped. Roughly we can divide the plan as represented by the foundations into two units, one positioned around an open court, 7-M.74, in which the main room is apparently 5-M.74, and a second unit with 1-L.74 as the central and principal room. The series of small rooms, 1-M.74 and 8-, 9-, and 10-L.74, formed a typical row of rooms similar to those usually found near the exterior wall of this type of building; they can equally be considered as part of the first unit or part of the second unit. Two similar rows of rooms existed against the northwestern and southeastern ends of the building. The largest room in the whole of this group was 1-L.74, a regular oblong room approximately 5 meters wide and 16 meters long. It was undoubtedly roofed. The only features of interest in it were two buttresses against each of its long walls. Those against the northwestern wall were approximately 1.50 meters long and projected about 25 centimeters from the surface of the wall dividing this wall into nearly three equal bays. Those against the southeastern wall were only 60 centimeters wide and were placed approximately 3 meters from the northeastern and southeastern corners respectively. Room 5-M.74 was of similar proportions but somewhat smaller. At the middle of its southeastern wall there was also a shallow projecting buttress similar to those against the northwestern wall of 1-L.74. At the northern end the brickwork of this building period was completely destroyed and the arrangement of the rooms here is uncertain. At the northern side small areas of a floor level, apparently the lowest floor belonging to the rebuilding, were found immediately below the surface in room 2-N.74. On the 2-N.74 floor (fig. 31, pl. 58a), which escaped detrition, we found a hoard of 112 tablets which obviously belonged to a temple archive.[3]

The Earlier Building Period

The plan of the central part of the earlier building period is the least clear since much of the brickwork was cut away by the trenches dug in preparation for the later rebuilding. The outer face of the northwestern wall was, however, preserved to a length of over 42 meters in an unbroken line decorated with regularly spaced buttresses. This indicates that the earlier building must have been roughly a square including the middle as well as the northeastern parts. The stumps of walls in rooms 1-L.74 and 5-M.74 with fragments of cross walls indicate that in some respects the later rebuilding followed the plan of the building below. Stumps of walls were also found in rooms 3- to 6-L.74 and rooms 10- and 11-L.74 contain wall fragments which are probably the remains of two long perpendicular walls. The brickwork in the other rooms to the east is more fragmentary and cannot be connected. The only feature of major interest in the eastern room 9-M.74 was an oven (pl. 59a).

The northeastern part of the building was fairly well preserved and in most cases the doorways between the rooms could be identified. Apparently no connection existed between the northeastern unit and the central unit of rooms for no doorway was found in the southwestern wall. The main entrance from the outside was in square M.73 through the vestibule 3-M.73. This main entrance could be approached from the long street through the small rooms 2-L.72 and 6-7-M.72 which seems rather inadequate considering the size and importance of the building. We may assume, therefore, that this was a secondary approach to the temple and that possibly an open space existed in front of the main entrance which was more easily accessible from the northeastern side. This main entrance served only the rooms to the south and east of it which probably were grouped around a small open court 7-M.73. A group of five rooms west of the entrance, though intercommunicating between themselves, was isolated from the group of rooms to the east and perhaps originally communicated with the central part of the temple. A third section of the building, which also was included in the area surrounded by a thick buttressed wall, seemed to have been isolated from the rest of the building and consisted in itself of two distinct parts. It would appear that a narrow passage existed between this southern section and the central part of the temple as both faces of the walls forming this passage were found intact at 6-M.75. A small pavement of kiln baked bricks was found at the southeastern end of the passage at 1-N.75 and a short stairway, also built of baked bricks, led from the passage into room 11-M.75. This room apparently served as an antechamber to a group of rooms forming roughly a rectangle 20 × 24 meters limited by the passage way in square M.75 to the north, the straight wall west of 13-M.75 and 4-M.76 to the east, a section of a buttressed wall with its corner at 2-L.76 to the south, and a wall running perpendicular to it and continuing east of rooms 14- to 16-L.75 to the west. A second unit was limited by this first unit to the east, by the central part of the building to the north, and a somewhat buttressed wall with a rounded corner at 1-K.75, which abutted against the western corner of the central part of the building at 3-K.74 and the first group

3. See Harris 1954, p. 9.

of rooms east of 3-L.76. The most interesting features in the first group of rooms were traces of large vaulted tombs built of specially made kiln baked bricks in rooms 1- and 10-M.75. Perhaps other rooms in the same group also contained such structures at a lower level which was not reached. Plate 58b shows the vaulted tomb in room 1-M.75. The tombs were destroyed and robbed in antiquity and no objects of any value were found in them. Area 1 in square M.76 probably was a small open court around which the other rooms were grouped. Against its southeastern corner there was a large pottery vat and a pottery drain which led through the wall and opened onto a small pavement of baked brick partly plastered with bitumen. Two entrances existed from the first into the second group of rooms, one was from the court 1-M.76 through a small vestibule 17-L.75, and the other connected the group of four rooms, 1-, 7–9-M.75, which had no communication with the main group of rooms to the east. The inner walls in this western part were considerably thinner and less carefully built than those in the first group. Most of the rooms, especially those near the western corner, were very small. Four large pottery vats, two of them in 13-L.75, one in 3-L.75, and one in 16-L.75, may indicate that at least some of these rooms may have served as store rooms, otherwise there is no clue as to their use since the rather irregular arrangement of the rooms themselves is not at all illuminating.

A third group of rooms south and east of the southern corner of the area included within the buttressed wall were apparently not connected with the temple. The excavations, therefore, were not continued here and no general plan was obtained. However, an interesting find occurred near 1-L.76 where both sides of a doorway leading into 6-M.76 were decorated by projecting buttresses forming two narrow niches on both sides. In the southern of these niches we found remains of a pottery lion with the lower part still in position (pl. 59b). Apparently a second lion decorated the other side of the entrance, for the fragments found in front of the doorway and at a distance from it as far as 2-L.76 certainly belonged to more than one beast. Plate 60 shows a restoration of one of the animals, the darker parts indicate the parts actually found, and the lighter parts are the artist's reconstruction made in the 1930s before similar figurines had been excavated elsewhere.[4] Other finds from the Sîn temple are illustrated on plates 61f, g, 62a, b, d-f, 65f, 66f, and 67a. See app. 5 and 6, pp. 225–35, for objects published elsewhere and other finds not illustrated here.

4. Cf. similar types from Tell Harmal. See Baqir 1946, pp. 23f. and "fig. 5" (= unnumbered plate), Basmachi 1975-76, no. 107, and Frankfort 1956, p. 57, figure 22 and note 28.

APPENDIX 5

CATALOGUE OF OBJECTS FROM KHAFĀJAH
MOUNDS B, C, and D BY SEASONS

Season / No.	Object	Mound / Locus	Plate / Reference

1935 EXCAVATIONS (The Oriental Institute of The University of Chicago)

Season / No.	Object	Mound / Locus	Plate / Reference
V:253	Plaque	D, Sounding (Surface)	62c

1935 / 36 EXCAVATIONS (The Oriental Institute of The University of Chicago)

Season / No.	Object	Mound / Locus	Plate / Reference
VI:72	Cylinder Seal	D, Sîn Temple	OIP 72, pl. 40:430
VI:73	Cylinder Seal	D, Sîn Temple	OIP 72, pl. 40:431
VI:74	Metal Plate	D, Sîn Temple	—
VI:75	Plaque	D, Sîn Temple	61g
VI:76	Beads	D, Sîn Temple	—
VI:77	Sculptor's Workpiece	D, Sîn Temple	66f
VI:78	Arrowhead	D, Sîn Temple	65f
VI:79	Plaque	D, Sîn Temple	62b
VI:80	Figurine Mold	D, Sîn Temple	61f
VI:81	Plaque	D, Sîn Temple	62a
VI:85	Spear Blades	C, (?)	64j
VI:86	Spear Blades	C, (?)	64k
VI:87	Metal Sickle	C, (?)	63f
VI:88	Metal Sickle	C, (?)	—
VI:89	Spear Blade	C, (?)	64d
VI:90	Spear Blade	C, (?)	64e
VI:91	Spear Blade	C, (?)	64f
VI:92	Spear Blade	C, (?)	64g
VI:93	Spear Blade	C, (?)	64h
VI:94	Spear Blade	C, (?)	64i
VI:95	Spear Blade	C, (?)	—
VI:96	Metal Hoe(?)	C, Sounding	63g
VI:97	Metal Axe	C, Sounding	63b
VI:98	Metal Axe	C, Sounding	63c
VI:99	Metal Bracelet(?)	C, Sounding	63j
VI:100	Beads	C, Not stratified	68i

Catalogue of Objects from Khafājah Mounds B, C, and D by Seasons (*cont.*)

Season / No.	Object	Mound / Locus	Plate / Reference
	1935 / 36 EXCAVATIONS (The Oriental Institute of The University of Chicago) (*cont.*)		
VI:101	Beads	C, Not stratified	67h
VI:102	Beads	C, Not stratified	67f
VI:103	Beads	C, Not stratified	68e
VI:104	Beads	C, Not stratified	68a
VI:105	Beads	C, Not stratified	—
VI:106	Beads	C, Not stratified	68c
VI:107	Beads	C, Not stratified	—
VI:108	Beads	C, Not stratified	—
VI:109	Beads	C, Not stratified	—
VI:110	Beads	C, Not stratified	68f
VI:111	Beads	C, Not stratified	67b
VI:111a	Beads	C, Not stratified	68h
VI:112	Beads	C, Not stratified	—
VI:113	Beads	C, Not stratified	67d
VI:114	Beads	C, Not stratified	67g
VI:115	Beads	C, Not stratified	—
VI:116	Beads	C, Not stratified	67e
VI:117	Beads	C, Not stratified	68g
VI:118	Beads	C, Not stratified	—
VI:119	Beads	C, Not stratified	68b
VI:120	Beads	C, Not stratified	68d
VI:121	Beads + Amulet	C, Not stratified	—
VI:122	Beads	C, Not stratified	67c
VI:123	Beads	C, Not stratified	—
VI:124	Beads	D, Sîn Temple	67a
VI:134	Statuette	C, (?)	—
VI:135	Cylinder Seal	C, (?)	—
VI:136	Cylinder Seal	C, (?)	OIP 72, pl. 40:428
VI:137	Amulet(?)	C, (?)	66k
VI:138	Cylinder Seal	C, (?)	66j
VI:139	Metal Axe	C, (?)	63d
VI:140	Metal Axe	C, (?)	63e
VI:141	Metal Hoe(?)	C, Sounding	63h
VI:142	Metal Hoe(?)	C, Sounding	63i
VI:143	Arrowhead	C, Sounding	65a
VI:144	Metal Tool	C, Sounding	65b
VI:145	Metal Needle	C, Sounding	65i
VI:146	Metal Needle	C, Sounding	65j
VI:147	Metal Needle	C, Sounding	65k
VI:149	Plaque	D, Sîn Temple	62d

Catalogue of Objects from Khafājah Mounds B, C, and D by Seasons (*cont.*)

Season / No.	Object	Mound / Locus	Plate / Reference
1935 / 36 EXCAVATIONS (The Oriental Institute of The University of Chicago) (*cont.*)			
VI:150	Figurine (Animal)	D, Sîn Temple	—
VI:152	Statuette	D, Sîn Temple	—
VI:154	Cylinder Seal	C, Surface	OIP 72, pl. 40:429
VI:155	Cylinder Seal	C, Surface	OIP 72, p. 55
VI:157	Plaque	D, Sîn Temple	62f
VI:158	Plaque	D, Sîn Temple	62e
VI:452	Gaming Board	D, Balk	66e
VI:453	Dagger	D, Balk	65c
VI:(?)	Lion Statues	D, Sîn Temple	59b, 60
1936 / 37 EXCAVATIONS (The Oriental Institute of The University of Chicago)			
VII:250	Cylinder Seal	D, Sîn Temple (Surface)	OIP 72, pl. 40:432
1937 EXCAVATIONS (The University Museum of The University of Pennsylvania)			
VIII:36	Duck Weight	D, Surface	66d
VIII:37	Cylinder Seal	C, Surface	66h
VIII:72	Cylinder Seal	C, Trench n.74-75	66i
VIII:73	Model Wheel	C, Trench n.74-75	—
VIII:74	Pot Rim	C, Trench n.74-75	66a
VIII:75	Vessel	C, Trench n.74-75	OIP 63, pls. 132a, 161:B.576.720a
VIII.76	Figurine (Human)	C, Trench n.74-75	62l
VIII:77	Bone Scraper	C, Trench n.74-75	—
VIII:78	Arrowhead	C, Trench n.74-75	—
VIII:79	Figurine (Animal)	C, Trench n.74-75	62m
VIII:80	Weight	C, Trench n.74-75	66c
VIII:81	Cylinder Seal	C, Trench n.74-75	OIP 72, pl. 40:427
VIII:82	Bone Pin	C, Trench n.74-75	—
VIII:83	Bone Needle	C, Trench n.74-75	—
VIII:84	Bone Needle	C, Trench n.74-75	—
VIII:85	Arrowheads	C, Trench n.74-75	64a-c
VIII.86	Arrowheads	C, Trench n.74-75	—
VIII:87	Metal Spatula	C, Trench n.74-75	—
VIII:88	Metal Pin	C, Trench n.74-75	—
VIII:89	Metal Needle	C, Trench n.74-75	65g
VIII:90	Metal Needle	C, Trench n.74-75	65h
VIII:98	Bone Needle	C, Trench n.74-75	—

Catalogue of Objects from Khafājah Mounds B, C, and D by Seasons (*cont.*)

Season / No.	Object	Mound / Locus	Plate / Reference
\multicolumn{4}{l}{1937 EXCAVATIONS (The University Museum of The University of Pennsylvania) (*cont.*)}
VIII:99	Vessel	C, Trench n.74-75	OIP 63, pl. 132b
VIII:100	Vessel	C, Trench n.74-75	OIP 63, pls. 132c, 161:B.576.720b
VIII:101	Cylinder Seal	C, Trench n.74-75	—
VIII:102	Statue	C, Trench n.74-75	—
VIII:103	Plaque	C, Trench n.74-75	61c
VIII:106	Beads	B, g.65 (gr. VIII-5)	—
VIII:107	Vessel	B, g.65 (gr. VIII-5)	OIP 63, pl. 132e
VIII:108	Vessel	B, g.65 (gr. VIII-5)	OIP 63, pl. 132d
VIII:109	Vessel	B, g.65 (gr. VIII-5)	OIP 63, pls. 132d, 163:B.656.720
VIII:169	Plaque	D, J.77	61o
VIII:170	Plaque	D, J.77	61m
VIII:171	Plaque	D, J.77	62j
VIII:172	Plaque	D, J.77	61m
VIII:173	Plaque	D, J.77	61n
VIII:174	Plaque	D, J.77	—
VIII:175	Plaque	D, J.77	62h
VIII:176	Plaque	D, J.77	61k
VIII:177	Plaque	D, J.77	—
VIII:178	Plaque	D, J.77	62g
VIII:179	Plaque	D, J.77	62i
VIII:180	Relief	D, J.77	62n
VIII:181	Vessel	D, J.77	OIP 63, pl. 153:B.237.200
VIII:182	Metal Sickle	C, r.80 house	—
VIII:184	Tablet	D, J.77	—
VIII:185	Tablet	D, J.77	—
VIII:186	Tablet	D, J.77	—
VIII:199	Tablet	D, J.77	—
VIII:213	Plaque	D, J.77	61i
VIII:214	Plaque	D, J.77	61j
VIII:215	Plaque	D, J.77	61l
VIII:216	Tripod Dish	C, r.80 house	OIP 63, pp.102 and 123:B.041.900
VIII:217	Vessel	C, r.80 house	OIP 63, pl. 159:B.547.320
VIII:218	Vessel	C, r.80 house	OIP 63, pl. 160:B.556.720
VIII:226	Cylinder Seal	C, r.80 house	OIP 72, pl. 40:426
VIII:227	Macehead	D, J.77	66b

Catalogue of Objects from Khafājah Mounds B, C, and D by Seasons (*cont.*)

Season / No.	Object	Mound / Locus	Plate / Reference

1937 EXCAVATIONS (The University Museum of The University of Pennsylvania) (*cont.*)

Season / No.	Object	Mound / Locus	Plate / Reference
VIII:229	Plaque	D, J.77	61h
VIII:231	Vessel	D, J.75	OIP 63, pl. 150:B.140.210
VIII:232	Vessel	C, r.80 house	OIP 63, pl. 166:B.757.320
VIII:239	Cylinder Seal	C, house	66g
VIII:241	Plaque	C, house	61e
VIII:242	Plaque	C, house	61d
VIII:243	Plaque	C, house	61b
VIII:246	Vessel	B, g.67	OIP 63, pl. 188:C.665.740
VIII:249	Bone Pin	C, house	—
VIII:250	Bone Pin	C, house	—
VIII:251	Metal Chisel	C, house	65e
VIII:257	Plaque	C, house	61a
VIII:274	Plaque	C, house	—
VIII:279	Plaque	C, house	—
VIII:280	Figurine (Human)	C, house	62k
VIII:281	Tablet	D, (?)	—
VIII:282	Tablet	D, (?)	—
VIII:(?)	Model Shield	D, (?)	OIP 63, pl. 106e

1937 / 38 EXCAVATIONS (The University Museum of The University of Pennsylvania)

Season / No.	Object	Mound / Locus	Plate / Reference
IX:66	Weight	B, (?)	—
IX:67	Clay Cylinder (Inscribed)	B, 1-e.66	—
IX:191	Figurine (Human)	B, (?)	63a
IX:218	Dagger Blade	B, g.66	65d

YEAR OF EXCAVATION AND NUMBER UNKNOWN

Season / No.	Object	Mound / Locus	Plate / Reference
—	Vessel	B, (?)	OIP 63, pl. 171:C.225.310b
—	Vessel	B, (?)	OIP 63, pl. 177:C.493.360
—	Vessel	B, (?)	OIP 63, pl. 186:C.606.320

APPENDIX 6

CATALOGUE OF OBJECTS FROM KHAFĀJAH MOUNDS B, C, AND D BY SITES

Plate	Object	Season/No.	Locus/Square	Material	Remarks	Museum
			Mound B			
—	Beads	VIII:106	g.65 (gr. VIII-5)	carnelian, paste stone	23 exx. (in cup VIII:107)	ND*
—	Vessel	VIII:107	g.65 (gr. VIII-5)	pottery (light green)	—	Baghdad
—	Vessel	VIII:108	g.65 (gr. VIII-5)	pottery (light brown)	—	P**
—	Vessel	VIII:109	g.65 (gr. VIII-5)	—	height 143, diameter 92 mm	Baghdad
—	Vessel	VIII:246	g.67	pottery (light brown)	—	Baghdad
—	Vessel	—	(?)	—	—	(?)
—	Vessel	—	(?)	—	—	(?)
—	Vessel	—	(?)	—	—	(?)
—	Weight	IX:66	(?)	hematite	30 × 10 cm (8 gm)	Baghdad
—	Clay Cylinder	IX:67	1-e.66	baked clay	inscribed, 133 × 76 mm	Baghdad
63a	Figurine	IX:191	(?)	lead	height 4.50 cm	Baghdad
65d	Dagger	IX:218	g.66	bronze/copper	181 × 37 mm	(?)
			Mound C			
64j	Spear Blades	VI:85	(?)	bronze	average length 13 cm	Baghdad
64k	Spear Blades	VI:86	(?)	bronze	average length 13 cm	OI: A17725
63f	Sickle	VI:87	(?)	bronze	length 18.40 cm	Baghdad
—	Sickle	VI:88	(?)	bronze	length 20 cm	OI: A17726
64d	Spear Blade	VI:89	(?)	bronze	length 13.50 cm	OI: A17727
64e	Spear Blade	VI:90	(?)	bronze	length 13 cm	Baghdad
64f	Spear Blade	VI:91	(?)	bronze	length 12 cm	OI: A17728
64g	Spear Blade	VI:92	(?)	bronze	length 11 cm	Baghdad
64h	Spear Blade	VI:93	(?)	bronze	length 9 cm	OI: A17729
64i	Spear Blade	VI:94	(?)	bronze	length 8.50 cm	OI: A17730

*   Not divided
**   The University Museum of The University of Pennsylvania

Catalogue of Objects from Khafājah Mounds B, C, and D by Sites (*cont.*)

Plate	Object	Season/No.	Locus/Square	Material	Remarks	Museum
			Mound C (*cont.*)			
—	Spear Blade	VI:95	(?)	bronze	length 8 cm	(?)
63g	Hoe(?)	VI:96	sounding	bronze	length 16 cm	Baghdad
63b	Axe	VI:97	sounding	bronze	8 × 17.50 cm	Baghdad
63c	Axe	VI:98	sounding	bronze	10 × 12 cm	OI: A17731
63j	Bracelet(?) with Rivet	VI:99	sounding	bronze	diameter 7 cm	OI: A17732
68i	Beads	VI:100	not stratified	alabaster/ hematite	—	OI: A17733
67h	Beads	VI:101	not stratified	lap la, hem, var	—	OI: A17682
67f	Beads	VI:102	not stratified	gra, cry, var	—	OI: A17734
68e	Beads	VI:103	not stratified	gra, cry, var	—	Baghdad
68a	Beads	VI:104	not stratified	car, var(?)	—	Baghdad
—	Beads	VI:105	not stratified	hem, sh, bo	—	OI: A17735
68c	Beads	VI:106	not stratified	alab, gra, ste, car	—	OI: A17736
—	Beads	VI:107	not stratified	alab, gra, sh	—	OI: A17737
—	Beads	VI:108	not stratified	alab, sh, var st	—	OI: A17738
—	Beads	VI:109	not stratified	car, lap la, var	—	(?)
68f	Beads	VI:110	not stratified	car, ste, frit, var	—	OI: A17739
67b	Beads	VI:111	not stratified	st, ob, var	—	OI: A17740
68h	Beads	VI:111a	not stratified	car, cry, ste, var	—	OI: A17740
—	Beads	VI:112	not stratified	ag, car, red stone	—	Baghdad
67d	Beads	VI:113	not stratified	lap la, gra	—	Baghdad
67g	Beads	VI:114	not stratified	alab, car, frit, lap la	—	Baghdad
—	Beads	VI:115	not stratified	lap la, shell	—	Baghdad
67e	Beads	VI:116	not stratified	car, lap la, st	—	Baghdad
68g	Beads	VI:117	not stratified	car, lap la	—	—
—	Beads	VI:118	not stratified	car, hem	—	Baghdad
68b	Beads	VI:119	not stratified	hem, lap la	—	OI: A17741
68d	Beads	VI:120	not stratified	car, lap la, st	—	Baghdad
—	Beads/Amulet	VI:121	not stratified	lap la	—	OI: A17742
67c	Beads	VI:122	not stratified	car, cry, st	—	OI: A17743
—	Beads	VI:123	not stratified	car, frit, lap la, st	—	OI: A17744
—	Statuette	VI:134	(?)	terracotta	—	(?)
—	Cylinder Seal	VI:135	(?)	clay	impression only	(?)
—	Cylinder Seal	VI:136	(?)	ivory	—	OI: A17747
66k	Amulet(?)	VI:137	(?)	bone	2 × 2.60 cm	Baghdad
66j	Cylinder Seal	VI:138	(?)	stone (gray)	—	(?)
63d	Axe	VI:139	(?)	bronze	lgh. 13 cm, ht. 5.50 cm	Baghdad
63e	Axe	VI:140	(?)	bronze	lgh. 11 cm, ht. 5.00 cm	OI: A17748

Catalogue of Objects from Khafājah Mounds B, C, and D by Sites (*cont.*)

Plate	Object	Season/No.	Locus/Square	Material	Remarks	Museum

Mound C (*cont.*)

Plate	Object	Season/No.	Locus/Square	Material	Remarks	Museum
63h	Hoe(?)	VI:141	sounding	bronze	wdh. 3.50 cm, lgh. 7 cm	Baghdad
63i	Hoe(?)	VI:142	sounding	bronze	wdh. 3.50 cm, lgh. 8 cm	OI: A17749
65a	Arrowhead	VI:143	sounding	bronze	length 7.40 cm	Baghdad
65b	Tool	VI:144	sounding	bronze	length 6 cm	Baghdad
65i	Needle	VI:145	sounding	bronze	length 15 cm	Baghdad
65j	Needle	VI:146	sounding	bronze	length 15.40 cm	OI: A17750
65k	Needle	VI:147	sounding	bronze	length 14.60 cm	(?)
—	Cylinder Seal	VI:154	surface	tablet clay	—	(?)
—	Cylinder Seal	VI:155	surface	stone (white)	—	OI: A17752
66h	Cylinder Seal	VIII:37	surface	hem (black)	OB style	P(?)
66i	Cylinder Seal	VIII:72	Trench n.74-75	paste (white)	—	Baghdad
—	Model Wheel	VIII:73	Trench n.74-75	marble (white)	—	Baghdad
66a	Pot Rim	VIII:74	Trench n.74-75	yellow ware	—	Baghdad
—	Vessel	VIII:75	Trench n.74-75	pottery	—	P
62l	Figurine	VIII:76	Trench n.74-75	clay (black)	human	ND
—	Scraper	VIII:77	Trench n.74-75	bone	$58 \times 17 \times 5$ mm	ND
—	Arrowhead	VIII:78	Trench n.74-75	bronze	$77 \times 20 \times 7$ mm	ND
62m	Figurine	VIII:79	Trench n.74-75	clay (green)	animal	ND
66c	Weight	VIII:80	Trench n.74-75	hematite	1.50 gm	ND
—	Cylinder Seal	VIII:81	Trench n.74-75	limestone	—	P
—	Pin	VIII:82	Trench n.74-75	bone	107×5 mm	ND
—	Needle	VIII:83	Trench n.74-75	bone	88×5 mm	ND
—	Needle	VIII:84	Trench n.74-75	bone	122×5 mm	ND
64a-c	Arrowheads	VIII:85	Trench n.74-75	bronze	3 exx., 154×25 mm	P 37-15-15
—	Arrowheads	VIII:86	Trench n.74-75	bronze	4 exx., tang and midrib ($103-122 \times 17-20 \times 4$ mm)	Baghdad
—	Spatula	VIII:87	Trench n.74-75	bronze	$95 \times 10 \times 4$ mm	Baghdad
—	Pin	VIII:88	Trench n.74-75	bronze	94×5 mm	Baghdad
65g	Needle	VIII:89	Trench n.74-75	bronze	141×5 mm	P 37-15-13
65h	Needle	VIII:90	Trench n.74-75	bronze	140×6 mm	P 37-15-14
—	Needle	VIII:98	Trench n.74-75	bone	rect. sect., 44×5 mm	ND
—	Vessel	VIII:99	Trench n.74-75	pottery	—	Baghdad
—	Vessel	VIII:100	Trench n.74-75	pottery	—	Baghdad
—	Cylinder Seal	VIII:101	Trench n.74-75	clay (black)	impression only, 35×15 mm	ND
—	Statue	VIII:102	Trench n.74-75	granite	skirt fragment, $101 \times 59 \times 36$ mm	ND
61c	Plaque	VIII:103	Trench n.74-75	terracotta (brown)	—	ND
—	Sickle	VIII:182	r.80 house	bronze	128×44 mm	Baghdad
—	Tripod Dish	VIII:216	r.80 house	pottery (lt red)	—	ND
—	Vessel	VIII:217	r.80 house	pottery (lt brown)	—	Baghdad

Catalogue of Objects from Khafājah Mounds B, C, and D by Sites (*cont.*)

Plate	Object	Season/No.	Locus/Square	Material	Remarks	Museum
			Mound C (*cont.*)			
—	Vessel	VIII:218	r.80 house	pottery (lt green)	—	Baghdad
—	Cylinder Seal	VIII:226	r.80 house	hematite (black)	—	Baghdad
—	Vessel	VIII:232	r.80 house	pottery (lt yellow)	—	Baghdad
66g	Cylinder Seal	VIII:239	house	serpentine	impression only	Baghdad
61e	Plaque	VIII:241	house	terracotta (green)	—	P
61d	Plaque	VIII:242	house	terracotta (brown)	—	Baghdad
61b	Plaque	VIII:243	house	terco (red buff)	—	Baghdad
—	Pin	VIII:249	house	bone	$55 \times 9 \times 3$ mm	ND
—	Pin	VIII:250	house	bone	$79 \times 8 \times 3$ mm	ND
65e	Chisel	VIII:251	house	copper/bronze	$166 \times 11 \times 11$ mm	P 37-15-12
61a	Plaque	VIII:257	house	terracotta (lt brn)	—	P 37-15-4
—	Plaque	VIII:274	house	terracotta	—	ND
—	Plaque	VIII:279	house	terracotta	fem., $106 \times 59 \times 20$ mm	ND
62k	Figurine	VIII:280	house	clay (lt brown)	—	ND
			Mound D			
62c	Plaque	V:253	sounding (surface)	terracotta	—	OI: A17104
—	Cylinder Seal	VI:72	Sîn temple	soft black material	—	Baghdad
—	Cylinder Seal	VI:73	Sîn temple	stone (gray)	—	OI: A17719
—	Plate	VI:74	Sîn temple	copper/bronze	diam. 8 cm × dph. 1.20 cm	Baghdad
61g	Plaque	VI:75	Sîn temple	terracotta	—	OI: A17720
—	Beads	VI:76	Sîn temple	—	50 exx., various shapes	ND
66f	Sculptor's Workpiece	VI:77	Sîn temple	stone	diameter 7 cm	Baghdad
65f	Arrowhead	VI:78	Sîn temple	flint	—	ND
62b	Plaque	VI:79	Sîn temple	terracotta	—	ND
61f	Mold	VI:80	Sîn temple	clay	figurine, 6×16 cm	OI: A17721
62a	Plaque	VI:81	Sîn temple	terracotta	—	Baghdad
67a	Beads	VI:124	Sîn temple	carnelian	43 exx., various shapes	OI: A17745
62d	Plaque	VI:149	Sîn temple	terracotta	—	Baghdad
—	Figurine	VI:150	Sîn temple	terracotta	lion fragment, 11 cm long	ND
—	Statuette	VI:152	Sîn temple	terracotta	seated human figure	ND
62f	Plaque	VI:157	Sîn temple	terracotta	—	Baghdad
62e	Plaque	VI:158	Sîn temple	terracotta	—	Baghdad
59b, 60	Lion Statues	VI:(?)	Sîn temple	terracotta	frgms of lower portions	ND
66e	Gaming Board	VI:452	Balk	clay	frgm, 4.50×3.50 cm	OI: A17872

Catalogue of Objects from Khafājah Mounds B, C, and D by Sites (*cont.*)

Plate	Object	Season/No.	Locus/Square	Material	Remarks	Museum
			Mound D (*cont.*)			
65c	Dagger	VI:453	Balk	copper/bronze	30 cm long	OI: A17873
—	Cylinder Seal	VII:250	Sîn temple (surface)	stone (green)	—	—
66d	Duck Weight	VIII:36	surface	hematite (black)	—	P
61o	Plaque	VIII:169	J.77	terracotta	—	ND
61m	Plaque	VIII:170 + 172	J.77	terracotta	—	Baghdad
62j	Plaque	VIII:171	J.77	terracotta (buff)	—	P
61n	Plaque	VIII:173	J.77	terracotta (drab)	—	P
—	Plaque	VIII:174	J.77	terracotta	cf. VIII:173	ND
62h	Plaque	VIII:175	J.77	terracotta	—	ND
61k	Plaque	VIII:176	J.77	terracotta	—	Baghdad
—	Plaque	VIII:177	J.77	terracotta	—	ND
62g	Plaque	VIII:178	J.77	terracotta	—	ND
62i	Mold	VIII:179	J.77	terracotta	plaque	ND
62n	Relief	VIII:180	J.77	terracotta	surface destroyed	ND
—	Vessel	VIII:181	J.77	clay	cup	Baghdad
—	Tablet	VIII:184	J.77	clay	cuneiform	ND
—	Tablet	VIII:185	J.77	clay	cuneiform	ND
—	Tablet	VIII:186	J.77	clay	cuneiform	ND
—	Tablet	VIII:199	J.77	clay	cuneiform	Baghdad
61i	Plaque	VIII:213	J.77	terracotta (green buff)	—	P
61j	Plaque	VIII:214	J.77	terracotta	cf. VIII:213	Baghdad
61l	Plaque	VIII:215	J.77	terracotta	—	Baghdad
66b	Macehead	VIII:227	J.77	marble (gray+white)	diameter 3.40 cm	P
61h	Plaque	VIII:229	J.77	terracotta (lt yellow)	—	P
—	Vessel	VIII:231	J.75	clay	small bowl	Baghdad
—	Tablet	VIII:281	(?)	clay (gray)	cuneiform	P
—	Tablet	VIII:282	(?)	clay (dark gray)	cuneiform	P
—	Model	VIII:(?)	(?)	—	chariot shield	(?)

PLATE 47

(*a*) Khafājah—Mound B Fortress of Dur Samsuiluna. General View of Northeast Wall and Buildings, Viewed from Northwest

(*b*) Khafājah—Mound B Fortress of Dur Samsuiluna. General View. (The Photograph Is an Extension of the View to the Right-Hand Side of pl. 47a.)

PLATE 48

(a) Khafājah—Mound B Fortress of Dur Samsuiluna. View from Outside of the Southwestern End
of the Fortification Wall to the Southeast

(b) Khafājah—Mound B Fortress of Dur Samsuiluna. Inscribed Clay Foundation Cylinder, Kh. IX:67,
in Northeast Corner of the Gate Room, 1-e.66, with Later Burial in the Foreground

PLATE 49

(b) Khafājah—Mound B. Impression of Inscribed Clay Foundation
Cylinder, Kh. IX:67, from Gate Room 1-e.66

(a) Khafājah—Mound B. Inscribed Clay Foundation Cylinder, Kh. IX:67, from Gate Room 1-e.66

PLATE 50

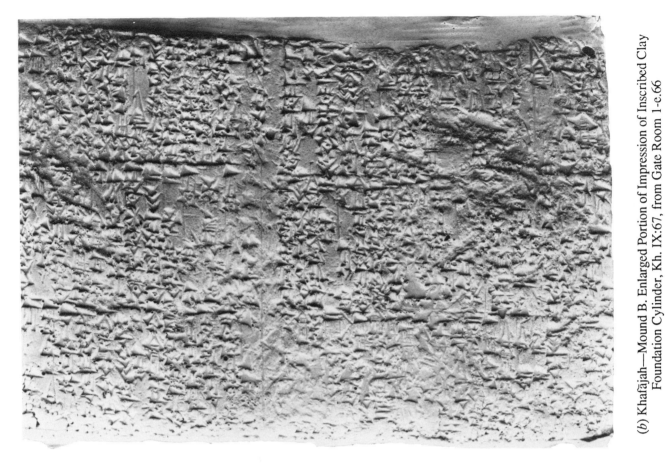

(b) Khafājah—Mound B. Enlarged Portion of Impression of Inscribed Clay
Foundation Cylinder, Kh. IX:67, from Gate Room 1-e.66

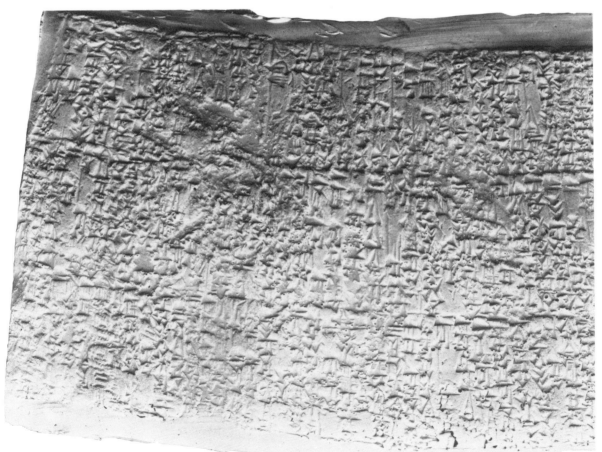

(a) Khafājah—Mound B. Enlarged Portion of Impression of Inscribed Clay
Foundation Cylinder, Kh. IX:67, from Gate Room 1-e.66

PLATE 51

(a) Khafājah—Mound D. Northeast Corner Tower of Enclosure Wall, Viewed from the Southeast

(b) Khafājah—Mound D. Main Gate and Drain in Center of Northeast Portion of the City Wall

PLATE 52

(a) Khafājah—Mound D. Eastern Side of Main Gate in the Enclosure Wall

(b) Khafājah—Mound D. Western Side of Main Gate in the Enclosure Wall

PLATE 53

(a) Khafājah—Mound D. Northwest Corner of Enclosure Wall with Secondary Wall Outside,
Viewed from the East

(b) Khafājah—Mound D. Northwest Corner of Enclosure Wall with Secondary Wall Outside,
Viewed from the Northeast

PLATE 54

(b) Khafājah—Mound D. Earlier Northwest Section of Enclosure Wall with Buttresses Near Northwest Corner

(a) Khafājah—Mound D. Northwest Section of Enclosure Wall with Buttresses, Viewed from the Southwest to the Northeast

PLATE 55

Khafājah—Mound D. Sin Temple. General Panoramic View from the Northwest

PLATE 56

(*a*) Khafājah—Mound D. Sîn Temple. Close-Up Panoramic View (East Side of pl. 55)

(*b*) Khafājah—Mound D. Sîn Temple. Close-Up Panoramic View (West Side of pl. 55)

PLATE 57

(*a*) Khafājah—Mound D. Sîn Temple. General View from the Southeast

(*b*) Khafājah—Mound D. Sîn Temple. Clay Maceheads and Sling Bullets Found When
Excavating the Outline of the Enclosure Wall Near the Main Gate (cf. pl. 52)

PLATE 58

(a) Khafājah—Mound D. Cuneiform Tablets in situ in Room 2-N.74 of the Sîn Temple

(b) Khafājah—Mound D. Brick Built Vaulted Tomb in Room 1-M.75 of the Sîn Temple

PLATE 59

(b) Khafājah—Mound D. Terracotta Lion Statue, Kh. VI:(?), in situ
South of Doorway, 1-L.76, to Room 6-M.76 of the Sîn Temple

(a) Khafājah—Mound D. Oven in Room 9-M.74 of the Sîn Temple,
Viewed from West to East

PLATE 60

Khafājah—Mound D. Reconstuction of the Terracotta Lion Statue, Seen in situ on pl. 59
(From water-color paintings by G. Rachel Levy)

PLATE 61

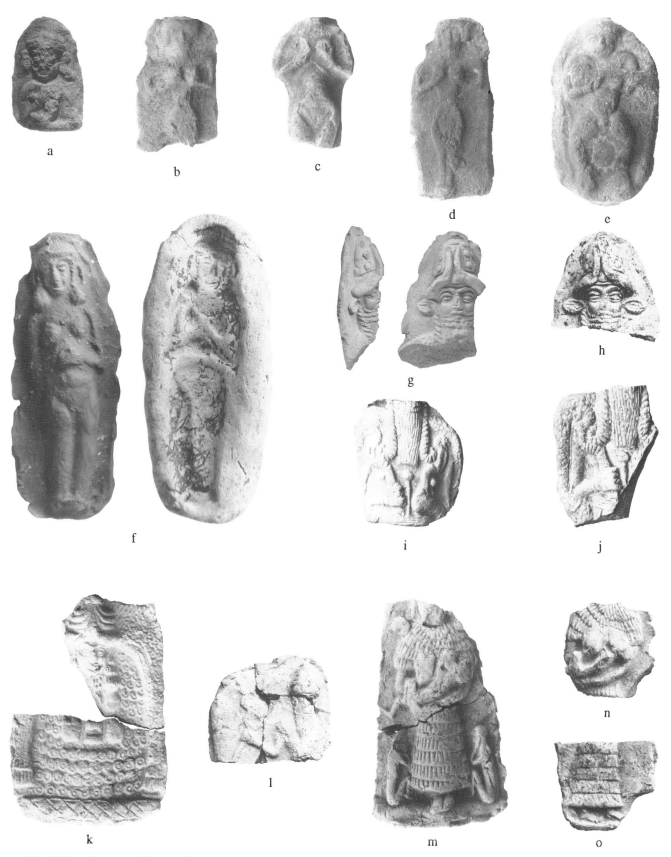

Khafājah—Terracotta Plaques (*a-e* and *i-o*) and Mold (*f*) with God-Like Images: (*a*) VIII:257, (*b*) VIII:243, (*c*) VIII:103, (*d*) VIII:242, (*e*) VIII:241, (*f*) VI:80, (*g*) VI:75, (*h*) VIII:229, (*i*) VIII:213, (*j*) VIII:214, (*k*) VIII:176, (*l*) VIII:215, (*m*) VIII:172 + 170, (*n*) VIII:173, and (*o*) VIII:169. Scale 1:2. From Mound C (*a-e*) and Mound D (*f-o*).

PLATE 62

Khafājah—Miscellaneous Terracotta Plaques (*a-j* and *n*) and Figurines (*k-m*) Depicting Various Scenes and Representations:
(*a*) VI:81, (*b*) VI:79, (*c*) V:253, (*d*) VI:149, (*e*) VI:158, (*f*) VI:157, (*g*) VIII:178, (*h*) VIII:175, (*i*) VIII:179, (*j*) VIII:171,
(*k*) VIII:280, (*l*) VIII:76, (*m*) VIII:79, and (*n*) VIII:180. Scale 1:2. From Mound C (*k-m*) and Mound D (*a-j* and *n*)

PLATE 63

Khafājah—Metal Objects: (*a*) Lead Figurine, IX:191, (*b-e*) Bronze Axes, VI:97, 98, 139, and 140, (*f*) Bronze Sickle Blade,
VI:87, (*g-i*) Bronze Hoes(?), VI:96, 141, and 142, and (*j*) Bronze Bracelet(?) with Rivet, VI:99. Scale 1:2.
From Mound B (*a*) and Mound C (*b-j*)

PLATE 64

Khafājah—Bronze Spear Blades: (*a-c*) VIII:85, (*d*) VI:89, (*e*) VI:90, (*f*) VI:91, (*g*) VI:92, (*h*) VI:93, (*i*) VI:94, (*j*) VI:85, and (*k*) VI:86. Scale 1:2. From Mound C (*a-k*)

PLATE 65

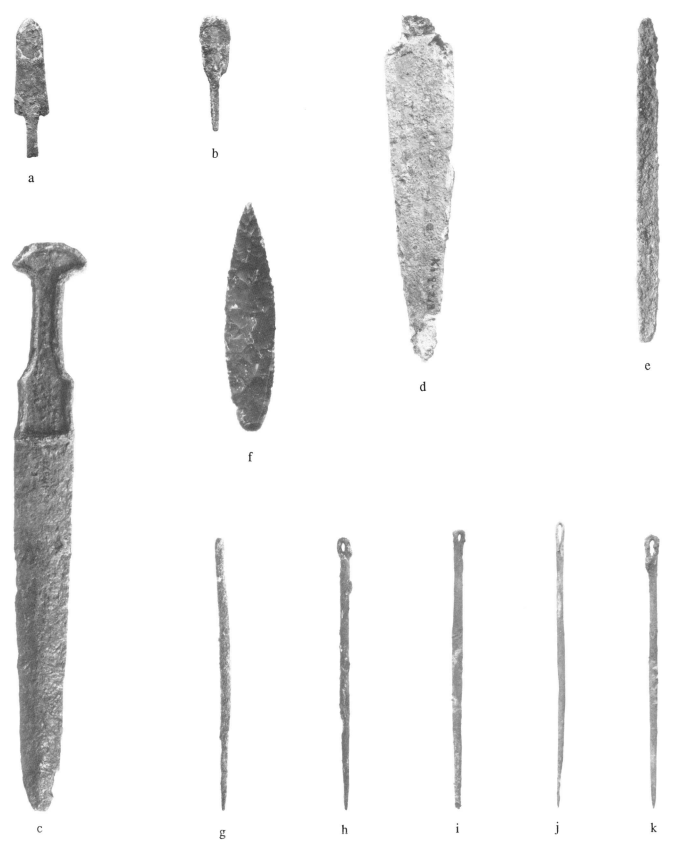

Khafājah—Metal and Flint Tools and Weapons: (*a*) Bronze Arrowhead, VI:143, (*b*) Bronze Spatula-Like Tool, VI:144,
(*c*) Copper / Bronze Dagger, VI:453, (*d*) Copper / Bronze Dagger, IX:218, (*e*) Copper / Bronze Chisel, VIII:251,
(*f*) Flint Arrowhead, VI:78, and (*g-k*) Bronze Needles, VIII:89, 90, and VI:145-47. Scale 1:2.
From Mound B (*d*), Mound C (*a, b, e,* and *g-k*), and Mound D (*f*)

PLATE 66

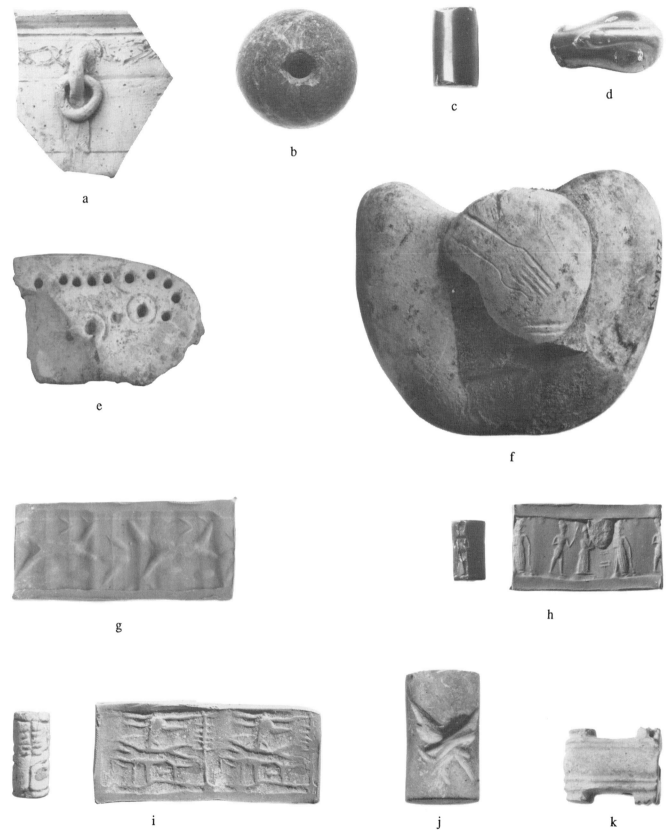

Khafājah—Miscellaneous Bone, Terracotta, and Stone Objects: (*a*) Pottery Bowl Fragment, VIII:74, (*b*) Marble Macehead, VIII:227, (*c*) Hematite Cylinder-Shaped Weight, VIII:80, (*d*) Hematite Duck-Shaped Weight, VIII:36, (*e*) Clay Gaming Board, VI:452, (*f*) Stone Sculptor's Workpiece, VI:77, (*g*) Serpentine Cylinder Seal Impression, VIII:239, (*h*) Hematite Cylinder Seal and Impression, VIII:37, (*i*) White Paste Cylinder Seal and Impression, VIII:72, (*j*) Stone Cylinder Seal, VI:138, and (*k*) Bone Amulet(?), VI:137. Scales (*a-d* and *g-k*) 1:2 and (*e, f*) 1:1. From Mound C (*a, c,* and *g-k*) and Mound D (*b* and *d-f*)

PLATE 67

Khafājah—Stone Beads: (*a*) VI:124, (*b*) VI:111, (*c*) VI:122, (*d*) VI:113, (*e*) VI:116, (*f*) VI:102, (*g*) VI:114, and (*h*) VI:101.
Scale 1:2. From Mound C (*b-h*) and Mound D (*a*)

PLATE 68

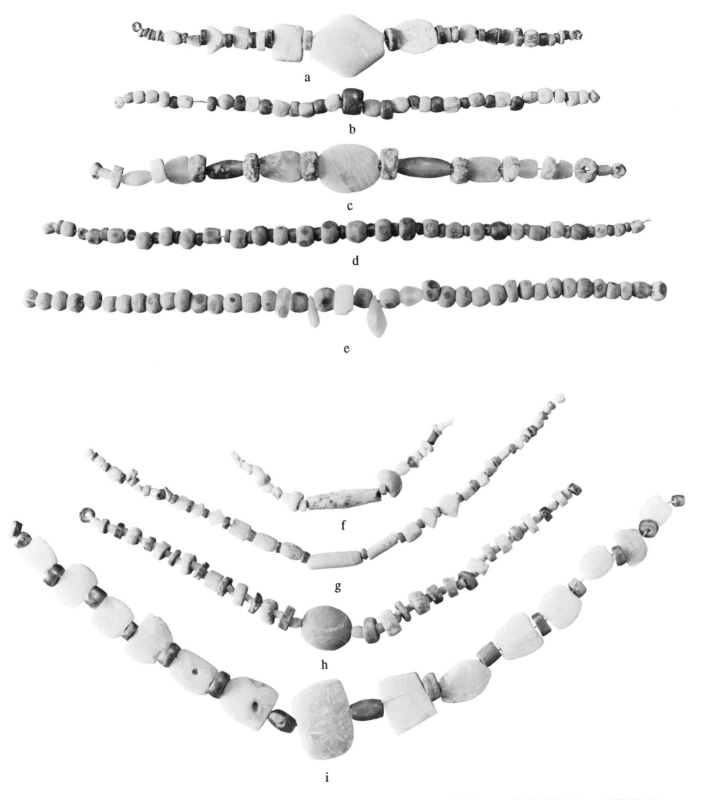

Khafājah—Stone Beads: (*a*) VI:104, (*b*) VI:119, (*c*) VI:106, (*d*) VI:120, (*e*) VI:103, (*f*) VI:110, (*g*) VI:117, and (*h*) VI:111a, and (*i*) VI:100. Scale 1:2. From Mound C (*a-i*)

ORIENTAL INSTITUTE PUBLICATIONS—VOLUMES IN PRINT

Available from the Oriental Institute, Publications Sales

1155 East 58TH Street, Chicago, Illinois 60637, Tel. (312) 702-9508, Fax (312) 702-9853

Available from The University of Chicago Press

11030 South Langley Avenue, Chicago, Illinois 60628. Tel. (1-800) 621-2736, (312) 568-1550
Telex: 28-0206 (answerback U C Press)

Europe, Middle East, Africa, and India
126 Buckingham Palace Road, London, SW1W 9SD, England, Telex: CHIBOOKS LDN